QUEEN OF CAPRICE

A Biography of Kristina of Sweden

Noel B. Gerson

QUEEN OF CAPRICE

Published by Sapere Books.

20 Windermere Drive, Leeds, England, LS17 7UZ,
United Kingdom

saperebooks.com

ISBN: 978-1-80055-505-1.

For Lucille and Edwin J. Harragan

TABLE OF CONTENTS

Kristina is a woman, and behaves as such — irrationally.
— POPE INNOCENT XI

I: 1660

LADY OF FORTUNE: PAST AND FUTURE

Night was falling. A cold November wind blew in from the North Sea and the frost was thick on the banks of the Elbe and the two branches of the little Alster River. But the citizens of the Free City of Hamburg ignored the weather and gathered by the hundreds outside the Summer Palace, an imposing stone building that stood near the Inner Alster, in the shadow of the walls that had protected the great port in medieval times. Even the pikemen, employed by the city to maintain order, were excited, although they had seen many of the world's great come and go. The Summer Palace, which had been built early in the sixteenth century, was the property of the city; distinguished visitors were lodged there by the City Council, free of charge; but when it was not occupied, the thrifty burghers willingly rented it to anyone who could pay for the privilege. It was rumored that the notorious woman who was making her temporary home there was being charged an exorbitant sum, but that she did not care, as money meant nothing to her. Officials of the Finance Board, who had rented the palace to her, maintained a dignified, discreet silence.

Men tugged their greatcoat collars more closely around their necks, women huddled beneath their shawls and stamped their feet, but no one went home. Instead, the crowd became larger, and eventually the pikemen were forced to clear a path for the carriages that passed through the gates and, drawing to a halt in the central courtyard, discharged their passengers. Rarely had the citizens of Hamburg seen so many distinguished ladies and gentlemen gathered, and they wondered why the nobles and bishops, university professors and generals had bothered to accept the invitations extended to them by a woman who, as she approached her thirty-fourth birthday, had become a political nonentity.

Hamburg was proud of its political acumen, and with good reason. The German states and, eventually, all of Europe had become embroiled in the ferocious struggle that was now known as the Thirty Years' War, but Hamburg, refusing to join one side or the other and maintaining an armed force to prevent an invasion, had remained neutral. As a consequence, she was prosperous, her houses were intact and her people were healthy. Elsewhere, the devastation had been staggering; some cities had lost seventy-five per cent of their residents, and areas where the fighting had been the heaviest had become barren wasteland. The people of Hamburg felt they could afford to be smug, for they had learned the secret of survival. Their Protestants and Catholics lived side by side peacefully and, although they detested each other cordially, they carefully observed an unarmed truce.

Oddly, the woman who was living at the Summer Palace was the symbol of the Thirty Years' War to most of Europe. Her father, King Gustavus II Adolphus of Sweden, had been the greatest of Protestant champions, and some students of military affairs claimed that no general since Julius Caesar was his peer. Even those who had fought against him admitted that he had been responsible for Sweden's rise from obscurity to the rank of a great power, and anyone who glanced at a map could see that he had vastly enlarged the boundaries of the domain that his daughter inherited when he met his death on the battlefield.

Kristina herself was an enigma. Trained to rule from birth, she had assumed power on her eighteenth birthday. Then, ten years later, she had startled the civilized world by abdicating, renouncing her faith, and embracing Catholicism. The Church of Rome had rejoiced, and her conversion had been regarded as a victory as great as any ever won on the field of battle. But most members of the College of Cardinals had subsequently entertained grave doubts which they found it inexpedient to voice publicly. The Cardinals had discovered what the people of Sweden had learned earlier: Kristina's intellect was extraordinary, but she was capricious, dissolute, and refused to tolerate discipline. Popes who had known her had commented privately that perhaps she was less than an asset to Catholicism.

Certainly, Sweden was relieved to be rid of her, in spite of the many farsighted benefits of her ten-year reign. She was in Hamburg now after making a brief journey to Stockholm, where she had tried in vain to regain her crown, and the incident produced the usual stories, rumors, and half-truths, none of which anyone bothered to verify. It was said that there had been riots in Stockholm when the people had learned of her presence there. According to another account, the Riksdag, or parliament, had been convened, and when she had learned that its members, many of whom she herself had given titles, had planned to imprison her in a fortress, she had fled from the country in disguise.

Hamburg knew only a few real facts. Kristina had arrived unexpectedly, and the City Council had welcomed her reluctantly, but she had paid in gold for the right to occupy the Summer Palace. She had been accompanied by a large suite, including three equerries, five ladies in waiting, several secretaries, and four priests. She had hired cooks and chambermaids, valets and grooms, and she paid high wages, which annoyed the wealthier citizens of Hamburg, who complained that servants would expect them to match her lavishness. She had remained in seclusion, and it had been assumed that she was nursing her wounds, but she had astonished everyone, including those who knew it was her habit to make unexpected gestures, when she had issued banquet invitations to more than one hundred ladies and gentlemen. Perhaps she was trying to prove that her abject failure at Stockholm had not discouraged her.

Few of the invitations had been refused, and the carriages arrived at the palace in a steady stream. The guests, like the common people who stood shivering in the cold, were curious about a woman who had become a legend in her own time.

A handsome, dark-haired woman of thirty-two in a brocaded gown greeted the guests at the entrance to the great hall of the palace, and explained graciously to those who thought she was Queen Kristina that she was the Baroness Mathilde von Echner, Her Majesty's principal lady in waiting. The guests, who had heard wild stories about the Baroness, were impressed by her aristocratic bearing, and wondered if some of the tales might have been exaggerated.

As a matter of record, virtually all of the whispers about Mathilde were false, but she was an obvious target of speculation. Although she was no beauty, many men admired her, and evil rumors flourished when she, like Kristina, remained single. It was odd, too, that a noblewoman who had clung to the Lutheran faith should follow her royal mistress into exile, and it was equally strange that someone who had been born in one of Sweden's German provinces should feel any sense of loyalty to a monarch who was loyal to no one but herself.

Fortunately for posterity, the Baroness von Echner kept a voluminous *Diary*, which she later supplemented with her

Memoirs, so her own motives are clear; history owes much of its knowledge of Kristina to the indefatigable Mathilde. The reasons for her association with the former Queen are simply explained in her own words: "I was selected as a companion for Queen Kristina when she was sixteen. It was believed that there were too few feminine influences in her life, and although I was only fourteen, I was even then conscious of my femininity. Her Majesty immediately accepted me as a comrade, and we spent many years together on terms of equality.

"The slanders that have linked our names have never bothered me. How obvious it is that I should prefer the companionship of Kristina and her court, that I should be free to choose lovers and discard them at will, than to marry some baron or knight (all whom I have ever met are dullards) and spend the rest of my days in a dreary provincial town, or, still worse, in seclusion on a desolate estate."

So much of Kristina's life is seen through the eyes of her lady in waiting that it would be wise to take the measure of the Baroness von Echner more carefully, and a brief line in her *Memoirs*, written after she had returned to Stockholm in her old age, gives a deep insight into Kristina's character and the nature of their relationship. "It is good to live my own life," Mathilde wrote frankly. "Only now that Her Majesty and I have quarreled and parted can I admit that our association was a contest of wills. She tried to dominate me and convert me to her Roman belief. I accepted the challenge and resisted successfully. Had we not duelled, we would have gone our separate paths long ago, yet I can truthfully state that I always found Her Majesty's company stimulating. She enjoyed mine because I, alone of all her followers, refused to dissemble and spoke my mind candidly to her. Others trembled when she became angry, but I did not fear her wrath. Behind her frown was the gentility of one who was and is, like me, a woman."

Mathilde does not reveal whether the guests who came to the Summer Palace at Hamburg on the raw November evening in 1660 were surprised to find their hostess absent. But she makes it clear, as does the correspondence of the Papal Legate, that the ladies and gentlemen were startled by the pagan sumptuousness of the great hall, where fires burning in three hearths removed the chill from the air. A small pond filled with scented water had been placed in the center of the hall, and in it floated laurel wreaths and paper flowers coated with wax.

The guests were astonished to discover that all of the hall's furniture had been removed, and that mattresses covered in bright silks were scattered on the stone floor. Mathilde announced that the banquet was being given in honor of the heroes and heroines of antiquity, and the gentlemen and ladies were urged to recline on the mattresses. A few of the more daring made themselves comfortable, and servants circulated through the hall, offering cups of potent wine which, Mathilde said, was made "from an ancient receipt."

The Papal Legate was aware of the potency of the beverage, however, and in his succinct report to the Vatican, stated: "The beverage was a mixture of brandywine and other strong spirits disguised by a blend of milder wines from the Palatine. Those who failed to perceive its insidious qualities soon became intoxicated."

At that stage of the evening, most of the guests drank cautiously. The prosperous burghers, who were members of the City Council, sat primly with their wives; the foreign envoys, aware that something out-of-the-ordinary was in the air, only sipped their drinks, and the clergymen carefully refrained from touching the concoction. The Lutheran ministers sat on one side of the pond, and were joined by Hamburg's few Calvinists. The Catholics, on the opposite side, clustered around the Papal Legate. The two groups pointedly ignored each other. Priests and ministers always avoided each other, and only someone very daring or very callous would have invited them to the same party.

Count Ludwig von Alster, the ranking nobleman present, became restless, as the self-conscious guests stared at each other and the hostess failed to make her appearance. Mathilde had been watching him surreptitiously, and although a few carriages were still discharging members of the gentry at the entrance, she waved her handkerchief in what was obviously a prearranged signal, and an orchestra stationed in an anteroom struck up a strange air. Cymbals crashed, lutes were strummed vigorously, and then the high, wailing sound of wind instruments filled the hall.

There was a stir behind the long draperies that concealed the dais at one end of the chamber, and a score of women moved down a flight of steps in single file. All were dressed like slave girls from the Ottoman Empire: semitransparent silk trousers clung to their hips, their midriffs were bare, and sheer, gauzelike layers of silk were draped over their breasts. Each wore a long metal chain, painted gold, attached to her left wrist and right ankle, and, writhing sinuously, they followed the leader toward the pond.

A single glance was sufficient to identify the first woman in the procession. Her shining blond hair hung in loose waves; artfully applied black antimony accented her intense blue eyes; and, although she would soon be thirty-four, her slender, almost boyish figure was that of a girl half her age. A diamond was pasted on her right cheekbone and she was clearly enjoying the sensation she was causing, for her rouged lips were parted in an ecstatic smile. A careful observer might have noted that her left shoulder was a trifle higher than her right, a result of an accident she had suffered in childhood, but no one was looking at her shoulders. Her Majesty, Kristina, former Queen of Sweden and daughter of the immortal Gustavus Adolphus, had rouged her nipples, and everyone present could see her breasts through the silk of the band that revealed more than it concealed.

Guests who had been reclining sat up abruptly, ladies gasped and some covered their faces. A number of the men recognized the pretty girls who followed the Queen: They were the most attractive courtesans and bawds in a city that was known for the beauty of its trollops. Some of the wenches waved boldly to erstwhile clients, and Count von Alster broke the shocked silence by laughing loudly.

The clergymen forgot their differences; had the occasion been notable for no other reason, it would be remembered because Protestants and Catholics reacted simultaneously and identically. Ministers and priests, including the members of the Queen's own entourage, rose hurriedly to their feet and stalked out of the hall. According to one totally unsubstantiated story, the Lutheran Bishop and the Papal Legate departed in the same carriage, but it is unlikely that even in a moment of stress these rivals for men's souls would have joined hands. Too much blood had been shed, too much bitterness had been engendered; only Kristina, who failed to understand the passionate convictions that had caused the Thirty Years' War, would have asked members of both factions to break bread with her and then disgrace herself. The outraged clergymen sought only to escape.

A few of the other guests left, too, but the majority remained, and the musicians played more loudly to distract attention from the departing prudes. An equerry carried a cushion to the side of the pool; Kristina stood on it, steadying herself by gripping the man's shoulder, and when the music stopped, she made a short speech of welcome. Her remarks were not recorded, but Mathilde states in her *Diary* that "Her Majesty's comments were applauded amiably."

There had been enough that was novel and bizarre to keep the royal courts of Europe buzzing for months, but the evening had just begun. Kristina announced that, as a pre-supper entertainment, a prize would be awarded to a fortunate lady. The "dancing girls" gave each woman a small square of parchment bearing a Latin inscription, and the Queen drew a square that matched one of them, from a silver wassail bowl. The prize, a valuable ruby, was awarded to the Countess von Alster, a Bavarian noblewoman several years Kristina's junior, who had given up Catholicism and become a Lutheran when she had married.

The Countess, whom Mathilde describes as a "modest lady of some beauty, with fine teeth and a pure skin," accepted the gem.

The courtesans passed out another set of parchment squares to the ladies, and the Queen herself received one. The men, she declared, would draw for their supper partners, and she asked them to approach the wassail bowl in a single line. It is difficult to imagine that the long arm of coincidence could have been responsible for developments that the more cynical and worldly of the guests predicted accurately: Count von Alster won Kristina as his partner, and they moved off together to a mat sufficiently near one of the hearths to permit the underclad Queen to dine in comfort. The Countess, who had been maneuvered into a position that forced her to remain silent, presumably had to be content with the expensive bauble she had been given.

A portrait of Count von Alster, painted in 1661, shows a broad-shouldered man with long, straight black hair and dark eyes, wearing various ribbons across his chest. Most of his honors must have been granted because of his title, for he played no noteworthy part in Hamburg's history, either as civic leader or statesman. Several of his ancestors were distinguished sailors, and a great-nephew, who inherited the title early in the following century, became a famous admiral, but Kristina's supper partner is remembered only because of his brief association with her.

Rare and exotic dishes were served, wine flowed in a never-ending stream, and the guests ate and drank for four hours. There is no account relating the nature of Kristina's discussion with the Count, so it must be assumed that they made no attempt to solve any of the grave problems facing the world. After the last course had been served, the musicians, who had been playing softly, broke into a lively air, and some of the courtesans danced for the edification of the guests.

During the exhibition, Mathilde notes: "Her Majesty and the senior noble of Hamburg absented themselves from the company for a time."

No mention is made of the Countess von Alster's reaction.

The party continued until dawn, and before it ended, the Queen and her partner slipped away a second time. At last, the weary revelers called for their carriages, and they departed hastily when they saw a crowd gathering outside the palace. Word of the depraved affair had spread through the city, and several hundred angry Lutherans, most of them armed with stones, marched up and down defiantly, demanding that the "whore of Rome" be deported.

Stones crashed through several windows before pikemen were able to disperse the angry mob. In the meantime, however, Kristina lost her temper, and although she was still dressed in her scanty slave-girl attire, she seized a pistol and would have fired it at the crowd, but, in her own words, "I was dissuaded by one of the gentlemen in waiting in my service at that time." It was fortunate that she did not fire, for she was a deadly shot and had she killed or injured one of the citizens, the furious mob might have caused great damage.

At last the Summer Palace was quiet, and most of the staff crept off to bed, exhausted. But Kristina detained Baroness von Echner and two other ladies in waiting, and, pacing angrily up and down the great hall, kicking silk mats and empty goblets out of her path, she delivered a lengthy tirade. The party had been a dismal failure, the guests had been totally lacking in wit and intelligence, and she had never met more boring people. Thanks to her efforts, Stockholm had emerged from the Dark Ages and had become a cultural and intellectual center, and might have rivaled Rome and Paris had her compatriots been sufficiently farsighted to restore her to the throne. But Hamburg was hopelessly dismal — the poets were less talented than court minstrels, university professors displayed no scientific curiosity, everyone was too timid to discuss theology, and the whole city seemed to be interested only in food and financial profits.

Ordering one of the ladies to bring her a jar of the soap that was made for her in Milan, according to her own formula, Kristina stripped off her tawdry harem silks and, plunging into the cold water of the pool, scrubbed herself vigorously, at the same time issuing furious commands. According to Mathilde, the other attendants scattered. One hurried to the stables behind the palace for the young stallion Her Majesty had purchased recently, and another brought the Queen's riding clothes to the hall.

The shirt and breeches, stout fustian coat, and heavy leather boots were men's attire, cut to Kristina's measurements, and when she twisted her hair into a knot, piled it on the crown of her head and pulled a broad-brimmed hat over her forehead, a stranger would have mistaken her for a man. Her long-legged, masculine stride bore no resemblance to the mincing, seductive walk she had affected earlier, and when she stamped into the courtyard where the horse was being held, she vaulted into the saddle with the agility of a cavalry officer.

She returned to the palace four hours later, and a groom led the exhausted stallion back to the stable. But the outing had improved Kristina's spirits and, not bothering to change her clothes, she ate a hearty meal, drank a mug of ale, and retired to her study, where she spent the afternoon dictating long letters to friends in Rome, Brussels, and Paris. After a light supper she played a game of chess with one of her equerries, read several pamphlets, including one that amused her because it attacked her viciously, and finally went off to her own chamber sometime after midnight.

Baroness von Echner noted in her *Diary* that, as always, the Queen slept soundly, although her financial situation was delicate because the Riksdag, to punish her for breaking her pledge never to return to Sweden, was deliberately holding up the semiannual payment of her pension. The scandalous banquet had cost a fortune, and she had too little cash on hand to pay the bills that tradespeople were presenting, but the knowledge that she was in debt did not disturb her.

Nor was she bothered by the fact that the Protestant and Catholic clergymen of the city were demanding that she be expelled from Hamburg, and that the City Council, which had been forced to double the guard outside the gates of the palace in order to prevent a repetition of the riot that had disturbed the peace, was seriously considering asking her to leave. She knew, too, that at least two reports had been sent to the Vatican and that she would receive an irate letter from the ascetic Pope Alexander VII, but she refused to admit that any man, even the Holy Father, had the right to chastise her. And she was completely undisturbed by the news that one of her chaplains, disgusted by the pagan banquet, had written an urgent request to his superiors in Rome, asking to be relieved of his onerous assignment.

Kristina believed that she was not bound by the laws and codes, the ethical standards and moral guides that lesser mortals obeyed. In her own mind she was no less a queen because she had given up her throne, and she was convinced she belonged to a tiny, exclusive set that stood far above the rest of humanity. Monarchs, even those who had abdicated or been driven into exile, made their own rules, and she agreed heartily with Louis XIV of France and young Charles II of England, who had recently regained the realm his father had lost to Oliver Cromwell, that the rights of royalty were divinely inspired.

Her pithiest comment on the banquet that has survived — a brief sentence in a letter to her good friend, Decio Cardinal Azzolino — perhaps describes her reaction more vividly than the shocked murmurs of her contemporaries. "I hope," she wrote, "that the Countess von Alster appreciates the ruby I gave her. It is a lovely little gem."

II: 1626–1644
THE BEGINNING

The story of Kristina does not begin with her birth on December 8, 1626. It is impossible to understand this complex, puzzling, and paradoxical woman without meeting her parents, who lived their lives in the shadow of the Thirty Years' War, 1618–1648.

It would be quite accurate to state that King Gustavus II Adolphus of Sweden was the most important figure on either side in that struggle. His many admirers claim, with considerable justification, that he was the greatest man of his age, and even a cursory study of his life reveals that he was the strongest Protestant leader of his century in Continental Europe. He was ambitious, proud, and gifted — he stands with Caesar and Napoleon as a general — and although he delegated considerable power to his able Chancellor, Axel Oxenstjerna, he acted as his own foreign minister and proved himself as capable as Talleyrand and Metternich, who may have imitated his techniques consciously.

Gustavus Adolphus had traveled through many parts of Germany in disguise, and had coveted the fertile farmlands he had seen in the Rhine valley. But his entry into the Thirty Years' War was caused less by his desire to expand his possessions than his need to protect the Swedish provinces on the Prussian side of the Baltic Sea. And, above all, religious considerations forced the King to enter the war. He was as devoted a champion of Protestantism as Cromwell, and it is no exaggeration to say that they shared the same fanatical zeal. When visiting the Rhineland he had been startled by the arrogance of Catholic bishops who, far removed from the influence of the Vatican and disinterested in spiritual matters, ruled as temporal potentates.

Gustavus Adolphus' comment at the time was prophetic: "If these priests were subject to me, I would long ago have taught them that modesty, humility, and obedience are the proper characteristics of their profession."

Sweden's declaration of war caused scarcely a ripple in the enemy camp. The land of the North was still shrouded in the fog of the Middle Ages, her soldiers were illiterate, untrained, and little better than a rabble. Ferdinand, the Holy Roman Emperor, expressed a commonly held opinion when he declared disdainfully, "We have got a new little enemy."

He soon learned, as did all of Europe, that he was mistaken. The leader of the Swedes was a military genius, a man who instinctively understood problems of strategy and tactics that other, lesser generals were forced to approach intellectually. Before leading his troops into the field, Gustavus Adolphus invented an improved musket and a better cannon than any that had ever been used. Forges burned brightly in the night sky of the North, and when the King left Stockholm, he declared solemnly, "We will show our enemies that we are honest men and honorable gentlemen."

He kept his word. Swedish troops were not permitted to loot, rape, or burn, and the rabble became transformed into a superb striking force. Gustavus Adolphus' religious fervor was as great as his military talent, and before each battle he led his troops in the singing of Protestant hymns. His name became a legend, and on several occasions the enemy fled in panic when they heard his legions chanting, "Fear Not Little Flock."

The mists no longer obscured Sweden by the time Gustavus Adolphus met his death on the battlefield in 1632. The

Lutheran "giant of the North" was a major European power, and only France and Spain were her peers.

Kristina's mother had no claim to fame other than her beauty. Princess Marie-Eleonore was the eldest daughter of the Elector of Brandenburg. Gustavus Adolphus, who had met her while traveling through the German states, fell in love with her at first sight, according to several of his companions. They were married in 1620, and the King took his lovely, fair-haired bride to Stockholm.

Kristina, who regarded her mother with amiable contempt, wrote of her parents' marriage with a critical detachment in which the element of romance was missing. Gustavus Adolphus, she declared, selected Marie-Eleonore as his wife because "she was the most eligible of the Protestant Princesses of the period, to whom his religion limited his choice. This Princess, who was not without beauty and possessed the good qualities looked for in her sex, lived with the King on sufficiently pleasant terms in a union which nothing marred except the lack of an heir to secure the succession."

This was a mild description of a tempestuous, legalized love affair. Gustavus Adolphus had not sought a woman of intellect, for he had more than enough for two. His wife's lack of ready wit did not disturb him, as he himself was solemn. But he worshiped Marie-Eleonore for her beauty and in return won her complete devotion. He dazzled her and was the center of her existence; she clung to him so fiercely that after he declared war she often insisted on accompanying him into the field.

Courtiers complained to one another that the Queen was a woman of unpredictable moods, but they carefully refrained from criticizing her to her husband. Gustavus Adolphus believed she was perfect, and if he became aware of her increasingly nervous disposition, her sulkiness, and eccentricity, he carefully kept his opinions to himself. Members of the Court did not blame Queen Marie-Eleonore for behaving strangely, for she had suffered two major disappointments: in 1621 and again in 1623 she gave birth to a daughter. Both babies died in infancy, and the nation mourned with her.

In 1626, Marie-Eleonore became heavy again, and astrologers in the capital, and in Malmo, Goteborg, and Landskrona, each prophesying independently of the others, predicted that the Queen would give birth to a son and that he would live. Sweden waited tensely and, it may be assumed, so did Gustavus Adolphus. The baby was delivered on the eighth day of December, and cried so loudly and lustily that the King was informed he had indeed sired a son. He hurried to his wife's suite, but the women who had attended Marie-Eleonore seemed curiously abashed, and each found some excuse to avoid going into the sitting room where Gustavus Adolphus paced up and down, waiting to see his son.

Finally his sister, Princess Katherine, summoned enough courage to face his wrath, and carrying the infant in her arms, went to the King. In all probability he was surprised to learn that the baby was a girl, and if he was disappointed, he soon became reconciled to the situation. Kristina, in her *Memoirs*, represents her father as having been delighted, and proceeds to quote what she purports to be his actual words: "Let us thank God, my sister. I hope my daughter will be as good as a son to me. Since God has given her, may God preserve her." She says the King stared at her gravely for a moment, then chuckled and added, "She ought to be clever, since she has taken us all in."

Kristina herself seems to have been far more concerned than her father about her sex, for she devotes herself to a vigorous self-defense in her *Memoirs*. In a passage addressed to the Almighty, she declares, "My sex has been Your means of preserving me from the vices and debaucheries of the country in which I was born. If it had been Your will that I should be born a man, perhaps the habits of the country and the example of my companions would have corrupted me. I might perhaps have drowned in drink, as so many others do, all the virtues and talents which You have given me. Very likely, too, my ardent and impetuous temperament would have led me into embarrassing relations with women from which it would have been difficult for me to extricate myself. At any rate, there would have been a danger that the society of women would have taken up the time which, having been devoted to study and the search for Truth, has brought me nearer to You."

These words were written in the final years of her life, when she had conveniently forgotten some of her more daring escapades. But even in her old age she remained hostile to Marie-Eleonore. "The Queen, my mother," she wrote, "who had the weaknesses as well as the virtues of her sex, was inconsolable. She could not endure me, she said, because I was a girl and was ugly — wherein she told the truth, for I was both. My father, on the contrary, was very fond of me, and I responded to his affection in many precocious ways. It seemed to me that I understood the differences between their qualities and their feelings and was able to do justice to both of them, even in the cradle."

Kristina's belief that she was unattractive was undoubtedly strengthened by an accident that occurred sometime during her first year. A nursemaid or governess dropped her on the floor, inflicting a slight but permanent injury to her left shoulder. Her clothes, even her low-cut gowns, which she favored as a woman, were designed to compensate for the difference in the height of her shoulders, but there is no evidence to indicate that the deformity was visible to anyone but her dressmaker.

The scars were psychological rather than physical; however, they were important in the formation of Kristina's character, and in her *Memoirs* there are several references to her conviction that she had been dropped deliberately. No explanation is given for such a vicious act, however, and had a servant committed it purposely, the punishment would have been severe.

Not even Kristina could exaggerate the genuine delight that Gustavus Adolphus felt when his daughter was near him, and he spoiled her so thoroughly that it would have been strange had Marie-Eleonore, to whom her husband had been devoted, not grown jealous. Kristina, in turn, worshiped her father, and a brief incident described in her *Memoirs* summarizes the intensity of her love for him and her strong desire to emulate him.

When his daughter was two years old, Gustavus Adolphus made an inspection of his garrisons and, not wanting to be separated from his family, took his wife and child with him. An unexpected complication developed when they approached the fortress of Calmar, for Kristina was the official heiress to the throne, and the commandant wanted to pay his respects to her by firing a nineteen-gun salute. Here, in Kristina's words, is what happened:

"There was some hesitation because of the fear of frightening a baby as important as I was, and the Governor, not wishing to fail in his duty, asked what were the King's orders.

"The King, after hesitating for a moment, said: 'Fire! She is a soldier's daughter, and must get used to the sound of guns.'

"So the order was obeyed, and the salute was duly fired.

"I was with the Queen in her carriage, and instead of being frightened, as children of that tender age generally are, I laughed and clapped my hands, and, not being yet able to speak, expressed my delight as best I could by signs, and indicated that I wanted them to fire again.

"My father's affection was greater than ever after that. He hoped that I was destined to be as brave as he was himself."

Gustavus Adolphus was not destined to watch his daughter grow to womanhood, however. When Kristina was four, he mustered the strongest army he had ever raised and, before marching off to Germany, ordered his troops to swear fealty to Kristina. Then he summoned the Riksdag, and when the parliament had convened, he appeared before the members, holding his daughter in his arms. Apparently he had a premonition of death, for he made a long, solemn farewell speech to the nobles, concluding by asking them to promise without reservation that they would accept Kristina as their ruler if he should be killed. The Riksdag responded by giving the royal father and daughter a rousing standing ovation.

Kristina's description of his departure is one of the more moving passages in her *Memoirs*. Her governess had taught her a little speech, and after her father had kissed her goodbye and tried to put her down, she tugged at his beard in order to force him to listen to her. She does not record what she said to him but declares, "He took me in his arms again and kissed me, unable to restrain his tears. Or so I have been told by persons who were present, who also assure me that I cried so bitterly for three whole days that I hurt my eyes and very nearly ruined my sight which, like his, was extremely weak. My tears were regarded as of evil omen, as I was a child who hardly ever cried."

Two years later, Gustavus Adolphus went to his death on a fog-covered field near Lützen, and the circumstances of his death have remained a mystery for more than three hundred years. One romantic account, which Kristina preferred to believe, was that a German officer, after shooting Gustavus Adolphus, called out to the dying man, "Who are you?"

The deep voice supposedly answered, faintly, "I *was* king of Sweden."

Kristina's conversion to Catholicism will be discussed in later pages, but it might be well to pause briefly to examine a situation that, at first glance, seems hopelessly contrary. Gustavus Adolphus was the strongest conscious influence in Kristina's life; she was so proud of him that she would permit no one to utter a single critical word in her presence. There is a story, which may or may not be true, that she boxed the ears of a cardinal who dared to refer to "the Lucifer of the North."

Yet she could hardly deny that Gustavus Adolphus had been the great champion of Protestantism. How could she, who gave up her throne in order to embrace the faith against which he had fought, admire him without reservation?

The solution to this seemingly insoluble conundrum does much to explain the ambivalence of Queen Kristina's character. She straddled the fence neatly. Her father was a very great man, who had fought on the wrong side, but that error in no way detracted from his greatness. She felt, in fact, that his achievements were all the more magnificent because he had opposed the omnipotent Almighty.

A line written in her *Memoirs* in 1688, the year prior to her own death, sheds light on her thinking: "It may be, Lord, that a ray of Thy triumphant grace may have descended to crown him at the last moment of his life."

In 1632, Kristina's career entered a new phase. Her father had provided for every emergency and had named five nobles to act as Regents for the six-year-old Queen, under the chairmanship of the energetic and wise Chancellor Oxenstjerna. Gustavus Adolphus had understood his wife well, for he wrote gently but firmly in his will that she was neither to serve as a regent nor be given any voice in the nation's affairs. Furthermore, he insisted, it would be the responsibility of the Regents to educate the little Queen, and he authorized them to take any measures they felt necessary to circumvent well-meant interference from his widow.

These instructions may seem harsh to a later era, but no historian has questioned Gustavus Adolphus' sagacity. Marie-Eleonore was a silly, moody woman, and the whole nation was aware of her instability. A small but vocal Republican party had been formed in some of the larger cities, and had the Dowager Queen meddled in affairs of state, it was probable that the ranks of those dedicated to the overthrow of the monarchy would have grown. But no patriotic citizen would try to undermine the throne when an innocent child sat on it, seemingly alone and helpless.

The move was shrewd and farsighted. The Republican party collapsed almost overnight.

The personal repercussions were even more violent. Marie-Eleonore became hysterical when she learned that her husband had been killed, and, leaving her daughter in Stockholm, made a journey to Germany to accompany his body to the capital. The lugubrious ceremonies dragged on for many weeks. Foreign envoys called at the royal palace to pay their respects, and protocol made it necessary for Kristina to receive them.

Although she was precocious, there may be a hint of exaggeration in her *Memoirs* when she writes about the visit of the Russian ambassadors.

The Regents told me not to be afraid of them. Their want of confidence in me hurt me, and I asked them indignantly, "What is there to be afraid of?"

They told me that the Russians were dressed quite differently from us, that they had long beards, that they were tall and terrible persons, and that there were a great many of them, but that I must not be frightened. It so happened that the Ministers with me on that occasion were the Grand Constable and the Grand Admiral, who, themselves, wore long beards.

So I laughed and said, "Suppose they have beards — what of that? You have beards, and I am not afraid of you. Why should I be afraid of them? Tell me what I have to do and leave the rest to me."

And I kept my word. I received my visitors, seated on the throne in the customary manner, with a demeanor so self-possessed and majestic that, instead of being frightened as other children are on similar occasions, I made the Ambassadors feel what all men feel when they are brought into the presence of the great; and my subjects were delighted and admired my manner, as people admire every trifling trait on the part of children whom they love.

Less biased journals indicate that even at six Kristina loved being the center of attention. She would have been deeply shocked had she known that, like her mother, she was becoming narcissistic and that in the years ahead she would behave even more erratically than the melancholy Marie-Eleonore, who had never exercised self-control and who behaved with such a lack of restraint when she returned to Stockholm from Germany that she disgusted people of every class. As far back as three hundred years ago, Sweden believed in the virtues of self-discipline.

Marie-Eleonore's grief was sincere, but there can be no doubt that she enjoyed her hysteria. She made a scene at the great state funeral she had ordered for Gustavus Adolphus, she insisted that his body should lie in state permanently in a church near the palace so she could visit the chapel daily, and she had his heart enshrined in a satin-lined silver box, which she placed at the head of her bed. She spent most of her time in her chamber, weeping, and Kristina's memories of the two-year period of official mourning were dismal. The gloom of those long, dreary months lives on in her *Memoirs*:

> My mother shut herself up in her apartment, which was draped with black hangings from the ceiling to the floor. The windows were covered with curtains of the same dark material. We could hardly see there, and the wax candles which burned there by day as well as night revealed only the symbols of her mourning. Day or night, she never ceased to weep.
>
> I had the highest respect for her and her tender affection, but I felt sorely troubled when, in spite of my tutors, she insisted upon monopolizing me. There were some disputes with the Regents on the subject, but they allowed her to do as she liked for some time, in view of their great regard for her, feeling that as she had been excluded from the Regency, this indulgence was her due.
>
> She loved me very tenderly, saying that I was the living image of the late King, but the very force of her love reduced me to despair. She insisted that I sleep with her and never let me out of her sight. She forced me to accompany her on her one daily outing, to see my father's coffin, and when, after visiting it many times, I no longer wept, she began to upbraid me. It was with the greatest difficulty that she could be persuaded to let me have a room to myself in which to learn my lessons.

As Marie-Eleonore became increasingly neurotic, her relations with her daughter deteriorated rapidly. The Dowager

Queen conceived the wild notion that she and her daughter would die if they drank water, so she forced Kristina to drink wine and beer exclusively. The child's palate was undeveloped, and she rebelled. Her mother retaliated by removing all drinking water, and Kristina stubbornly refused to drink at all. She could not conquer her thirst, however, and desperation made the little girl cunning. Each night after dinner Marie-Eleonore went into her private chapel to pray, leaving Kristina alone in the depressing atmosphere of the bedchamber. The child investigated every corner and was delighted when she found a phial that the palace gardeners filled every day with dew. It was one of the Dowager Queen's foolish conceits that her skin was extraordinarily delicate, and that she could use only dew as toilet water.

Kristina happily raided the phial every night for a week; presumably Marie-Eleonore was so distracted that she neglected to use toilet water during that period. Eventually, however, she missed the contents, spied on her daughter, and caught her in the act. Kristina was whipped with a birch rod, but refused to succumb meekly. She flew at her mother, scratching her face and tearing her gown. Thereafter she was permitted to drink water.

There were other torments, too, which she related in detail in the *Memoirs*: "My mother liked to surround herself with jesters and dwarfs, as is the fashion in Germany. Her rooms were always full of them. It was intolerable to me, for I have always had a perfect horror of these ridiculous freaks. So I was delighted when lessontime called me to the schoolroom. There was never any need to urge me to study. I went to my lessons with unimaginable joy even earlier than the appointed time and studied for six hours in the morning and another six in the evening, taking holidays only on Saturdays and Saints' days."

Marie-Eleonore prolonged her mourning in the most extravagant manner. Indifferent to the hard fact that Sweden needed every copper for the prosecution of the war, she spent vast sums replacing the black draperies every month, buying huge quantities of black silk for new gowns, and at every opportunity, ordering expensive memorial services for her late husband. Chancellor Oxenstjerna showed incredible patience, but when he returned from a long, grueling tour of inspection that had taken him to every fighting front in Germany, Marie-Eleonore pushed him too far. She demanded that two Regents should wait on her at table at every meal, and that at least one member of the Grand Council of State should stand behind her chair to pour her wine.

Oxenstjerna refused curtly, and when she began to rave, he reminded her forcibly that the husband she claimed to revere had placed her under the authority of the Regents. She wept, fainted, was revived and screamed, but the Chancellor did not stay to witness her histrionics. Wasting no more time, he summoned the Regents to a formal meeting, and the official records of that session, which Kristina later copied and reproduced in her *Memoirs*, attacked the problem vigorously.

The Chancellor stated the matter tersely. "It is necessary," he said in his written charge, "for the young Queen to be educated in royal virtues. This cannot be done while she lives with the Queen-Dowager. Therefore she must be separated from her mother."

The other Regents were asked to express their views on paper, and their opinions were equally unequivocal:

"It is better to stem the brook than the flood. The general welfare is the supreme law. I vote for the separation."

"We have left the young Queen with the Queen-Mother in the hope of seeing some improvement, but there is none.

Kristina is brought up, if not in actual bad habits, at least not in such a way, or among such men, as she ought to be. Neither fear of God nor love of her country is instilled into her mind, nor is she taught the duties of government. She must, therefore, be taken away from her mother. I vote for the separation."

"We often see parents, out of love for their children, send them away for their benefit. Even monkeys do so with their young. I vote for the separation."

Oxenstjerna acted swiftly, ruthlessly, and thoroughly. He permitted Marie-Eleonore to remain in Stockholm for a final ceremony, in which Gustavus Adolphus' coffin was placed in a vault. Then she was banished to one of the royal estates in the country. The captain of the guard was ordered to keep her there by force, if necessary, and to permit her to leave the grounds only with the written consent of the Regents. The black draperies and curtains were removed from Kristina's living quarters, plain furniture was installed, and a new regime began. The Chancellor was determined to obey the instructions of his late master to the letter, and, hiring new tutors, riding and fencing masters, he made it clear that the Regents would enforce the late King's commands.

Kristina describes those regulations in pungent terms: "My father had enjoined the Regents to educate me as a man and to teach me everything that a prince ought to know if he is to reign worthily. He declared with great emphasis that he did not wish me to be inspired with any of the characteristic sentiments of my sex, except insofar as honor and modesty were concerned. For the rest, he wished me to be a prince and to receive the instruction which is proper for princes."

So the young Queen was torn from a melancholy feminine world and thrust into one in which masculinity was stressed in every possible way. Her wardrobe was burned; the royal tailors made her boy's clothes; the royal cobblers fashioned male boots for her; and her long blond hair was cut short. Generals and colonels lectured her on military affairs, hard-headed male tutors taught her mathematics, foreign languages, science, and diplomacy. She learned the history of her country, the obligations of a monarch, and the intricacies of finance. The physical side of her education was not neglected, and her fencing and riding instructors were so zealous they even forced her to endure physical hardships.

Her reaction to this abrupt and complete change in her whole way of life is related in one of the most significant pages in her *Memoirs*. Certainly it does much to explain the impulsive, ambivalent acts that marked her adult life. "My personal inclinations," she wrote, "seconded my father's designs in the most marvelous manner, for I had an unconquerable antipathy to all women's sayings and doings. Women's clothes and women's ways were alike insupportable to me. I never wore their headdresses. I never took any care of my complexion, my figure, or my person generally; and save in the matters of cleanliness and honorable conduct, I cherished a profound contempt for everything appertaining to my sex.

"I could not endure dresses with trains, but much preferred breeches. When visitors were present, I wore short skirts, especially when I visited one of my lodges in the country. I was so clumsy at all kinds of needlework that it was quite impossible to teach me how to do it. But, on the other hand, I was marvelously quick at learning languages and lessons of every kind."

A twentieth-century student, armed with the insights of Freud, finds it easy to understand Kristina's rejection of the feminine at this stage of her development. Her father-image was almost overpowering, and the years of enforced mourning she had spent with her mother caused her to loathe women. Certainly she tried hard to behave like a boy. She developed a masculine stride, she became an expert duelist and pistol shot, and she could handle any horse. Deliberately hardening herself, she kept her rooms cold in winter, and on the warmest summer days engaged in violent exercise. She spent her free time at the royal stables with the horses and dogs, she developed stamina by taking long walks and, scorning the elaborate meals prepared by the royal chef, she ate the food of the army: bread and cheese, dried beef, and salt herring.

She developed the mind of a logician, she cursed like an artilleryman, she argued with the skill of a rhetorician, and her manners were those of the cavalry troopers who had formed the backbone of Gustavus Adolphus' elite corps. She studied her father's military campaigns in detail and asked endless questions of his staff officers. One strong principle emerged — he had always favored a bold attack, striking hard before an enemy was prepared for battle and defending himself only when absolutely necessary. She resolved to emulate him. She became brusque, and the ladies of the court, whom she frequently reduced to tears, avoided her.

Some nobles were disturbed, feeling that the Regents were going too far, and that the late King would have been appalled if he could have known that his daughter was turning into a creature who was neither male nor female. And Marie-Eleonore, whom Kristina visited infrequently, became alarmed. But the one woman who was influential in Kristina's life, her aunt, Princess Katherine, was wise and discerning. She saw her niece daily and finally wrote a soothing letter to her distracted sister-in-law. "Fear not," she said firmly, "that the Regents are creating a monster. All children live in a world they fabricate from their own lively imaginations, and Kristina is no exception. She plays at being a boy and she enjoys herself immensely. But I have never seen a more feminine being, yourself included. Even when she tries to behave like a rough lout, she is conscious of her growing beauty and she flirts with everyone, her tutors, the sergeants of the palace guard, even the conscientious Oxenstjerna, whom God has seen fit to endow with all good qualities but the saving grace of humor."

Princess Katherine died when Kristina was thirteen, and Marie-Eleonore promptly applied for permission to return to Stockholm. But her plea was worded so hysterically, and she referred so frequently to her late husband, that the Regents knew she had not changed and they refused her request. Crushed and despondent, she made a journey to foreign lands, visiting her relatives in Brandenburg for a year, then going to Denmark, where she remained for an even longer period.

Kristina's training became more strict, with a committee of clergymen, professors, and generals advising the Regents. Her aptitude for foreign languages was remarkable, and she mastered French, German, Italian, Dutch, and Spanish. She became so proficient in Latin and ancient Greek that her tutors could teach her no more, and she read Livy and Homer, Tacitus and Aristotle, Cicero and Plato in the original.

She began to develop an independent, inquiring mind, and her refusal to take anything for granted caused troubles with her tutors in theology. She dutifully learned what they taught her, but she argued with them, refusing to accept dogma on faith. One day she became highly indignant when she asked a number of explicit directions regarding the Lord's precise program for the Day of Judgment, and when her poor tutor floundered, she remarked acidly that as he could not reply adequately, it was likely that mere mortals had erred and misunderstood God's intentions.

"The tutor administered a severe rebuke," Kristina notes in her *Memoirs*, "saying that it was an awful sin and an act of impiety even to entertain such thoughts, and that if ever I said anything of the sort to him again he would birch me."

She states that she made the following reply, "I promise not to say anything of the sort again, but I am not a small child any longer and I am not going to be birched. If anything of that kind is done to me, you will all be sorry for it. I am the Queen, and he who forgets my rank or would take advantage of my tender years does so at his peril."

Kristina's arrogance was an inevitable result of Oxenstjerna's policy, for the Chancellor actually encouraged her to assume an imperious air. He was unwilling to permit anyone else to teach her the intricacies of international affairs, and although he was working long hours governing the country, holding dissident factions together, and trying to recoup the losses Sweden had been suffering in the Thirty Years' War, he spent at least an hour each day with the young Queen from the time she was ten years old.

Kristina could have had no better tutor in politics. Oxenstjerna was so shrewd, clever, and farsighted that Cardinal Richelieu of France, the master diplomat of the age, paid him the supreme compliment when he said, "The Chancellor of Sweden is the only man in Europe who knows what is in my mind. When we communicate, each of us understands the nuances that lie behind the words of the other."

No ruler could have been trained by a greater man, and Oxenstjerna made Kristina conscious of her destiny. He taught her to think in terms of "my army" and "my navy, my policy of state and my people." The final transition to "my glory" and "my greatness" was easy to achieve.

"I took the keenest pleasure in hearing him talk," Kristina notes in her *Memoirs*. "There was no other lesson and no amusement which I did not gladly leave in order to listen to him. He, on his part, if I may say so without doing violence to modesty, took the greatest pleasure in instructing me. We often spent three, or four, or more hours together. More than once this great man had to express his admiration for a child in whom You, O Lord, had implanted such talents, such a desire to learn, and such an aptitude for learning — qualities which he admired without understanding them, for they are very rare at such a tender age."

Kristina's sixteenth birthday was a memorable occasion. She spent the better part of the day working with her tutors, as was her custom, then went for a long gallop. When she returned to her apartment at the palace, she was astonished to see her mother waiting for her. The Regents, relenting for the moment, had allowed Marie-Eleonore to pay a brief visit to Stockholm, and a surprise dinner party had been planned for the young Queen. But not even Oxenstjerna could have predicted the results of the meeting between mother and daughter. They were not strangers, as Kristina paid several brief visits to the Dowager Queen's estate each year, but this was the first time since Marie-Eleonore had been banished from the capital that she had seen her daughter in her own home.

When Kristina, her boy's clothes reeking of the stables, walked into the sitting room of her private suite, threw off her hat and tossed her riding crop onto a chair, Marie-Eleonore burst into tears. The Regents, waiting in an antechamber to join the celebrators, tried to make peace, but the Dowager Queen was inconsolable. "You have made my lovely daughter into a freak," she told the abashed Chancellor, and Oxenstjerna was forced to agree that perhaps he had obeyed Gustavus Adolphus' instructions too literally.

He reversed his policy after Marie-Eleonore told him that no ruler in Europe would want to marry a woman who looked like a man and, even worse, behaved like one. Since the most powerful weapon in the Chancellor's arsenal was a young queen whom he could marry to a powerful monarch of some other nation and thus form a binding alliance, Oxenstjerna embarked on a new campaign. Kristina was instructed to wear women's clothes at all times except the period she devoted to exercise each day. Two new governesses, both noble ladies of high station, were assigned to instruct her in the art of becoming more feminine, and Mathilde von Echner was brought to Stockholm to serve as the Queen's companion. Kristina protested violently, but the Chancellor ignored her temperamental scenes and she was forced to obey his wishes.

She made the adjustment far more quickly than any of her apprehensive tutors had believed possible. She let her hair grow long again, took an interest in cosmetics, and although she claimed that she despised women's attire, she accumulated a large wardrobe. But her arduous training had marked her character, and she could find no real peace within herself. "Men," she told Mathilde, "are fools, and I delight in ripping aside their flimsy cloaks of pretentiousness and exposing them naked in all of their foolishness."

When her eighteenth birthday approached, she shocked the Regents — with whose services she would dispense when she began to rule in her own right — by informing them that at the coronation ceremony she intended to wear a uniform like her father's. Even Chancellor Oxenstjerna failed to realize that she was teasing and begged her to reconsider. However, she continued to insist that she had made up her mind, and not until she appeared for the coronation, wearing a cloth-of-silver gown that complemented her fair hair, did the worried Regents finally understand that they had been the victims of a hoax.

Thousands of citizens from every province lined the streets of the capital to see the Queen in her coronation robes, and although the weather was bitterly cold, she rode in an open carriage. The wind whipped her hair, but she did not care, for Gustavus Adolphus' iron crown sat on her head for the first time, and the people cheered until they were hoarse. Kristina had made few public appearances, but she behaved with the dignity of a monarch accustomed to public acclaim, and someone coined the name, "Minerva of the North" for her.

She appeared before the Riksdag and made a brief, simple speech in which she promised to serve the interests of the nation at all times. In return, she said, she required the unalterable loyalty of all of her subjects. Members of the diplomatic corps glanced at each other in discreet amazement when, without preamble, she said she was opposed to "wars that cause so much death and misery, that impose a burden of taxation on our subjects and hinder our attempts to attain the destiny that the Lord has ordained for us."

Sweden was involved in two wars at the time: the Thirty Years' War was still dragging on, and a "minor" conflict with Denmark made it necessary to divert some funds, troops, and supplies from the principal fronts in Germany. The diplomats saw that some of the Regents, all of them members of the Council of State, also were surprised by the young Queen's unexpected declaration, which hinted that she was willing to negotiate for peace terms. Chancellor Oxenstjerna, who was seated at the left of the throne, remained impassive, however, and neither his own colleagues nor the foreign envoys knew that he was as astonished by Kristina's declaration as anyone else.

She concluded her speech by stating that she was asking the Chancellor to keep his post, in which he had served for so many years with distinction, and as the ceremony came to an end and they left for the reception at the palace, the members of the Riksdag felt reassured. With Oxenstjerna at the helm, they thought, there would be no major, abrupt changes in state policy. They did not know Kristina.

Her mother was the first to realize that the Queen intended to reign firmly in her own right. Marie-Eleonore foolishly hoped that she would be invited to return to Stockholm, and in the days immediately following her daughter's coronation, she spoke at length with the royal chamberlain about the decoration of a suite of rooms she planned to occupy. Kristina bluntly disabused her of the idea, and on the morning after the last coronation banquet was held, the Dowager Queen was riding back to her isolated country estate.

The daughter of Gustavus Adolphus had studied long and hard for her new role, and she was determined to rule her realm without interference from anyone.

III: 1644–1650
MINERVA OF THE NORTH

The Reverend Samuel Bochart, one of the great seventeenth-century students of language and philosophy and well known as pastor of a Protestant church at Caen in Norman France for many years, became rhapsodical when he spoke in the same rhyme of Kristina and the Queen of Sheba. At the time he penned the verse, he was a member of the Court of Divines and Scholars that had gathered at Stockholm.

But early in her rule, Kristina faced a number of immediate problems, and she threw all her energies into solving them before she allowed herself to relax with intellectuals and artists. The problems were closely intertwined; war and high taxes plagued Sweden, and the young Queen was determined to do something about both. Chancellor Oxenstjerna deluded himself into believing that he was still master of the nation's affairs until he learned, to his horror, that Kristina was negotiating with Sweden's enemies behind his back. In 1645, less than one year after her coronation, she concluded a peace treaty with Denmark. It was difficult for the Chancellor to complain, as she had obtained terms that were not harmful to Sweden, and it was a relief to be able to concentrate on the major struggle.

But success went quickly to Kristina's already inflated head, and, again intriguing in secret, the Queen entered into protracted negotiations that led to the Peace of Westphalia, which was signed in 1648. Kristina had been fortunate when she concluded the war with the Danes; Oxenstjerna's brilliant planning and the superb leadership of the troops in the field by General Lennart Torstensson had made Copenhagen even more eager to end hostilities than the Minerva of the North, so Kristina had been able to strike a favorable bargain. The Peace of Westphalia, however, was infinitely more complicated.

Since virtually every nation of consequence on the Continent had taken part in the Thirty Years' War, every country had suffered great losses and each one hoped to emerge with concrete benefits. Kristina, a child playing in a game with adults, signed away all that her father's military genius and the Chancellor's patient statesmanship had won. When the war ended, Kristina was hailed throughout Sweden as "the dove of peace." The people rejoiced and cheered their Queen more vociferously than ever, but Oxenstjerna was as angry as he was shocked. He knew, as did ministers in every chancery of every European capital, that the capriciousness of his young Queen had nullified his life's efforts. Sweden might have become the most powerful nation on the Continent had the Chancellor's plans prevailed, but Kristina preferred peace and paid a high price for it.

Her financial reforms were equally drastic, but here she accomplished more good than harm. Tax collections had fallen off badly, principally because both the peasants and the city artisans were almost penniless. The nobles paid no taxes, claiming exemption because of their exalted status, and the clergy also avoided making payments, on the grounds that their spiritual usefulness would be impaired if they were forced to part with money, which they considered a grubby necessity.

Cautiously, Kristina interviewed members of every class, summoning some to her study, riding out into the country to see others, and thus she formed her own conclusions. Then, confiding in neither the Chancellor nor the members of the council, she wrote a royal edict, composing it herself and publishing it on the first anniversary of her reign. The nobles and clergy were presented with a flat order: henceforth they would pay the greater share of taxes, and the poor would pay correspondingly less.

Kristina's popularity with the common people soared, but she made enemies of the most influential men in the land. Eventually, although she claimed that she did not care what they thought of her, their opposition forced her to adopt policies so radical that she was compelled to abdicate. That, however, is moving too far, too fast. The significant fact to note at this stage of her career is that she realigned the tax structure on a more equitable basis, and the principles she enunciated were so sound that even under her successors, neither the nobles nor the clergy were able to regain their privileged status.

Her personal life was far more important to her than the welfare of the nation, however, and as soon as she obtained freedom from supervision, she flaunted her liberty by engaging in a series of love affairs. Her long, repetitious statements on the subject in her *Memoirs*, considerably abbreviated here, are one of the most curious mixtures of truths, half-truths, and lies ever concocted. Perhaps at the time she wrote she believed what she said, for she had practiced self-deception for so many years that it had become difficult, if not impossible, for her to tell the difference between black and white.

> My ardent and impetuous temperament inclined me to love, not less than to ambition. [Her opening words hint at candor, but she could not compel herself to speak frankly.] To what disasters might not this inclination have brought me, if Thy saving grace had not employed my very faults for my correction! But my ambition and my pride, which made me incapable of submitting my will to that of another, but inspired me with scorn for everybody and everything, have preserved and protected me...
>
> Thou knowest that, whatever envy and slander may say, I am innocent of all the secret sins with which they have charged me in order to blacken my character...
>
> I solemnly declare that if I had not been born a girl, the tendencies of my temperament would assuredly have caused me to lead a shockingly disorderly life, but Thou hast made me prefer honor and glory to pleasure. You have guarded me from the disasters and temptations to which that ardent temperament of mine and the opportunities of indulgence which my position commanded exposed me...
>
> If I had felt myself too weak to resist temptation, I should have married ... but, finding that I could dispense with even the most legitimate pleasures, I did not attempt to overcome my unconquerable aversion to marriage.

Kristina protested too much.

The record speaks even more vehemently than her *Memoirs*. Her first love, or, to be more charitable, her first infatuation, struck when she was seventeen and still under the care of the Regents. The young man was her cousin, Charles Gustavus, the son of Princess Katherine. They had known each other all their lives, and when the young prince went off to the wars,

Kristina's sense of the romantic overwhelmed her. A letter she wrote to him on January 5, 1644, tells its own adolescent story:

> Beloved Cousin,
>
> I see by your letter that you do not venture to trust your thoughts to the pen. We may, however, correspond with all freedom if you send me the key to a cipher, and compose your letters according to it, and change the seals, as I do mine. Then the letters may be sent to Maria [Princess Maria, Charles Gustavus' sister]. You must take every precaution, for never were people here so much against us as now, but they shall never get their way so long as you remain firm. They talk a great deal of the Elector of Brandenburg, but neither he, nor any one else in the world, however rich he be, shall ever alienate my heart from you.
>
> My love is so strong that it can only be overcome by death, and if, which God forbid, you should die before me, my heart shall remain dead for every other, and my mind and affection shall follow you to eternity, there to dwell with you.
>
> Perhaps some will advise you to demand my hand openly, but I beseech you, in the name of our love and all that we deem holy, to have patience for some time, until you have acquired some reputation in the war, and until I have the crown on my head. I entreat you not to consider this time long, but to think of the old saying, "He does not wait too long who waits for something good." I hope, by God's blessing, that it is a good thing we both are waiting for.
>
> Ever thine, K.

By no stretch of even an adolescent girl's romantic imagination was Charles Gustavus a Lancelot. A heavy-set young man with a ruddy complexion, he was ambitious, coarse, and direct. He was valiant in war, but in the early stage of his life he displayed no other good qualities. He overindulged in beer and ale, he could not speak without injecting vulgar oaths into the simplest sentence, and, above all, he relished the soldier's prerogative of taking his love where he found it. Every military bivouac had its quota of camp followers, and Charles Gustavus was irresistibly drawn to a bold eye, a slender waist, and a trim ankle. Reports of his repeated infidelities drifted back to Stockholm, and within a few months Kristina's attitude changed sharply. A short time before her cousin returned for her coronation, she wrote him primly:

"Do not fear that the expression of your feelings will displease me; as a proof of your regard they are pleasing to me so long as you keep them within the bounds which are prescribed by your cousin and friend, Kristina."

The first real love of the Queen's life was a young man she had also known since childhood, Magnus Gabriel de la Gardie, the son of the renowned General Jacob de la Gardie and the lovely Ebba Brahé, with whom Gustavus Adolphus had been in love. According to a story that was commonly told, the young warrior king had paid court to Ebba, who, upon discovering that he was keeping a mistress, had refused his suit and married De la Gardie. The following year Gustavus Adolphus had married Marie-Eleonore.

Never one to allow personal feelings to stand in the way of duty, Gustavus Adolphus had used Jacob de la Gardie's talents frequently, and the General had become an important figure at the court before Kristina's birth. Magnus, two years her senior and one of her earliest playmates, had now grown into a handsome, accomplished young gentleman. He danced with the Queen frequently on the night of her coronation ball — the first time anyone had become aware of an attachment between them — and people immediately began to gossip.

Two weeks later, Mathilde von Echner made the first significant comment in her *Diary*. "This evening," she wrote,

"Her Majesty and I were reading aloud to each other, but were interrupted by the arrival of milord Magnus, surely the most dashing man in Stockholm. I was dismissed summarily, and they embraced before I finished curtsying, so anxious were they to kiss. My bedroom is located on the far side of the corridor from the main room of Her Majesty's apartment, so it has been impossible for me to ignore what has transpired since I was told to leave. The candles in the main room were extinguished at least three hours ago, but Magnus has not yet departed from the Queen's suite. I prophesy that Her Majesty and I will not read to each other again for many evenings to come."

The following week she made another, briefer notation: "I was right. When I read, I read alone."

Kristina showed little discretion and made no attempt to hide her feelings for Magnus. The crown was the largest landowner in the country, and one of the Queen's first official acts was to give Magnus de la Gardie a large estate on the Baltic and raise him to the rank of count. Others were far more deserving of honors, but she unhesitatingly heaped rewards on her favorite, and although the whispers became louder, she defied them by appointing him to one of the most important diplomatic posts in her service. A young man in his early twenties, with no experience, became the Swedish Ambassador to France.

Magnus was indiscreet, too, and Madame Françoise de Motteville, one of the inveterate gossips at the Louvre, was soon writing to a friend in Stockholm: "The Ambassador spoke of his Queen in terms so passionate that it was easy to suspect in him a feeling more tender than that which he owes to her as a subject. He has even hinted that, should she follow her own inclination, she would marry him."

The Queen's new love, rather than Charles Gustavus' infidelities, was responsible for the abrupt termination of her childhood romance with her cousin — or so she told him in later years. Bulstrode Whitelocke, the British Ambassador in Stockholm, sent a report to London which indicated that Magnus deserved "credit" for the rupture. Whitelocke said that a ranking member of the Riksdag had told him that Magnus had been responsible for the break between the royal cousins. "My source may not be reliable, although it has proved so in the past," the envoy wrote. "In this instance he swears that young De la Gardie, trying to improve his own position, poisoned the mind of the Queen before she was crowned, by whispering to her that Prince Charles Gustavus was too familiar with some ladies in the German states."

In any event, the romance between Kristina and Magnus was short-lived. The son of General de la Gardie was not considered sufficiently important to become the consort of a reigning monarch, and although there is no evidence today to suggest that various members of the council hinted to him that he would serve his own best interests if he forgot the Queen, it was widely believed at the time that various ministers had intervened. The facts speak for themselves. Magnus returned to Stockholm after spending a year in Paris and immediately began to pay court to Princess Maria, Charles Gustavus' sister, the girl Kristina had suggested as an intermediary during her adolescent flirtation with the warrior prince. No member of the royal family could be married without receiving written approval from the Queen. Apparently Kristina bore Magnus no grudge, for she granted her cousin permission to become the ambitious young nobleman's bride, and brushing aside plans for a quiet ceremony, insisted on giving the couple a state wedding.

In the meantime, pressure was being exerted on her from all sides to consider marriage herself. Oxenstjerna was corresponding with every Protestant court in Europe, negotiating for the most favorable terms. The nobles reminded the Queen frequently that the succession to the throne had to be made secure, and a group of eminent clergymen submitted a curt plea to Kristina. "Celibacy," they informed her, "is inconvenient to the individual and the State." Suitors appeared almost overnight, and Kristina was kept busy receiving foreign ambassadors. Princes from Denmark, the German states, and Poland were anxious to share her throne with her, but King Philip IV of Spain, although charmed by her miniature, took a more pragmatic view. He was a mature man, he informed her in a blunt letter, and if she preferred someone younger, his son was also available. He generously offered her a choice, saying that in either case she would sooner or later become Queen of Spain.

Philip's ardor cooled quickly, however, and he withdrew the proposal hastily when Oxenstjerna told the Spanish Ambassador that His Majesty and the Infante would be required to give up Catholicism and embrace the Lutheran faith before the offer could even be presented to the Queen.

Kristina found the furor boring. She had discovered that she was free to live as she pleased, and after having been dominated for so many years, she refused to submit again to the authority of any man. When she chose a lover he would have to be the suppliant, and she could dismiss him when he became tiresome. She would be deprived of her precious liberty if she married, and she gradually concluded that she would emulate Elizabeth of England.

To the distress of the Chancellor and the council, she made no secret of her decision. She held a ball, with the principal entertainment a masque in which she herself appeared, lightly clad as the goddess Diana. At the climax of the pantomime she broke Cupid's bow and arrow into small bits. Her meaning was clear to everyone present.

Late in life she had a medal struck, which offers a significant insight into her character. On one side was an idealized version of her profile as a young, beautiful woman, and on the other, the inscription, "I was born, lived and died free."

At first her advisers thought her attitude toward marriage was a passing whim, but they took her at her word when, at the age of twenty-two, she told the French Ambassador in all seriousness that she would rather die than marry. On the other hand, she made no secret of her preference for the company of men, and she confided in Mathilde that she could not tolerate more than one or two women at a time. "I dislike them in the lump," she said.

One of her jests on the subject became so famous that she repeated it frequently, and it appears in the correspondence of at least seven or eight prominent persons of the period. "I like men," she declared, "not because they are men, but because they are not women."

Her ridicule became sharper in her *Aphorisms*, which she wrote throughout her life for her own amusement. Inasmuch as she revised them frequently, copying them and changing their order, it is impossible to determine when she wrote either of the following passages:

> One needs more courage to expose oneself to the misfortunes of marriage than to face those of war. I admire the courage of those who marry, but people enter into this terrible contract, as they do so many other things in the course of their lives, without realizing its significance or the engagements to which it commits them.

Socrates, one of the wisest of men, said, "Whether you marry or refrain from marrying, you will be sorry." For my own part, I think that everyone who marries will infallibly be sorry, but I see no reason why anyone should be sorry for not having married. I speak from experience, so I do not offer this observation lightly.

It was not easy for a queen to turn her back permanently on the prospect of marriage, and the council made Kristina's life miserable. Charles Gustavus, who was so near to the throne yet so far from it, added his voice to the clamor. He paid court to her assiduously, and as he was heir presumptive to the throne, some of the nobles favored his cause. For a short time, Kristina appeared to give in to the pressures and said that she would allow an announcement of a formal betrothal to be made.

But she changed her mind before the necessary documents could be published. Charles Gustavus became so angry that he announced he would leave Sweden permanently, offer his sword to some other nation, and absent himself from his native land for the rest of his life. Maria stood next in the line of royal succession, but no one wanted a child of the upstart Magnus de la Gardie to sit on the throne. Oxenstjerna, who had little admiration for Charles Gustavus and was beginning to lose his enthusiasm for the young woman he regarded as his protégé, was forced to seek a diplomatic solution.

He spent the better part of a day alone with Kristina, and in the end he succeeded in establishing once more the relationship of tutor and pupil. The Queen, who had known what was in his mind from hints in his correspondence, and had opposed his scheme before he came to her, finally consented to it gracefully. She was determined to remain single, she said in an official pronouncement from the throne, but in order to safeguard the succession, she was officially naming her beloved cousin, Prince Charles Gustavus, her heir.

The nobles accepted the compromise because they were given no choice. Oxenstjerna admitted that he was unhappy, but he saw no alternative. Only Charles Gustavus was pleased, and although he had to face the strong possibility that he would die without being crowned, for Kristina's health was perfect, he stopped talking about going into exile.

The Queen's conduct caused incessant, although contradictory, comment throughout the courts of Europe. It was said in one breath that she was a libertine, and in the next that she had "neither the beauty nor the natural inclinations of a woman." The talk did not arise from idle curiosity, for Sweden was a powerful nation and the character of her ruler important to the monarchs and diplomats engaged in the endless tug of war of international politics. So Anne of Austria, Queen of France, instructed the Comte de Chanut, the French envoy to Stockholm, to submit a full report on Kristina. His account is probably the clearest and most impartial portrait of the controversial young Queen that has survived.

I have not presumed to stare at the Queen or to pay particular heed to the beauty with which she endowed [he began discreetly]. One in my position cannot afford to become known as a lecher. Nevertheless, I have observed Queen Kristina carefully.

The expression of Her Majesty's countenance, whatever may be passing in her mind, is always serene and agreeable. Yet it is true that, occasionally, when she is displeased with what is said to her, clouds, as it were, gather on her brow, to the alarm of those on whom she fixes her gaze.

Her voice, as a rule, is soft and low — a voice which, however firm her utterance, is unmistakably that of a girl. Now and again, without apparent cause, she adopts a tone rather louder than is usual with her sex, but she soon, and sensibly, relapses to a more ordinary modulation.

Her Majesty's height is a little below the average, but this would hardly have been noticeable if she consistently followed the custom of wearing the high-heeled shoes which ladies generally wear. She does not, however, and wears them only when it pleases her. At other times, in order that she may be able to go about the Palace, or to walk or to ride more conveniently, she only wears shoes with a sole and a little black heel, like those of a man.

I have been taxed to discover whether Her Majesty's nature is religious, and I cannot speak as her confessor nor as her counselor in matters of theology. However, as nearly as I can judge, she has a loyal attachment to Christianity, but she does not make any great public display of it, which may be the cause of so many vicious rumors about her beliefs. It is commonly known that she views the theological bickerings of hostile sects with a toleration which almost amounts to indifference, and the elaborate ceremonies of Lutheran public worship obviously bore her.

With my own eyes I have seen her at play with her black spaniel during prayer services at Church, and on one occasion I observed her reading Virgil during the Sermon. But I do not believe that these incidents prove that she lacks piety. Rather, I think they show that she is more interested in philosophy than in theology.

None who have conversed with her can doubt the excellence of her scholastic achievements. I, myself, have heard her speak Latin, Greek, French, German, Flemish, and Polish, as well as Swedish. Learned persons converse with her, in her leisure hours, of all that is most abstruse in the various sciences. Her intellect, eager for all kinds of knowledge, seeks information about everything. Hardly a day passes without her reading Tacitus — an author whom she calls her game of chess, and whose style is absolutely intelligible to her, or so she claims, though perplexing to many of the erudite.

Her Majesty's power and influence in the Council Chamber are enormous, and although it be true that only those who attend the meetings that take place behind the closed and guarded doors of the Chamber are privy to its secrets, the Grand Admiral, a blunt man, has said in the presence of several fellow Ministers without contradiction that when Her Majesty makes a decision, it is irrevocable, and her strength is even greater than that of Count Oxenstjerna. Some people, it is true, attribute the deference of her Ministers to the fact that she is a woman, believing that the attraction of her sex compels involuntary submission to her will, but the truth is that her great authority is due to her great qualities, and that a king who evinced the same qualities would wield an equal influence.

The discerning Comte draws a clear picture of Kristina's social life, too. "She hardly ever speaks to the ladies of her Court," he writes. Apparently unable to believe her own frequent complaint that she found members of her own sex dull, this French gentleman — who thought all women charming — discovered other reasons for her attitude. "Her addiction to sport and her interest in affairs of State leave her no time to engage in the small talk that is the spice of feminine life. She does not seek the society of ladies; they only pay her formal visits; and then, after the interchange of the ordinary civilities, she leaves them to themselves in a corner and converses with the men."

But she was impatient with men who had nothing of importance to say, and De Chanut notes, "When one babbles, Her Majesty cuts him short. It is her joy to dwell in the high realm of the intellect, and she states to all that her preoccupation with the mind of man makes sleep less necessary for her than for ordinary beings. She spends no more than five hours out of each twenty-four on her couch, unless it should happen that she is acting as hostess to a favored friend, in which instances, it may be fairly assumed, she enjoys even shorter periods of slumber. Lest it be imagined that she possesses extraordinary powers of physical endurance, it must be said that she invariably retires alone to her suite for two hours after dinner every evening. All activity at the Palace ceases during this time and resumes after Her Majesty has rested."

The Comte, who admired Kristina openly, based his conclusive judgment on her femininity, and here he praised and chastised her in almost the same breath. "When it pleases Her Majesty to shine more radiantly than other women, she is truly the Minerva of the North!" he exclaims. "On occasion, it amuses her to submit to the ministrations of her ladies, her hairdresser and other skilled persons who comprise her personal staff. Men who have seen her for the first time when she appears in all her glory invariably fall in love with her instantly.

"But," he continues sadly, "they are usually disillusioned the following day. Her Majesty takes her beauty for granted and attaches no importance to it, save when she becomes attached to a new friend. Ordinarily the adornment of her person means nothing to her — her division of the day assigns no time to her toilet. I am informed on the best of authority that it takes her only a quarter of an hour to dress; and, except on occasions of great ceremony, or at such times as those previously mentioned, she merely runs a comb through her hair and ties a bit of ribbon in it."

Grudgingly, he felt compelled to give Kristina her due, however: "Untidy hair, it is true, does not suit her badly. But she cares so little for her complexion that neither in the sun, nor in the wind, nor in the rain — neither in Stockholm nor in the country — does she ever wear either hat or veil. When she goes riding, a man's hat with a feather in it is her only protection from the weather; and no one who sees her in the hunting field, in her rough Hungarian riding habit, with a man's collar round her neck, would ever take her for a Queen."

His appraisal is balanced, and he tries to be fair. "Unquestionably Her Majesty carries this sort of thing too far — there are times when one fears it may be injurious to her health; but all these little eccentricities are as nothing when one thinks of her love for her country, for her nation's honor and virtue. Her great ambition, one may justly say, is to achieve fame through her personal merits rather than by her conquests, which appear to be only passing moments of fancy. As she has so often said, she would rather owe her reputation to herself than to the personal valor of her subjects."

A more jaundiced report was written several years later, probably in 1648 or 1649, by Father J.M. Mannerschied, a German Jesuit who was the Spanish Ambassador's confessor. Whether the priest was writing his own impressions or merely setting down on paper the views of the envoy is not made clear. Therefore, his observations are somewhat less valuable, for the Spanish Ambassador, having been made to look foolish when his sovereign proposed marriage either for himself or for his son, had reason to inspect Kristina with considerable prejudice.

In all probability, the words are those of the envoy and not the Jesuit, for Kristina at this period had not yet given serious consideration to renouncing her faith for Catholicism, so there would have been very little opportunity for the priest to see her, speak to her, or analyze her. The envoy, on the other hand, attended her daily at court, as did all other members of the diplomatic corps. "I have known the Queen for some years," the report begins, "and I will set down nothing except those facts which I have observed with my own eyes." So it is fairly safe to assume that the Ambassador, who may well have been a poorly educated grandee, dictated his thoughts to the priest.

The report itself opens on a lavish Iberian note. "Her Majesty of Sweden is a prodigy and one of the incomparable marvels of our age."

He proceeds to tear apart the image he has just created, however, and his touch is less than subtle. "Her brow is as broad as that of a philosopher, her nose resembles that of an eagle, and the look in her eyes is as piercing as that of an Inquisitor. There is nothing feminine about her except her sex. Her voice, her manner of speaking, her walk, her style, her ways are all quite masculine. Though she rides on a side-saddle to avoid ridicule, she holds herself so well and is so light in her movements that, unless one were quite close to her, one would take her for a man."

The detailed description of her person is still less flattering to the Minerva of the North.

> Her riding habit is a very cheap costume. I doubt whether it can have cost more than four or five ducats. At Court, too, she is usually very quietly dressed. I have rarely seen her wear any ornament of gold or silver in her hair or round her neck, nor is there any gold or silver embroidery on her clothes. In fact, her only article of jewelry is a ring, which she changes infrequently. She owns a variety of rare gems, among them diamonds, emeralds, rubies, sapphires, and other precious stones, but her favorite is a signet ring which belonged to her father, and which, I have been told, was removed from his finger after she ascended the throne. It is asserted that she ordered his crypt opened for this purpose.

Her Majesty of Sweden wears no rouge, powder, velvet face patch or other artifice favored by ladies here, as everywhere. Her hair is only dressed once each week, like that of merchants' wives. On Sundays she devotes half of an hour to her toilet, on week days, only a quarter of an hour. Often, when conversing with her, I have noticed that her chemise was splashed with ink, and I have sometimes observed that her linen was torn. Her companion, the Lady von Echner, has reminded her in my hearing that she ought not to be so careless; she replies that she leaves that sort of thing to people who have time for it. It is my opinion that she behaves as she does in order to shock the members of her Court, who, after the custom of the Swedes, are fastidious.

She boasts that she only allows herself three or four hours' sleep, going to bed very late and getting up very early. If any man knows otherwise, and there are many who would speak were it prudent, he remains silent. She says that for eighteen months she has done with no more than three hours' sleep a day. I have confirmed her claim that as soon as she is awake she devotes five hours to reading.

According to the Spanish report, Kristina was unable to find relaxation in the company of others. "It is a penance for her to dine with guests. When she dines alone, as she does most frequently, she spends barely half of an hour at table. She drinks nothing but water, and serves spirits to others reluctantly." Obviously, her antipathy to wine and beer was a direct consequence of the unfortunate experience she suffered in her childhood, although neither the Ambassador nor his confessor seems to have heard of her furious battle with her mother.

"There are French and German cooks in her kitchens, and she recently brought another to Stockholm from Warsaw. But they prepare meals to tempt the palates of others; Her Majesty of Sweden rarely glances at her plate, and is never heard to criticize her food or to remark that it is well or badly cooked.

"Her mornings are devoted to public affairs, and she regularly attends the meetings of her Council. Several Ministers have resigned their posts, and others threaten to follow. All make the same complaint; the Queen, they say, knows little or nothing about affairs of the State, yet she meddles in all things, upsets plans that have required great labor, and issues decrees without explaining the reasons for her orders to those Ministers charged with the responsibility for carrying out her wishes."

Twentieth-century knowledge of the human mind and emotions may suggest that Kristina was a guilt-ridden obsessive. Her pattern, as described in the Jesuit's words, might have been taken from the annals of a psychiatric journal: "One morning, in spite of the fact that she had been bled after suffering a rare disorder, she spent five hours at a Council meeting. Sometime later, when she was suffering from a fever which lasted for a month, she nevertheless continued, regularly, to attend to public business. God, she tells all who urge her to spare herself, has intrusted to her the government of her kingdom, and she will discharge the task to the best of her ability, in order that, even if she is not always successful, at least she will have no cause to reproach herself."

It was no wonder that the men who were trying to serve Sweden were annoyed, if Father Mannerschied's picture is correct.

> All public affairs pass through her hands, and she makes all
> final decisions. She settles all problems at once, taking no
> one's counsel; and when she harangues ambassadors, which is
> one of her favorite sports, she permits no interruptions from
> those who would urge her to speak more diplomatically.

Great generals, at whose names the German States tremble, stand mute and intimidated in the presence of their Queen, who takes delight in humiliating them and making them appear foolish. She reads all State Papers, all Treaties, and all Documents pertaining to the national welfare. It is her special joy to find a Latin phrase and explain its meaning at length to all who attend her. Her manner is frequently that of a tutor reprimanding refractory pupils.

Yet, in spite of her severity, she is cosmopolitan in her sympathies and informal in her manner. She frequently says she loves all nations and esteems virtue wherever it may be found. There are good and bad people in every nation, and she does not hesitate to expound the radical doctrine that many who do not espouse Christianity are good. Socrates, Plato, and Aristotle were not Christians, she tells those who would dispute her contention.

Her Majesty cannot endure the idea of marriage. Nothing can induce her to give herself to a husband because, she says, she was born free and intends to remain so. In ordinary conversation she is of such an easy familiarity that no one would take her for a great lady, not to say a Queen. Her informality and her use of words that are unseemly coming from the lips of one of high estate have led many who attend her to complain that she would be more at home in one of the city's public houses than in the palace of Gustavus Adolphus. There are some who secretly call her "Marta" because in appearance and manner she resembles a serving-woman at one of the city's wayfarer taverns.

She is the first to accost those with whom she wishes to converse, running up to them, taking them by the hand, and laughing and chaffing with them. She has maids of honor at her Court because the exigencies of pomp require her to do so, but she takes little notice of them and only converses with men. All men are of interest to her, and she cannot refrain from flirting with them, regardless of how high or low their station. When one is newly arrived at her Court, she sallies forth as from a castle to bend him to her will and she does not relax in the vigilance of her pursuit until he has succumbed to her charm. She is, it cannot be doubted, the only woman now alive, and perhaps, in all history, who is capable of captivating members of the other sex in eleven languages.

Kristina found time to explore every avenue of thought that attracted her, and she was drawn to virtually every aspect of government, the arts, and philosophy. Even had her personal life not been bizarre and her tastes erotic, she would have won a permanent place in history because of her contribution to the cultural development of a backward nation. The Renaissance had been in full bloom for one hundred and fifty to two hundred years when she ascended the throne, but Sweden continued to live in the Middle Ages. Kristina, whose education had been broader than that of many of the great scholars of her century, was appalled by the ignorance and illiteracy of her subjects, enraged by the complacent stupidity of the nobles, and shocked by the inability of the clergy to deal with the problem.

Gustavus Adolphus had made a clearing in the forest of darkness when he founded a Swedish university and systematically looted the libraries of cities he had conquered in order to secure books for the institution. But there were few schools in the country, and it was almost impossible for anyone except the sons of aristocrats to learn even the rudiments of reading and writing. The realization dawned on Kristina when she was seventeen that she was living in a cultural wilderness. It was impossible for her to discuss literature, science, or philosophy with any of her countrymen, and while the leading members of the clergy were learned men, they knew only one subject, theology.

The Comte de Chanut, the French Ambassador, became aware of her intellectual loneliness, and when she discovered that he was acquainted with many of the authors, artists, sculptors, and philosophers of France, England, and the Italian states, she bombarded him with questions about them. It was De Chanut who suggested that even the greatest scholars would be flattered to correspond with a queen, and Kristina began to write the first brief notes that were to have far-reaching consequences.

With De Chanut's assistance she composed shy, admiring letters to great men and was astonished when they replied at length. She became bolder, and by the time she attained her majority at eighteen, her correspondence with authors, scientists, and philosophers kept two secretaries busy. She sent expensive gifts to those who wrote her faithfully, and as there were no artists in Sweden capable of making objects of artistic value, she began to order gifts from Paris and Rome. Great men, she was beginning to learn, were human beings who responded to flattery, and by the time she was nineteen she began to deluge them with invitations to visit her court.

Most of them declined, for her reputation had preceded her invitations, and poets and essayists, philosophers and artists were reluctant to be drawn into a savage, iniquitous life. There were a few who expressed themselves bluntly: they were married, they said, and their wives, who had not been invited to accompany them, were opposed to their making the long journey. Others fell back on less obvious excuses: they were suffering from various ailments at the moment, the climate of Sweden was too severe, they could not afford to spend time away from their labors.

Nevertheless, a number of men of consequence did respond to Kristina's repeated invitations and visited her for periods ranging from a few weeks to many months. Her salon of scholars gradually gained renown and at least a measure of respectability, so it became easier as the years passed to attract intellectuals. At no time during Kristina's reign were less than ten scholars living at her court, and frequently more than twenty were her guests. Of these, the greatest star in the galaxy was Descartes.

During his lifetime, no intellectual was more revered than René Descartes, the French philosopher, metaphysician, and scientist, who spent many years wandering about Europe, finally settling in Holland. There the English princess, Elizabeth of the Palatine, granddaughter of James I and sister of Prince Rupert, the most renowned warrior in Christendom, became his patroness. Kristina opened her correspondence with Descartes when she was twenty years old. She was annoyed because Rupert, who had fought brilliantly in England against Cromwell, had achieved a reputation that was beginning to eclipse that of her father. And she asked Mathilde, "Is Elizabeth more learned than I? Is she more attractive to a scholar? Does she possess greater wit?"

The battle was joined, but Elizabeth, whose relationship with Descartes was completely innocent, was unaware of it. The middle-aged scholar had no idea that he was the object of a tug of war, but when Descartes showed her the Queen's letter, Elizabeth realized instantly that Kristina was trying to woo her favorite and deprive her of glory. It was a subtle, seemingly innocent little document. Kristina blandly stated that she was vexed by a problem she could not solve. Did the abuse of hatred or the abuse of love open the door to more perilous possibilities?

Amused and mildly flattered, Descartes replied briefly that the subject was too complicated to be answered in a few paragraphs.

This was precisely what Kristina had hoped he would say, and she promptly invited him to visit Stockholm.

His reply was a masterpiece. "Madam," he wrote gracefully, "if a letter had come to me from Heaven, and I had seen it fall from the clouds with my own eyes, I could not have been more surprised or have received it with more respect and veneration than the communication which Your Majesty has deigned to send me inspires. I feel myself so little worthy of the expression of thanks contained in it that I can only accept it as a favor and an act of grace for which I shall always owe Your Majesty a debt which I shall never be able to pay."

After continuing in the same vein for several pages, he finally came to the point. "I regret that my present infirmity makes it impossible for me to make the long journey to Sweden. I am unable to ride more than a short distance at a time, and am not able to spend whole days in the saddle."

Elizabeth had intervened neatly and had expressly forbidden Descartes to leave. As he was satisfied with his life, he was content to remain in Holland. But he failed to reckon with Kristina's tenacity and determination. Her next letter was sweet and short. It would delight her, she said, to send a Swedish warship to Holland. Nothing would please her more than to place the vessel at the disposal of the most distinguished scholar of the age, who would thus be spared even a short ride on horseback.

But Elizabeth remained adamant, and again Descartes declined. Kristina enlisted the aid of the Comte de Chanut, who wrote to the philosopher, urging him to accept. The power of France was being thrown into the struggle, and

Descartes began to reconsider. The fortunes of Elizabeth's family had dwindled considerably. Her uncle, Charles I, had lost his throne and his head, Prince Rupert was in exile, and Elizabeth's mother had offered to sell her jewels in order to aid the cause of her nephew, who would eventually return to England as Charles II.

Kristina sensed Descartes' hesitation, and, wasting no more time, sent the newest and best-appointed frigate in her navy to Holland. A Swedish admiral in full uniform presented the Queen's urgent invitation, and Descartes capitulated. His farewell meeting with Elizabeth was painful, and he assured her that the principal concern of his life was to achieve a reconciliation between the two "most scholarly women of our century."

Descartes, arriving in Stockholm on a blustery autumn day in 1649, immediately regretted his decision to leave the comforts of Holland. As soon as he was shown to the suite which had been made available to him, he wrote to Elizabeth, assuring her fervently that "neither change of air nor change of climate can diminish my devotion to you."

Kristina was eager to see her guest, but their first two meetings were dismal failures. The Queen received him in a private audience, and her personality irritated the philosopher. He found her informal manner annoying, and he was outraged when she tried to argue with him. His views had been accepted without question for many years by everyone whom he had seen and corresponded with, and the young woman who impertinently harangued him caused him to lose his patience, his sense of humor, and his perspective.

But he could not admit to Elizabeth that he had made a mistake and after his second meeting with the Queen, he wrote to his former patroness, "Her Majesty has all the virtue and more than the merit which common report attributes to her."

In an attempt to soothe the princess' ruffled feelings and smooth the path for his return to Holland, he wrote, "One of the first questions which Her Majesty asked me was whether I could give her news of you, and I allowed no affectation to hinder me from setting forth my high opinion of Your Highness." Having been told that Kristina felt such a proprietary interest in the scholars who came to her court that all of their correspondence was read and reported to her, he added another sentence for his hostess' benefit. "I had remarked Her Majesty's magnanimity and was sure that she would not be jealous, just as I am sure that Your Highness will feel no jealousy in reading my account of this great Queen's sentiments."

Descartes tried valiantly to make the best of a situation that he detested. He was horrified when he discovered that Kristina was not satisfied merely to house scholars under her roof, but wanted to show them off before her court. Naturally she was anxious to exhibit the prize she had finally won after angling so long and carefully, and the philosopher was obliged to attend several receptions and levees. At these functions he wore his best wig which, he said, "sat heavily on my head"; and his new shoes, which had been made for him before he had left Holland, "were so pointed that they pinched my toes."

He had no use for sycophants; pseudo intellectuals irritated him; and the few men he could genuinely admire — members of the royal council — were pragmatists who were dealing with day-to-day problems. He tried to establish a rapport with them, and they made an effort in return, but Descartes could not speak their practical language, and his abstract thought soared above their heads. He was lonely, restless, and bored.

Kristina, on the other hand, was hurt and bewildered. She was proud of her learning. Other visitors had taken care to flatter her, and apparently she was incapable of realizing that her brilliance might fail to dazzle a man of Descartes' stature. She was stunned when he rebelled and sent word to her through Mathilde that he would not attend a diplomatic reception. No one had ever treated her in such a cavalier fashion and, unwilling to let others see she had been snubbed, she canceled the affair.

Descartes began to think seriously about leaving the barbaric northern kingdom, but was reluctant to make a journey either by land or sea as the weather was becoming colder each day. He reconciled himself to the thought that he would be compelled to wait, but, no longer caring whether his hostess read his mail, he wrote recklessly to Princess Elizabeth, "I do not think I am likely to be detained in this country after next spring."

The appalled Kristina summoned the Comte de Chanut to an emergency meeting. Her reputation as a scholar would be destroyed if Descartes continued to sulk until he left the country, and in desperation she appealed to the French Ambassador for help. His advice was blunt: she, who submitted to no discipline except her own, would have to meet Descartes on his terms. She was not his equal, and it was absurd to pretend that their relationship could be anything but that of tutor and pupil.

Mathilde von Echner recounts the Queen's surrender in a single line in her *Memoirs*: "She swallowed her gall and surrendered."

Descartes could not refuse to meet his hostess in a private audience, and Kristina capitulated to him. She would not ask him to attend any more public functions, she said, and she gave him her royal word that all their future meetings would be informal. She was anxious to learn all he was willing to teach her, and would be grateful if he would consent to spend three mornings each week instructing her in philosophy and science. He had made her conscious of her ignorance, and she would not argue with him in the future, but would listen attentively and make every effort to acquire wisdom.

Relieved and mollified, Descartes accepted the conditions. Kristina enjoyed a fleeting triumph when she informed him that since her duties occupied the ordinary working day, he would be obliged to come to her at five o'clock in the morning for her lessons. Descartes, trapped, was forced to agree.

Each Monday, Wednesday, and Saturday he appeared, shivering, at her private suite before dawn, and spent four hours discussing the intricacies of his abstruse metaphysical beliefs with her. She was an apt student, but Descartes, unaccustomed to the raw cold, the chill that crept through every room, and the ever-present dampness that ate into his bones, was miserable. And Kristina, having won a minor victory, tried to enlarge it. She decided to give a grand ball to celebrate the Treaty of Münster, which had just been initialed, and she invited Descartes to dance in the ballet that she planned to direct.

He stalked out of her suite, and she was compelled to go to his rooms, apologize, and humbly retract the suggestion. Perhaps, she said, he would write a few appropriate lyrics for the occasion. Realizing that this spoiled young woman held the power of life and death over everyone in her realm, he agreed reluctantly, performed the task, but refused to attend the celebration. The relationship again became strained, and he made no secret of his desire to return to Holland as soon as the weather permitted.

But the winter and the early hours were too much for him, and on February 1, 1650, he became ill. Three royal physicians examined him and agreed that he was suffering from congestion of the lungs. In their anxiety to cure the great man they prescribed three different courses of treatment for him, meanwhile squabbling incessantly. On February 10, Descartes died.

There is a brief, unsavory postscript to his tragic sojourn in Sweden. When the grief-stricken Princess Elizabeth learned, through De Chanut, that her friend and mentor was dead, she replied that she wanted all her letters to him returned. Kristina became obstinate and refused. De Chanut, his diplomatic talents strained to the breaking point, informed Elizabeth that he wanted to present the letters to the Queen, who, "moved by the spectacle of virtue unaffected by jealousy, would be very glad to be confirmed in the singularly high opinion which she has formed of the character of Your Royal Highness."

Elizabeth could be stubborn, too, and she repeated her demand, hinting broadly that if she failed to receive every letter intact, she would be inclined to believe her worst suspicion, that the Queen had been responsible for Descartes' death. De Chanut used all of his persuasive powers to convince Kristina that if she remained adamant, Elizabeth would ruin her good name. The Queen saw the sense of his argument and gave in, but, showing her ire, sent the letters by ordinary post rather than by special messenger.

Kristina's relations with other scholars were prickly, too. Few of the distinguished men who came to her court enjoyed themselves, and the nobles, resenting the superior learning of the foreigners, made no secret of their contempt for the intellectuals.

One of the most distinguished men whom Kristina lured to Stockholm was Claude de Saumaise, the Burgundian scholar and historian whose knowledge of the ancient world was so great that he Latinized his name and was known as Claudius Salmasius. He held a professorship at the University of Leyden, at the time one of the leading institutes of learning in Europe. A vigorous man with definite opinions, he thrived on controversy, attacking the Vatican with such fervor that Protestants everywhere took up his cause, and then, to prove his versatility, he published a defense of Catholicism that left many of his former friends gasping.

A man of such a mercurial temperament inevitably appealed to Kristina, and she sent him repeated invitations to visit her, using the same technique she employed with Descartes. In Salmasius' case also, a woman tried to thwart her; her foe, who was formidable, was the historian's wife. The former Anne Mercier was a member of a noble French family, a lady whose opinions were as decided as those of her husband and whose will was as strong as Kristina's. She had made her husband something of a laughing stock by designing a gaudy costume that, she felt, was in keeping with his rank as one of the greatest scholars on earth. Aware of his lack of social poise, she attended all of his lectures, permitted him to attend no dinners or other functions without her, and generally kept him on a tight leash.

Kristina's invitation was, as usual, extended only to the husband, and Madame Salmasius balked. But there was a weak spot in the good lady's armor: she entertained social ambitions, and when the Queen sent her husband letter after letter, made him a gift of a chased gold cup and an embossed silver dish, she finally relented. She permitted him to obtain a six months' leave of absence from the university and allowed him to go off alone to Sweden.

He was so clumsy and ill at ease and lived in such dread of his wife's next letter that Kristina was bitterly disappointed in him. He wrote like a lion but lived like a mouse, she said, and he was so awkward that "He knows the name for the word 'chair' in at least eighteen languages, but he is incapable of sitting on one with grace." His reliance on his absent wife also irritated Kristina, and she said that his patience in putting up with her was even more exemplary than his learning.

Gilles Ménage, a French scholar who was visiting Stockholm at the same time and who quarreled with Salmasius, is responsible for a story that Mathilde corroborates. One day, Ménage writes, Salmasius remained in bed, having drunk too much strong Swedish wine the previous evening at dinner, but, afraid of offending the Queen, sent word merely that he was indisposed. Kristina, accompanied by Mathilde and Ebba Sparre, the prettiest and youngest of her ladies in waiting, promptly called on him.

> Her Majesty [Ménage says], found the noble scholar in bed. He was reading a book which, out of respect for her, he closed as soon as he saw her enter. She asked him what book it was, and he admitted that he was enlivening the tedium of his illness by reading a collection of stories which were, he was bound to admit, not suitable for the eyes of a lady.
>
> "Aha!" said the Queen, "I must look at it. Show me the good things."
>
> M. Saumaise showed her one of the stories, and she read it through to herself, smiling as she did so. Then she said to the beautiful Mlle Sparre, her favorite maid of honor, who knew French, "Come, Sparre, look at this handsome work of devotion entitled *How to Become Friendly with Ladies*. I want you to read this page aloud to me."

The fair maiden had not read three lines before she stopped and blushed, startled at the improprieties, but as the Queen, who was holding her sides with laughter, peremptorily ordered her to continue, her modesty did not save her. The poor girl had to read every word.

The Queen enjoyed the discomfort of M. Saumaise even more than she relished the embarrassment of the maid of honor, and when Mlle Sparre at last completed her odious assignment, the Queen seized the hand of M. Saumaise and declared that he was suffering from a chill. She said, "I am not a physician, but I can prescribe a remedy for you."

Before the maids of honor could dissuade her, she opened the sash of her gown and entered the bed. M. Saumaise tried to escape from her by retreating to the far side, but the Queen caught hold of him with a firm hand and pulled him close to her. Then she dismissed the maids of honor and remained to heal the ailment from which M. Saumaise was suffering.

When Ménage published the account of the incident some years later, Kristina, then in Rome, denied the story vehemently. But Mathilde, reading it while preparing her *Memoirs*, states succinctly, "I had forgotten the occasion, as there were many of the sort at that time. But M. Ménage has not told an untruth. He has omitted only to say that Her Majesty first tried to persuade me to crawl into the bed, and when I refused, told Ebba to crawl in, knowing that she would not."

Salmasius was rewarded for his services to the Queen, and when he returned to Leyden and his wife, Kristina gave him a handsome pension. The Swedish government continued to honor the obligation after her abdication, and Salmasius received a purse every year until he died. Perhaps it was not accidental that Kristina ordered the payment made on the anniversary of the day when she visited his sickroom.

Her sense of humor found various other outlets, too, and most of her pranks were rough, bawdy, and distinguished by a quality strongly reminiscent of an army barracks. Perhaps the most famous incident, which increased her notoriety throughout Europe, occurred on her twenty-second birthday. She held a reception that afternoon, and the palace was crowded with members of the diplomatic corps and Swedish nobles. Kristina accepted their congratulations, and then announced that she had prepared an unusual expression of thanks. She had assembled a number of young girls, all of them less than twelve years of age, daughters of courtiers, and had taught them a song which she hoped her guests would appreciate.

The children filed into the throne room, formed three rows and began to sing in French, which none of them understood. Few of the Swedish court present knew the language, either, but all of the foreign envoys spoke it, and Kristina watched their faces as the girls sang a vividly off-color song about the adventures of a courtesan. The Swedish nobles realized that something out-of-the-ordinary was happening when the Queen rocked back and forth on her throne, laughing silently, and the diplomats stood, red-faced and frozen, until the "concert" ended. The practical joke was successful, but Kristina made a number of bitter enemies that day, for the parents of the children who had been tricked were furious, and some never forgave her.

Gerhard Vossius the younger, son of a distinguished German clergyman and classical scholar, was another of Kristina's intimates and was associated with her for a longer period than most of the intellectuals she brought to Stockholm. Vossius was a man of considerable talent, and the Queen enjoyed conversing with him in classical Greek. She took pleasure in insulting him publicly, too, but he accepted her abuse with a cheerfulness that some of his contemporaries considered remarkable. But, contrary to the impression he created, Vossius was no meek weakling; he was a rogue, a shrewd opportunist, and an unprincipled but clever thief. It might be noted, parenthetically, that many years later, Charles II of England appointed him canon of Windsor, remarking facetiously at the time that he thought Vossius was particularly well qualified for the post because "he is a credulous person who believes everything except the Bible."

During the years of his sojourn in Stockholm, he shared Kristina's passion for manuscripts and books, and she gave him large sums to purchase his library. After he won her confidence, he persuaded her to appoint him custodian of her library, too, and thereafter purchased all of her books. Not until some years after she abdicated did it become known that he had pocketed considerable sums, sometimes charging her two or three times the price he had paid for a book, and that he had calmly expanded his own library at her expense and without her knowledge. She thought she was demonstrating her superiority when she treated him with condescension, but Vossius enjoyed the last and heartiest laugh.

A bibliophile of a different sort who visited Kristina was Pierre Daniel Huet, a French priest who was not only a theologian, but a mathematician, astronomer, classicist, chemist, and author. His learning was as prodigious as his education had been unorthodox. A Jesuit, he had studied for some years with Protestant instructors, and it was said of him that he could argue any side of any subject with equal facility, pungency, and brilliance. Later in his career, Louis XIV made him tutor to the dauphin, and subsequently he was appointed bishop of Avranches.

He was a somber man who refused to lead the double life that Kristina expected of her scholars. During the months he visited Stockholm, he spent most of his time in the royal library, and to this extent, scholarship in general is in Kristina's debt, for he found some fragments of the *Commentary on St. Matthew*, written in approximately 240 A.D. by the most distinguished of ancient Christianity's theologians, Origen.

Father Huet was fascinated, and although Kristina complained bitterly that he ignored her and spent all of his time in the library, he prolonged his stay until he had read all of the fragments. It was during this time that he conceived the idea of editing all of the works of Origen and translating them into French, a monumental task which he finally completed in 1668. He was regarded during his lifetime as one of the great thinkers of the century, but Kristina was still irritated when she wrote about him in her *Memoirs*, in 1686.

"Fr. Huet," she said, "was a rude, busy little man who showed scant regard for the common courtesies that civilized people hold dear. His eyesight was poor, which made it difficult to converse with him on the few occasions when he could be persuaded to leave my library. When I spoke to him, I found it impossible to judge whether he was looking at me or blinking away tears that had accumulated as a result of too much reading."

Nikolaes Heinsius, son of one of the most gifted classicists of the Dutch Renaissance, Daniel Heinsius, was a scholar more to the Queen's taste. A poet and also a translator of classics, he was given a post on the staff of the University of Leyden because of his father's reputation. But he had no aptitude for a life devoted to teaching, and a notice on the door of his lecture hall marked the abrupt end of his career. "Professor Heinsius," the statement said, "regrets to announce that the consequences of last night's debauch prevent him from lecturing this morning."

Soon afterward he began to travel from one country to another, searching for classical manuscripts, and to the astonishment of the scholars who had turned away from him in despair, he reformed. He became honest, conscientious, and hard working, and his poems were universally recognized as gems of classical purity. It was inevitable that he should find his way to Stockholm, where he and the Queen discovered they were kindred spirits. They drank nothing stronger than water, they discussed the ancients by the hour, talking in either Latin or Greek, depending on which was the more appropriate, and they explored metaphysical problems at length. Then, tiring of the exercise of their minds, they delighted in concocting practical jokes together, they went for long rides in the country, they fenced with sabers, much to the alarm of the Queen's staff, and they sang ribald songs in Latin.

Heinsius' admiration for Kristina was genuine, and he seems to have been one of the few people who understood her mercurial temperament. She had decided to enlarge the university her father had founded, and when Heinsius left Sweden, she commissioned him to purchase books for the institution. He agreed, refused to accept any fee for himself, and in the course of his travels fulfilled his mission faithfully and fervently. After visiting Milan, Florence, and Rome, he wrote to the Queen, "The Italians are complaining that ships leaving their shores are laden with the spoils of their libraries, and that all of their best aids to learning are being carried away from them to the remotest North."

Certainly, Kristina's interest in learning was real, in spite of her increasingly eccentric behavior. She gave large sums of money to the university, imported professors whom she paid high wages, and donated a valuable tract of crown land for another university, at Uppsala. Her talks with visiting scholars made her aware of the glaring deficiencies in Swedish education, and after brooding on the unfortunate situation for several years, in 1649 she issued an edict, a document unique in its day, that laid the foundations for the remarkably high educational standards Sweden subsequently achieved.

Under its terms, anyone in the land who wanted an education would be given the opportunity to obtain one, regardless of class or wealth. She established large numbers of primary and secondary schools, imposed a tax on all her subjects to support them, and gave such large sums from the crown purse for the purpose that her ministers became alarmed. Sensitive to the preferential treatment given to boys, she decreed that girls also were to be educated, if they showed intellectual promise. When she issued her order, it was considered revolutionary.

Perhaps her greatest achievement in education was to insist that the school system be organized by an expert, and at her insistence Chancellor Oxenstjerna brought Jan Komensky, a Bohemian-born, German-educated scholar, to Stockholm. Following the custom of the period, Komensky adopted a Latin name, and, calling himself Comenius, resigned his position as a bishop of the Bohemian Protestant church and came to Sweden in 1642.

His ideas were even more revolutionary than Kristina's edict, but the Queen approved of his plans and gave him her full support. It was Comenius' theory that education had become almost meaningless, that the revival of interest in the classics, an important feature of the early Renaissance, had been reduced to meaningless rote. He believed that a man was truly educated only if he knew something about the world in which he lived, and he insisted that courses in economics, geography, science, and history be included in every school's curriculum. He believed it important for children to know the history of their own country, and he felt that since not everyone was endowed with the intellect to receive a higher education, those students who would not benefit by attending universities should be taught useful trades.

Kristina gave Comenius a free hand, and although many of the nobles protested, she held her ground so firmly in the face of their opposition that succeeding monarchs could not change the pattern that she and Comenius established. The task of pulling Sweden out of the Dark Ages into the sunlight was complicated by other than members of the nobility, however. The clergymen, with a few notable exceptions, were opposed to change, and the peasants, in their ignorance stubbornly clinging to their old ways, resisted advances. The students themselves often created problems, for a feeling of national pride had begun to develop during the reign of Gustavus Adolphus, and young men who attended the universities resented the foreign instructors who had been engaged by the Queen.

Comenius was aware of the problem, and in a report to Kristina he wrote that the ideal situation would be one in which all professors were natives. Unfortunately, however, few men of Swedish birth were qualified to instruct their compatriots, and those who had studied abroad encountered hostility when they joined the faculties that Kristina was establishing. The troubles that vexed a professor named Georg Stiernhielm were typical. A scientist and classicist, Stiernhielm returned to Sweden after a long sojourn in Germany, and the Queen immediately gave him a position at Uppsala. The university there was an unusual institution. It had been founded in the fifteenth century, had flourished for a time as a school of theology and gradually, over the course of two centuries, had fallen into decay. Kristina granted it a new charter and poured gold into its coffers, but she discovered that it was impossible to transform it into a modern school overnight.

Professor Stiernhielm brought the microscope and the burning glass home from his travels, and in his classroom he demonstrated their marvels. He showed his students a flea under the microscope, and in a dramatic demonstration of the power of the glass, burned the long beard of a peasant. He was arrested, thrown into prison, and tried before a provincial court. The peasant declared that he was a sorcerer, and a pastor who had been present when the flea had been exhibited under the microscope, testified that the professor was an atheist. Stiernhielm was sentenced to burn at the stake. The case was called to Kristina's attention, and she hastily reversed the order, restored the professor to his former position and rebuked the court.

But a few months later, Stiernhielm's life again was threatened. He made the statement in a lecture that Hebrew was an older language than Swedish, and this startling pronouncement so infuriated his students that they rioted. A detachment of royal cavalry saved the professor's life and escorted him to Stockholm, where Kristina expressed her opinion in terms that no one could misunderstand: she made Stiernhielm a noble and expelled the rioters from the university.

Life was even more hazardous for the foreigners, as Jean Boecler, a distinguished Latin scholar from Strasburg discovered. He had been recruited by one of the Queen's agents, and, unable to resist the lure of extraordinarily high wages and the promise of numerous honors, he came to Uppsala with his wife. He was given a comfortable house, Kristina sent him a letter urging him to teach as he saw fit, and he threw himself into his work enthusiastically.

But he soon found that his students were surly and suspicious; they were reluctant to accept anything he told them, they made no secret of their loathing for foreigners, and although attendance at lectures was compulsory, they frequently sat in his classroom with their arms folded, obstinately refusing to take notes. Boecler finally lost his temper, and terminating a lecture on Tacitus abruptly, declared imprudently, "I would say more if the wooden heads of the Swedes could comprehend it."

The infuriated students ran to the podium, caught Boecler before he could escape, and after ripping off his academic gown, stripped him naked. Several of the young men laid him across his desk, and the rest of the class took turns beating him with a birch rod until his screams attracted the attention of the troops who were now stationed permanently at the university. The students, still dissatisfied and determined to obtain further vengeance, attacked Boecler's house that night, breaking all of the windows and terrorizing his wife.

The angry, humiliated scholar went to Stockholm the following day and resigned his post. Kristina tried to soothe him and gave him a purse of four thousand pounds and a magnificent gold chain. She offered him the position of official court historian, but Boecler wanted no more of Sweden, and he and his wife returned to Strasburg immediately. The students were imprisoned and flogged, but the incident had international repercussions and it was impossible to find a scholar willing to take Boecler's place.

The Queen was discovering that it was extraordinarily difficult to lead people who would not follow her.

During the early years of her reign, Kristina's domestic policy was sound. Her studies of economics had convinced her that Sweden could not become a great power unless the nation was prosperous, and she issued a large number of decrees that strengthened the economy. She encouraged the export of timber and the development of the mining industry, she abolished old laws that restricted the growth of towns, and she used the royal treasury liberally to help the artisans' guilds establish themselves on a sufficiently sound basis to compete with the weavers and carpenters and masons of Germany, France, and the Low Countries.

The lower chamber of the Riksdag approved her edicts without question, but the senate, which was composed of nobles and high-ranking clergymen, was more conservative and occasionally tried to block her reforms. She settled the problem briskly and in her own manner. Ignoring the protests of the irritated Oxenstjerna, she enlarged the ranks of the nobility, creating counts and barons until her followers outnumbered the old aristocracy. Most of those to whom she gave titles were foreign military officers who had served under her father. They were willing to allow her a free hand in domestic affairs, but the established families were horrified when she gave thousands of acres of crown lands to the new lords.

The country became stronger, and after the end of the Thirty Years' War, Sweden enjoyed an unprecedented era of prosperity. The reports that foreign envoys sent back to their chanceries were written in the same vein: fisheries and the timber industry were booming, Swedish ships were carrying her raw materials to other lands in ever increasing numbers, and new mines were being opened. Sweden was emerging from the Middle Ages in spite of herself, and in 1649, the Queen's popularity reached its zenith.

But Kristina displayed increasingly frequent signs of frivolousness, and gradually her behavior became even more irrational. When the Reverend Samuel Bochart sat down with her in private audience to discuss theology, the Queen ordered him to amuse her by playing the flute. He was too astonished to protest and could only mutter that he was not a musician. She thought his reply was hilarious, and offered him an alternative: she challenged him to a game of battledore and shuttlecock and suggested that he decide the stakes. When he courteously informed her that he was a student, not an athlete, she burst into tears, dismissed him, and spent the rest of the day sulking in her apartment.

She, who had usually enjoyed perfect health and had been ill only rarely, began to complain of fevers, and occasionally she suffered from fainting spells. The royal physicians examined her daily, much to her annoyance, but could find nothing wrong with her. Yet her eccentric behavior was becoming scandalous; she could not concentrate on problems of state for any length of time, she treated the members of her council like lackeys, and delighted in playing practical jokes on everyone.

In brief, the neurotic pressures to which she had been subjected all of her life had been intensified by overwork, and she developed a severe nervous condition.

It was at this critical period in Kristina's life, in 1650, that the notorious "Doctor" Bourdelot entered her life.

IV: 1650–1654
THE UNHAPPY REVELER

"Doctor" Bourdelot, son of a French barber, was born in the town of Sens. He was apprenticed to his father and, since barbers in the seventeenth century sometimes performed operations, he had a tenuous right to call himself a surgeon. However, he had never studied medicine, had virtually no knowledge of the subject, and was branded a charlatan by the most eminent physicians of the age, in France, in the Italian states, in Brandenburg, and in Sweden. He conveniently changed his Christian name wherever he traveled, taking a local name in order, as he said, "to give my patients greater confidence in me." In Germany he was known as Johann, in Rome he called himself Giovanni, and when he came to Stockholm in 1650, it pleased him to refer to himself as Gustavus Bourdelot.

He was such an inveterate liar that it is difficult, if not impossible, to distinguish truth from fiction in that portion of his career that preceded his sojourn in Stockholm. He claimed that he had been the personal physician of the Prince de Condé, but it is more likely that he served for a time as an assistant apothecary in the Prince's household and there learned a few rudiments of medicine. He enjoyed a vogue in Rome for a time, returning to Paris with the preposterous story that he had administered to the Pope, who had been gravely ill. He had cured His Holiness, he said, and had been offered a cardinal's hat, but was so devoted to his own profession that he had declined.

There can be no question that Bourdelot was a rogue, but he was evidently a man of considerable charm, and he had acquired a smattering of learning in his travels. Apparently he amused various scholars, among them Salmasius, at whose suggestion he was invited to Stockholm. Kristina did not summon him to become her physician. Salmasius, as nearly as can be determined, merely described his friend as a man of wit and intelligence. No other recommendation was required, and the Queen sent a letter to Bourdelot, who wasted no time in setting out for Sweden from Paris.

A few days after his arrival in Stockholm, Kristina was stricken again and went to bed. Her complaint was as vague as it was general, and the royal physicians prescribed an elixir which, they said, would restore her to perfect health in a few days. A short time after the physicians had departed, Bourdelot appeared unbidden at the royal suite, and Kristina granted him a brief audience. She had imagined that the purpose of his visit was social, but he assumed a professional air, examined the palms of her hands and her fingernails, looked into her eyes, and felt her forehead.

The treatment that had been prescribed for her was wrong, he said, and he threw out the bottles of elixir. The physicians, warned by a lady in waiting, returned, and a violent battle of words was fought in the Queen's presence. The learned doctors accused Bourdelot of being a charlatan. He, in return, attacked them vigorously, saying they lacked imagination and were the slaves of a pernicious professional routine. Their medicine could not cure Her Majesty, he insisted; what she needed was a complete change in her style of living.

Her curiosity aroused, Kristina dismissed the physicians and asked Bourdelot to remain. He described his regimen in a few words, which Mathilde von Echner dutifully notes in her *Diary*:

"You spend all of your days and nights at work, Your Majesty; I recommend a diet of frivolity."

Kristina admitted that she had never learned to relax, and Bourdelot offered to become her tutor. His own disposition was frivolous, he said, and he sent a page to his room for his most precious possession, a lute. Kristina was enchanted, and he spent the rest of the afternoon playing and singing light, romantic airs.

Three days later a radiant Queen appeared at a reception in her throne room, Bourdelot close beside her. She announced his appointment as her personal physician, and they became inseparable. Anyone who wanted to see Kristina was compelled to make the appointment through Bourdelot, who refused to permit his "patient" to spend more than two hours each day at work. In his first flush of power he made only one error, but it was so grave that it almost ruined him. Chancellor Oxenstjerna presented himself at the royal suite with some documents requiring the Queen's signature and found the "doctor" sitting alone in the drawing room, strumming his lute.

Bourdelot casually told Oxenstjerna to return the following afternoon, as he had composed some new songs for Her Majesty and she planned to spend the rest of the day listening to them. The Chancellor rarely lost his temper, but he made it clear that he would tolerate no interference in state affairs. He would see the Queen when it served the interests of Sweden, and anyone who came between him and his duty would be banished. Bourdelot, in spite of his pretensions, was a sensible man and realizing he had erred, he apologized, retired to an antechamber, and made no attempt to interrupt the Chancellor's meeting with the Queen.

Having learned his lesson, the French charlatan profited accordingly. When foreign envoys came to him, asking him to use his influence with Kristina, he replied that he was concerned with her health, but as a foreigner, he would not presume to offer her advice in matters pertaining to the government of her realm or to her relations with other powers. The council, which had been trying to find some subtle way to get rid of the upstart, decided it was the lesser evil to let him remain. His influence was personal rather than political, and the ministers obviously hoped that Kristina would recover from her infatuation and settle down again.

No member of the council understood the depth of Kristina's passion, and it is unlikely that even Bourdelot himself realized that he had appeared at precisely the time when Kristina was eager to abandon the responsibilities from which she had never before escaped. The Frenchman sought no power for himself but was content to enjoy his position as the royal favorite, and Kristina, who had rarely laughed, now gave herself completely to a life of pleasure.

Most of the crude practical jokes she perpetrated were instigated by Bourdelot, whose sense of humor was as primitive and adolescent as the Queen's. One incident marred her reputation as a serious student, and thereafter she found fewer scholars who were willing to visit her. Bochart was strong enough to refuse to play the flute, but other men lacked his courage, and the whole court was shocked when Kristina mocked two of the most distinguished scholars she had ever entertained.

A German professor named Marcus Meibom, who was considered the greatest authority of the age on the music of the ancients, was visiting Stockholm, and by good fortune, the expert on ancient dances, Naudaeus, happened to be there at the same time. The two scholars eagerly compared notes, and although most of their discussions were technical, there had been a time when their erudition would have fascinated Kristina. Now, however, she was impatient, and responding to Bourdelot's whispered suggestions, she ordered Meibom to sing and Naudaeus to dance. The request was absurd, and no one knew it better than Kristina, who was well aware that both men were scholars, not performing artists.

However, she ignored their pleas to be excused and repeated her command in a loud, threatening voice. Meibom began to croak, Naudaeus tottered around the throne room, and, while the embarrassed courtiers watched in silence, Kristina laughed until she wept.

The humiliated scholars managed to control their tempers in the Queen's presence, but when she finally took her leave Meibom invited Bourdelot to join him in the library. The two men walked out of the throne room together, Meibom's manner almost jovial, but when the door of the library closed behind them, he turned on the man who had been responsible for his torment and beat him until Bourdelot fell to the floor unconscious. Not waiting for the inevitable order expelling them from the country, Meibom left Stockholm immediately, and Naudaeus departed for Brandenburg the following day.

Some of Kristina's advisers tried to tell her that she had succeeded in making Sweden appear ludicrous, but as Mathilde remarks in her *Memoirs*, "Her Majesty's passion for Dr. Bourdelot was so intense that she would listen to no one, and after attending to his comforts with her own hands, she threatened to have any who molested him in the future put to death."

Obviously, Bourdelot enjoyed no popularity with the professors who were teaching at the Swedish universities, and the medical men, outraged by his conduct, spread the malicious rumor that all of his previous patients had died. The clerical hierarchy was disturbed, too, for Bourdelot enjoyed flaunting his affair with the Queen. The clergy began a systematic campaign to discredit him, claiming that he was an atheist. At a later date the Lutherans insisted that it was Bourdelot who had undermined Kristina's religious convictions and converted her to Catholicism. There is no evidence to suggest that there is any truth in either charge. It is sufficient that Bourdelot encouraged the Queen's vices and transformed her court from one of the most serious in Europe into one that mocked the very institution of royalty.

Kristina, who had never paid any attention to her wardrobe, now squandered huge sums on gowns and jewels, and when a gallant visitor pleased her, she rewarded him by granting him an estate. Mathilde sums up this hectic period in her *Diary*: "Fortune seekers from many lands appear daily in the throne room, knowing that they will become wealthy in return for speaking a few cheap compliments that will please Her Majesty. In the past month she has given titles to thirty-seven men of no standing."

The Queen's behavior on the Sabbath began to create an ugly reaction throughout the nation, but she took particular delight in shocking her subjects on Sunday mornings. She attended services regularly at the Storkyrka, the great church dedicated to St. Nicholas, and each week she made an exhibition of herself. Her pew was lined with silk cushions, and she was always accompanied by several of her dogs. She paid no attention to the services, disdainfully ignored the sermons, and either played with the dogs or lolled on the cushions.

When Bourdelot began to accompany her to church and they sat with their heads close together, giggling, the council decided that something had to be done. Obviously the ministers were desperate, or no one would have thought of sending for Marie-Eleonore, who was living quietly in retirement. The Dowager Queen arrived in Stockholm unannounced, and, appearing in her daughter's suite, tried to deliver a stern lecture on the subject of God and duty. Kristina listened for a time, apparently out of sheer curiosity, and then began to ask seemingly innocent questions. Her knowledge of theology was infinitely greater than that of her mother, and after Marie-Eleonore had become thoroughly confused, Kristina lost her patience.

"I told her," she informs us in her *Memoirs*, "that as she obviously had some difficulty in understanding theological detail, she should leave such matters to the theologians. She wept, as I thought she would, for it was her custom to take refuge in tears. I could not refrain from remarking that her trouble was of her own making. She agreed, whereupon I relented, and after embracing her, sent her back to her own house. She was relieved to be rid of her errand, and I, as usual, was bored."

The rumbles of discontent became louder, and when citizens in every part of the realm criticized the Queen's conduct openly, the ministers decided to launch a more aggressive attack on Bourdelot. They called on Magnus de la Gardie who, by virtue of his marriage to Charles Gustavus' sister, was considered a member of the royal family, and Magnus readily agreed to lead the assault. He had attained a certain dignity because of his affair with Kristina in the early days of her reign. Now her playful romp with Bourdelot was ruining his own standing, so he had personal reasons for taking part in the attack.

Careful preparations were made, and then Magnus struck, publicly accusing the Frenchman of slandering him behind his back. Bourdelot, knowing he was innocent, demanded proof.

The nobles were ready and produced several witnesses, all of whom swore that Magnus had been vilified. Kristina attended the hearing as a witness, but suddenly she became a principal and demanded the right to examine the witnesses.

The court was forced to submit to the unusual request, and Kristina, defending her lover with the ferocity and cunning of a trapped animal, proved that the witnesses were lying. They were forbidden to appear at her court again, and she wrote a long letter to Magnus, who was ordered to retire to one of his country estates.

> Do not imagine that I am angry with you [she wrote]. I assure you that I am not. The only sentiment which I can henceforth feel for you is that of pity; and that cannot help you, seeing that you have, by your own act, rendered my feelings of good will for you useless. You are unworthy, on your own showing.
>
> Were I capable of changing my mind, I should regret ever having formed a friendship with a soul so feeble, but such weakness is unworthy of me, and having always acted in accordance with the dictates of reason, I ought not to blame myself for throwing a veil over the course of events.
>
> During these past years I have done too much for you in always blindly taking your part against everyone. But now that you are false to your truest interests, there is no reason why I should give any further thought to them or to you.
>
> You have yourself betrayed a secret which I had resolved to keep all my life, by showing that you were unworthy of the fortune I built for you.

If Magnus betrayed a secret, as the Queen charges in her last sentence, time has obscured it. Scholars have puzzled over her enigmatic statement for centuries, but have found no real clues, and the mystery remains. The most obvious explanation is the least likely, that Kristina was annoyed because her affair with Magnus had become public knowledge. It is impossible to believe that she could have been so naïve, for people had been gossiping long before she had heaped honors on him and sent him to Paris. Another possibility is that he may have been unfaithful to her and that she was preserving her pride by pretending to remain his friend until he joined the party trying to get rid of Bourdelot. This, however, seems remote.

An even more spectacular theory is that Magnus was actually Gustavus Adolphus' illegitimate son, and therefore Kristina's half-brother. Some students who have advanced this view feel that if it is true, the Queen and Magnus had merely pretended to become romantically attached to each other, and that she had heaped honors on him because of their close relationship. Others have said that the affair was genuine, but that blood ties made marriage impossible, and that disappointment over this love formed the basis of Kristina's determination never to marry.

Today's biographer can add nothing new; no documents have been found that might clear up the mystery. The few facts speak for themselves: Magnus, forced to obey the Queen, retired with his wife to one of the larger estates Kristina had given him, and Bourdelot won a triumph that seemed to make his position even more secure than it had been. However, he had won at battle only to lose the war.

The most powerful men in the country, among them the elderly Chancellor, realizing they had given their foe too little credit, pooled their forces to get rid of him. Oxenstjerna visited the Queen frequently, and was closeted alone with her for long periods. According to Mathilde, writing in her *Diary*, "Her Majesty often weeps after the day's audience with the Chancellor has ended. She is inconsolable and dines alone."

The nobles enlisted the services of the Comte de Chanut, who still exerted considerable influence on Kristina, and he added his voice to the rising clamor of opposition to the charlatan who had made a shambles of the court's dignity. Kristina held out as long as she could, but generals who had served her father faithfully, admirals of the new navy, and professors for whom she had expressed admiration in the past, lost no opportunity to tell her their blunt opinion of Bourdelot. Even the new counts and barons were disturbed and came to Stockholm from the estates Kristina had given them. The whole world was laughing at Sweden, they said, and the Minerva of the North, who had been praised everywhere for her erudition and wisdom, was being called a stupid, emotional woman.

The pressures were too great for Kristina. Her pride was wounded and at last she faltered. She proposed that inasmuch as Bourdelot spoke perfect French, he should be sent either to France or to Savoy as the Swedish ambassador. The council, in its first act of complete defiance, refused to grant her request. She threatened to appeal to the Riksdag, but when friends and foes alike told her that she would suffer an even more humiliating defeat, she accepted the inevitable gracefully.

Bourdelot left the country quietly on board a Swedish warship. It was rumored that the hold was filled with parting gifts from the sorrowing Queen. No complete record of Kristina's largesse is available, but the captain of the frigate, Lars Goeden, made an inventory of at least a portion of Bourdelot's loot:

16 bolts, cloth of gold.
11 bolts, cloth of silver.
23 bales of precious furs.
9 cases of chased cups and plates from the royal treasury.

6 bolts, cloth of kings.

14 crates of furniture.

The captain adds, "There were numerous other boxes, all of them tightly sealed and bound with cords which were cleverly knotted in such a way that they could not be opened without breaking the wax impression made by the Queen's own signet ring of state. My crew wanted to open these boxes, and my own curiosity was aroused, but we feared the Queen's wrath and consequently left the boxes as we found them."

Bourdelot, now a wealthy man, disappeared from Kristina's life and from history.

The council members and statesmen, who had hoped the Queen would recover her regal qualities, were disappointed. On the surface, Kristina seemed to resume her old ways; she put aside her expensive finery and dressed as carelessly as she had in the days before the charming Frenchman had disrupted her court. She attended council meetings regularly again, took up new studies, and sent scores of letters to scholars who had not yet visited Stockholm. But her reform was only skin-deep; she had acquired a taste for caprice, and although she behaved seriously one moment, she became frivolous the next. No one could predict what she might say, do, or decide, and she frequently issued contradictory decrees on the same subject in a single day.

When she chose to exert herself, her mind was as sharp as it had been earlier in her reign, but she frequently acted like a giggling schoolgirl or gave in to the appetite for practical jokes that Bourdelot had whetted. Perhaps the clearest picture of her during this period is given by the British Ambassador, Bulstrode Whitelocke. Of necessity he was a firm supporter of the "Lord Protector," Oliver Cromwell, and was therefore a sober man of high religious principles. But he had been a member of the gentry before the Great Rebellion in England, he owned a large estate near Henley-on-Thames, and, a graduate of Oxford, he had practiced law for a number of years.

He had been sent to Sweden because he was something of a thorn in Cromwell's side. Whitelocke had opposed the execution of Charles I, and the arguments he presented in the House of Commons had been so brilliant that he was totally acceptable at royal courts of other nations, an asset possessed by only a few of England's Roundheads. He seems to have been a rather merry Puritan, a man who held firmly to his beliefs but was not rigidly fanatical. Fortunately for posterity he was a discerning judge of character.

He created a sensation at the Swedish court on his first appearance, a public banquet Kristina gave in the great hall of her palace. It was the custom to drink numerous toasts at the beginning of a meal, and even though Kristina herself, after Bourdelot's departure, refused to touch wine or the stronger, distilled "water-of-life," she could not curb her subjects' habit of tossing off drink after drink at the beginning of a banquet. Whitelocke endeared himself to the Queen immediately when, as the newcomer to the diplomatic circle, he made the first toast.

Rising to his feet, he spoke briefly. As he himself recounted in his report to London, "I enjoy a cup of sack or a tumbler of ale on occasion, but I have no stomach for the drinking of toasts. It is an insult to Her Majesty, as her abhorrence of spirits is known to all. Therefore I shall eat a toast to her. God bless the Queen!" He picked up a strip of pickled herring and ate it.

The following day he was summoned to a private audience at the palace, but refused, thus making an even deeper impression on the Queen. He sent word that he engaged in no business on the Sabbath, explaining that he intended no offense or discourtesy, but that he and his staff always spent the day at devotional exercises. He and his chaplain alternated in preaching sermons, leading prayers, and reading from the Bible, and even though he had been sent to Stockholm for the express purpose of establishing cordial relations and, if possible, persuading the Swedes to sign a treaty with his government, his convictions would not permit him to leave the British legation on the Sabbath.

Kristina made another appointment with him for the following morning, and the Ambassador appeared in a black suit, unadorned except for "a row of fair rich diamond buttons." Kristina received him in the throne room, "sitting at the upper end of the room upon her chair of state of crimson velvet, with a canopy of the same over it."

Her own attire, Whitelocke noted at once, was even plainer than his. "Her dress was of plain grey stuff, surmounted with a jacket such as men wear of the same stuff. Round her neck was a black scarf, tied before with a black ribbon, as soldiers and mariners sometimes used to wear. Her hair was braided at the crown and hung loose upon the back of her head. She nevertheless had much of majesty in her demeanor."

Kristina, according to Mathilde's *Diary*, had hoped to inspire awe in the envoy. The Spanish Ambassador had been speechless when he had presented his credentials to her, and she wanted to create the same effect on the Englishman, but Whitelocke had too much strength of character to be afraid of anyone on earth. "The Queen," he said in his first report, "was very attentive whilst I spake of the good relations between our nations that I wished to establish. She came up close to me, wishing to daunt me by her looks and gestures, or so I supposed; but those who have been conversant in the late great affairs in England are not so soon as others appalled with the presence of a young lady, who, regardless of her high station, is no more and no less than a young lady."

Kristina was attracted by his boldness and invited him to return whenever it pleased him. Whitelocke responded by attending court receptions regularly, and although he was a Puritan he proved himself a shrewd man of the world by going out of his way to become friendly with the Queen's new favorite, a handsome and gallant young gentleman named Grave Tott, who was helping Kristina forget her heartache over Bourdelot.

A question of protocol and Whitelocke's decisive manner of settling it, further cemented his friendship with the Queen. The Master of the Royal Household sent word to the British envoy that the Danish Ambassador would be given precedence at a private dinner to which Kristina had invited both men, because the Dane was the representative of a crowned monarch and the Englishman was not. Whitelocke's reply was explosive. He held no personal grudge against his colleague, he said, but if the representative of a small nation was given precedence over the envoy of a great power, he would consider the slight a personal as well as a national affront. He would not hesitate to lay violent hands on the Danish Ambassador, even if the Queen herself should be present, and would throw the man out of the palace. What was more, he declared, honor would require him to challenge the unfortunate Master of the Royal Household to a duel.

Kristina read the letter with delight. The Danish envoy received no invitation, and Whitelocke dined alone with the Queen. He lost no time in taking up an urgent and delicate matter: He had learned, through espionage agents, that Charles

II, son of the unfortunate king who had been executed by Cromwell, had proposed marriage to Kristina. Charles, who was living in France on the revenues he received from his cousin, Prince Rupert, was desperate. The French, wanting peace with England, were anxious to be rid of him, and Rupert's method of obtaining money was, to say the least, unorthodox. Demonstrating the versatility of his genius, the soldier had become an admiral and commanded a fleet of Stuart supporters who raided English merchant ships on the high seas. In brief, he was a pirate, and Cromwell's navy couldn't catch him.

A marriage to Kristina would give Charles a base of operations and, equally important, Rupert — who was still regarded as the great champion of conservative Protestantism on the Continent — would be in a position to recruit and train a new army. Cromwell's Roundheads, shuddering whenever they recalled Prince Rupert's exploits during the Great Rebellion, were deeply concerned.

"I taxed the Queen with the matter," Whitelocke states flatly in his report to the "Lord Protector."

Kristina, in spite of her escapades, knew how to handle herself in an emergency. "The Queen remained very calm and thoughtful; she smiled and asked me how it had come about that I was privy to her correspondence."

Whitelocke gambled on his judgment of her character, and although he could have saved face with an evasive reply, he hoped that his candor would compel the Queen to speak honestly, too. "Your government and mine rely on similar sources of information, Madam," he said.

Kristina was silent for a moment, and the Ambassador must have wondered whether she intended to order his expulsion from the country and break diplomatic relations with England.

But, he says in his report, she finally said, "I confess that letters have passed between King Charles and me."

"I am sorry to hear it, Madam," the forthright envoy replied.

Kristina made an earnest speech that reflected the consistent attitude she had displayed for years. "I assure you, I will not marry that King; he is a young man, it is true, and in a condition sad enough; though I respect him very much, I shall never marry him, you may be well assured."

The Ambassador relaxed, and it is obvious from the turn the conversation took that Kristina also was at ease. Curious about this direct man who refused to play the subtle games of diplomacy, she asked him, "How many wives have you had?"

"I have had three, Madam," he told her frankly.

"Then you have been divorced, sir?"

"Twice have I been widowered, Madam."

Perhaps Kristina had heard that Whitelocke was the father of twelve living children and that others had died early in life. She certainly knew that childbearing killed many women, and she minced no words. "Have you had children by all of your wives?"

"Yes, by every one of them," the Ambassador told her.

She smiled again, and her manner became roguish. The conversation had been conducted in English, but suddenly she switched to French. *"Pardieu! Vous êtes incorrigible!"*

Later in the meal, Whitelocke's report states, the Queen's attitude changed again, and suddenly she appeared to be brooding. England, she said, had made a remarkable economic recovery from the Great Rebellion, but Sweden was still suffering from the sacrifices she had made in the Thirty Years' War. The English had more than enough money to spare, she said unhappily, but she had none and was, in fact, virtually poverty-stricken.

Whitelocke promptly showed that when necessary he could be the perfect diplomat. "I do not see Your Majesty waste the revenues of your Crown in gallantry of clothes for your person."

"I am the least curious in clothes of any woman," Kristina replied.

"Your wearing of plain clothes makes them rich," the Ambassador said.

Perhaps he disappointed her by flattering her, or it may be that the subject bored her. Whatever the reason, she changed abruptly to another topic and said that her Chancellor, who had been resting in the country for a few days, would return to Stockholm shortly. Whitelocke answered politely, "Your Majesty is happy in such a servant of so great wisdom, experience, and fidelity."

The Queen did not reply and, rising from the table, stalked from the room. Whitelocke, uncertain whether he had offended her in some strange way that he did not understand, repeated every scrap of the talk in his report to London. If he had erred, he said, he hoped his successor would study what he had written and thus avoid making the same mistake. It was clear, at that early stage of his relationship with Kristina, that he had no idea whether she looked on him favorably or wanted nothing more to do with him.

Oxenstjerna, with whom he became acquainted in the next few days, gave him no real help. The Chancellor, disillusioned and tired after many years of hard work, indicated that Swedish policy was no longer consistent; it was the nation's misfortune, he said, that the Queen allowed her capriciousness rather than her superb intellect to dictate the affairs of state. The Chancellor was able to make the envoy only one hard, unconditional promise. Sweden, he said, was committed permanently to the camp of the Protestant nations.

It was significant that at Whitelocke's next meeting with the Queen, she raised the subject of theology. She asked many questions about the various sects in England and examined him closely on the differences in their creeds. She also displayed a lively interest in his views on the subject of transubstantiation, and here we have the first written word that she was thinking about Catholicism. But the clue was a slim one and disappeared completely when Kristina invited him to attend a court ball.

In spite of her complaints about money, the decorations in the great hall had cost a vast sum, and she was dressed in a cloth-of-gold gown that Whitelocke estimated had cost at least one thousand guineas. Kristina was in one of her giddy, teasing moods and, knowing that the Roundheads condemned dancing, she addressed the Ambassador in a loud voice, inviting him to dance with her.

Whitelocke politely begged to be excused.

Laughing, she came down from her throne and insisted.

He immediately proved that a diplomat had to shed at least some of the outward manifestations of his beliefs when the occasion gave him no choice. He danced with the Queen for a quarter of an hour, and she complimented him warmly, saying, "The Hollanders reported to me, a great while since, that all the nobles of England were of the King's party and none but mechanics of the Parliament party and not a gentleman among them.

"Now I thought to try you and to shame you if you could not dance, but I see that you are a gentleman and have been bred a gentleman and that makes me say that the Hollanders are lying fellows."

Whitelocke seized the opportunity. "Parliament," he replied, "would not have given the honor to any but a gentleman to kiss Your Majesty's hand. I was bred up in the qualities of a gentleman, and, in my youth, was accounted not inferior to others in the practice of them."

Kristina could be gracious, too, and after thanking him at some length, added, "I take it as a favor that you were willing to lay aside your gravity and play the courtier upon my request, which I see you can do so well when you please."

Their friendship ripened, and several months after Whitelocke arrived in Stockholm, he entertained the Queen and her ladies in waiting at a banquet. "Her Majesty," he informed London, "was tempted to eat and drink more than she used to do in three or four days at her own table. She was full of pleasantness and gaiety of spirit both in suppertime and afterwards."

His report to London carefully — and understandably — omits any mention of the guests' diversions. Cromwell would not have approved of a middle-aged ambassador playing kissing games with a group of attractive young women, but Mathilde von Echner gives a clear picture of the evening in her *Diary*: "Among other frolics, the Queen commanded Whitelocke to teach her ladies the English salutation, which, after some pretty defenses, their lips obeyed. Her Majesty's discourse was all of mirth and drollery, wherein Whitelocke endeavored to answer her, and the rest of the company did their parts."

Neither Whitelocke nor Mathilde says whether Kristina learned "the English salutation."

The envoy was no lecher, however, and when he learned some weeks later that the Queen had danced on the Sabbath, he felt it his solemn duty to lecture her severely. She was the reigning monarch of a prominent Protestant power, he told her, and when she behaved in a manner offensive to God and man, she did incalculable harm to the Protestant cause everywhere. Not even Oxenstjerna had rebuked Kristina as sharply since she had mounted the throne, but instead of flaring up, she accepted his censure meekly.

Then suddenly she surprised him by saying, "There is a matter that I intend to communicate to you, but it must be under secrecy."

Whitelocke's reply indicates that he believed she wanted to discuss some trifling romantic affair. "Madam," he said, "we that have been versed in the affairs of England do not use to be surprised with the discourse of a young lady. Whatsoever Your Majesty shall think fit to impart to me and command to be under secrecy, shall be faithfully obeyed by me."

The Queen was pleased and, lowering her voice, said that what she intended to tell him had been kept secret from everyone else.

The Ambassador had no way of knowing that she was baldly lying. She had taken the Comte de Chanut into her confidence three weeks earlier, and he had sent a long report to the Louvre by special messenger. She had also talked to several of her ladies in waiting, among them Mathilde von Echner and Ebba Sparre, both of whom had gone to the Chancellor in alarm. Oxenstjerna had held four or five private meetings with the Queen and had discussed her "secret" at length with her. So it can only be presumed that she had not been able to reach a firm decision. There is a suspicion, too, that she enjoyed creating a dramatic effect for its own sake.

In any event, she said to Whitelocke, "I have it in my thoughts and resolution to quit the Crown of Sweden, and to retire myself into a private life, as much more suitable to my contentment than the great cares and troubles attendant upon the government of my kingdom. What think you of this resolution?"

The envoy, deeply shocked, spoke at length of a queen's duty to her subjects. Kristina listened, but when he was finished, she replied that Charles Gustavus was far more competent than she to discharge the duty. And, she added, eventually her cousin would sire children, so the succession would be assured.

Whitelocke, who considered duty a sacred obligation, tried another approach. The Queen was accustomed to great luxury and if she abdicated, her income would certainly be greatly reduced. She was also accustomed to living in the midst of people who showed her great respect at all times. If she put aside her crown, she might be surprised and dismayed to discover that many of her subjects, including some who were close to the throne, would treat her with indifference.

Kristina answered each of his arguments. "My tastes are simple," she said. "I can content myself with very little. A small house in a quiet country place will satisfy me, and for servants I have need only for a lackey and a chambermaid. Indifference and disrespect do not dismay me. I look upon such things as these as the course of the world and shall expect such scorns and be prepared to contemn them."

Whitelocke soon discovered that the whole court was whispering about the "secret," but Kristina did not mention the subject to him again for several weeks. Then she summoned him to another private audience, to make a suggestion that was typical of her nature. The terms of the treaty that would bind Sweden and England in an alliance had been hammered out by the Ambassador and Oxenstjerna; only a few minor questions had not been resolved. Kristina proposed that a secret article be added, giving Cromwell the right to abrogate the agreement if the Swedish government failed to pay the retired Queen's pension promptly.

The envoy could not be a party to such a thoroughly feminine arrangement, and he respectfully declined. The friendship cooled perceptibly, and Kristina did not confide in the Englishman again.

In the meantime, Chancellor Oxenstjerna had not been idle. He considered Charles Gustavus a crude, headstrong boor, a man totally unsuited to wear the crown, and he used all his powers of logic to persuade Kristina that her abdication would mean the ruin of Sweden. The crisis was so grave that he finally brought the matter into the open at a meeting of the council, and all of the great men of the land added their pleas to his. Magnus de la Gardie was called from his country estate, professors whom the Queen respected, visited her and urged her to reconsider, and pressure was applied from every source. Even Charles Gustavus was persuaded to see her and ask her to do nothing rash, but it may be assumed that his arguments were less than cogent and his manner somewhat lacking in enthusiasm.

At that period, in 1651 and 1652, Kristina had no real reason to abdicate other than her own selfish desire. Her interest in Catholicism was mild, and since she still knew almost nothing about the religion, her logic was weak and her arguments lacked force. So as last she succumbed, gave the Chancellor her word that she would put thoughts of abdication out of her mind and devote herself seriously to her subjects.

Instead, she did the opposite, and her behavior was as frivolously unstable as it had been during the months that Bourdelot had been her favorite. She created so many new nobles and gave away so much crown land that members of both chambers of the Riksdag became alarmed. She gave lavish entertainments at the palace and at her country houses, showered expensive gifts on her favorites, and the Chancellor, afraid that she would drive the country into bankruptcy, refused to give her free access to the treasury.

Kristina made a scene, claiming that monarchs of Sweden had always owned the treasury and that no man had the right to deprive her of her own property. But Oxenstjerna held firm, and the council supported him unanimously. The Queen, determined to have her own way, went behind his back to private bankers and mortgaged several large parcels of crown property, including valuable forests, some undeveloped mines, and one of her father's favorite hunting lodges. The council was stunned, but could do nothing; her signature was legally binding, and she had already received large sums of money from the bankers and was spending the gold crowns rapidly.

She dressed one day in an elaborate costume, then remained in her suite, refusing to see anyone, and on her next public appearance reverted to her old, careless habits. She was completely unpredictable, and refused to listen to advice from any source.

She committed one impulsive act that might have had serious consequences had Oxenstjerna not reacted promptly and somewhat harshly. Confiding in no one, Kristina had conferred on several occasions with the Spanish Ambassador and had secretly signed a treaty in which she promised to join Spain in a new war against Portugal. The action was illogical, unreasonable, and actually contrary to Kristina's own beliefs. She had always loathed war and had gloried in the title, "Queen of Peace" — yet she had committed her nation to take part in a war in which Sweden had no real interest! Both Spain and Portugal were distant lands whose policies and difficulties had little effect on the North. Swedish trade with these countries was negligible, and she maintained only thin diplomatic ties with them.

Oxenstjerna learned about the treaty by accident and refused to believe that Kristina had signed it. He went to her immediately, and she calmly confirmed the news, producing a copy of the document for him to read. He was old and very tired, but he loved his country so much that he lost his temper. Sweden, he declared, had no reason to squander lives and money on the perennial quarrels that disrupted the peace of the Iberian peninsula.

Kristina waited until he stopped shouting, then informed him that it was her prerogative, as Queen, to sign any treaty she wished. Oxenstjerna challenged that right and summoned the council. The members supported him unanimously, but Kristina stubbornly refused to budge, so the Chancellor went to the Spanish Ambassador and informed him that Sweden would not supply one soldier or one piece of gold for the war. The envoy was chagrined, but pointed out that the treaty had been signed and would remain in effect until Sweden formally abrogated it. Oxenstjerna had no choice; he went to Kristina again and told her that although he had no wish to humiliate her publicly, having served the throne all of his life, he would call the Riksdag into session, inform the members of her rash act, and request a vote.

The Queen's reply, according to Mathilde's *Diary*, was confident. "My people," she said, "will support me in any venture I choose to undertake."

Both houses of the Riksdag repudiated the treaty by an overwhelming vote, and that night there were riots in the streets of Sweden's major cities. The daughter of Gustavus Adolphus had lost her popularity; she undoubtedly heard the mob that gathered outside the palace, calling, "Abdicate! Abdicate!"

Soldiers dispersed the throng, and a surface quiet was restored. But a sense of uneasiness pervaded the nation, and for the first time the nobles began to think seriously of Charles Gustavus as their future king. He apparently felt the change in the political climate, for his own manners changed. He became less boorish, stopped cursing and roistering in public, and, for the first time, began to attend council meetings, where he carefully studied every document relating to the nation's welfare.

Kristina seemed indifferent to the stir she had caused, and, continuing to behave capriciously, spent her time giving extravagant parties or going off alone, dressed as a man, on long, hard rides in the country.

The people began to blame her for all of Sweden's ills, and as the country was still recovering from the Thirty Years' War, her waste of money deepened their hostility. Paradoxically, at the universities she had struggled so hard to create and improve, the students now turned against her, and pamphlets appeared throughout the country, condemning her in imaginary dialogues.

One, allegedly a conversation between the Queen and the Master of the Royal Household, is typical. "How much," Kristina is supposed to have asked, "does a ballet cost?"

"About ten thousand crowns, Your Majesty."

"What? Is that all? Get the money from the Treasurer at once, and I will have a ballet performed for my amusement."

Another broadside was even more vicious. In it the Queen was allegedly talking to the palace chamberlain. "What are the people talking about in the city?"

"They find that the time hangs heavily and tediously, Your Majesty."

"My subjects and I feel as one! Why are they sad? Is it because bread is so dear?"

"No, Your Majesty. It is because Your Majesty no longer dances."

"Then something must be done at once!"

"What shall I do, Your Majesty?"

"Fool, prepare a ball for the amusement of the people, and I will dance. Then the city will be happy again."

"It will be done, Your Majesty."

"How much does a ball cost?"

"About twenty thousand crowns, Your Majesty."

"I will not permit a paltry twenty thousand crowns to come between me and my people. They must be happy, regardless of the cost. Tell the Treasurer to give you the money at once. And prepare a new decree for my signature, increasing the tax on bread."

Kristina was beginning to reap a harvest of contempt she partly deserved.

Kristina's decision to give up the faith of her father and her country in order to become a Catholic was not made suddenly, and the closest study of the process of her conversion reveals glaring inconsistencies. Writing in her *Memoirs* late in her life, she reveals: "In 1648 I endured a spiritual crisis. I suffered from a serious illness, and it was in this sickness that I made a vow to quit all and become a Catholic if God would save my life."

It is impossible to check the authenticity of this bold statement, but the known facts make it somewhat less than credible. In the first place, there is no record that the Queen was seriously ill in 1648. And if she did make such a vow, it is odd that she waited five years before beginning to fulfill it. Not until 1653 is there any sign of an active interest in Catholicism.

In fact, only eighteen months before her abdication and conversion, she wrote a letter to Prince Frederick of Hesse, who was thinking of giving up the Protestant faith for Catholicism. "You must be aware," she told the prince, "how much converts are hated by those they leave, and you must know from many famous examples that they are despised by those whom they join. Consider how the belief in his constancy affects the reputation of a prince, and be assured that your fame will suffer if you are guilty of such a fault."

These words fail to sound like the thoughts of a woman considering conversion.

In Kristina's own day, the Comte de Chanut and Descartes were believed responsible for her change of mind and heart, but it is difficult to believe that either exerted much influence in the matter. Her relationship with Descartes was as troubled as it was brief, and he had more than enough to occupy his mind during his fatal sojourn in Sweden. De Chanut was close to the Queen, so it is possible that his religious attitudes might have aroused her curiosity and made her amenable to the idea of becoming a convert, but there is not one word in his voluminous reports to Paris to indicate that he addressed her on the subject. An ambitious man who held a good opinion of himself, De Chanut never concealed his accomplishments from his superiors, and if he had played a role in winning the daughter of the great Protestant champion to the cause of Catholicism, he undoubtedly would have said something to the Dowager Queen, Anne of Austria, and to Cardinal Mazarin, the real ruler of France.

De Chanut's first mention of the subject was in 1653, after the Queen had told him, again in confidence, that she was thinking of abdicating. In 1651, when she had told him the same "secret," she had spoken of retiring to an estate in the Swedish countryside, a declaration of intention which casts even more doubt on the romantic statement written in an old lady's *Memoirs*. Now, however, in 1653 she informed the French envoy that she was seriously entertaining the idea of becoming a Catholic, and from that time until she actually left the throne, the Comte never failed to mention the subject in his reports.

A Jesuit priest, Father Macedo, is probably the man who aroused Kristina's interest in Catholicism. The priest was the confessor and chaplain of the Portuguese Ambassador, who spoke no language except his own, and as Kristina's knowledge of Portuguese was limited, the priest frequently accompanied the envoy to court and acted as interpreter. Father Macedo spoke Latin fluently, and the Queen undoubtedly enjoyed talking with him. Kristina's will and intellect were so strong however, that it is unlikely that any one person was responsible for her conversion. She made her own decision, and the process was long, gradual, and frequently painful.

It was difficult for Father Macedo to meet the Queen without arousing suspicion, but their caution was such that even the Portuguese Ambassador had no idea that talks of any sort were taking place. Kristina delighted in debating theological questions, and the priest found himself thrashing about in dialectical waters that were too deep for him. The situation was less than satisfactory to both parties, and Kristina asked Father Macedo to undertake a private mission for her; she wanted him to go to Rome and send two learned theologians to debate with her. The priest agreed and asked the

Ambassador for a leave of absence. Having been sworn to secrecy, he could not explain his reasons for wanting a holiday, and the Ambassador refused his request. Father Macedo considered his duty to the Church infinitely greater than his obligation to the nobleman who employed him, and he decided to absent himself without leave. Intrigue always appealed to Kristina, and she secretly provided the priest with a ship. Through a misunderstanding, Father Macedo was forced to wait all night on a rock at the waterfront for the vessel to appear, where he was seen by several fishermen and two naval officers. Finally the ship kept its rendezvous, and he sailed away.

A few hours later, the Portuguese Ambassador, alarmed because his chaplain had vanished, appeared at the palace. Before noon he learned from the fishermen that Father Macedo had been waiting for a ship; and one of the men, obviously agitated, declared that a woman had been waiting with him.

Lutheran Stockholm was in an uproar, and several shipowners decided to set out in pursuit of the fugitive. Kristina, enjoying the adventure, acted first. She announced that she would send a navy frigate to capture the priest, and the warship sailed a short time later. The Queen received the captain of the ship in private audience before he sailed. Not until Kristina finally abdicated and openly embraced Catholicism did he reveal that she had ordered him not to capture Father Macedo under any circumstances.

In the latter part of 1653, two affluent Italian scholars appeared at the Swedish court. One was Francesco Malines, professor of theology at Turin, the other was Paul Casati, professor of mathematics at Rome. So many scholars had visited Stockholm that their arrival created no stir of any kind.

No one, including Kristina herself, realized that they were the two priests who had been sent to debate with her. They wore the clothes of laymen, and nothing in the manner of either indicated that two very nervous clergymen were afraid they would be attacked by a savage Protestant mob if their true mission became known.

They visited the court several times before Kristina discovered that these were the emissaries for whom she had asked. How she learned their identity has not been revealed, but Mathilde records a brief conversation in her *Diary*. "Her Majesty held a spirited debate this day with two Italian scholars, and one of them said something that disturbed her. She drew them into the small room behind her throne room, taking only me with her. 'Are you the gentlemen whom I have been expecting?' she asked them.

"The scholar from Turin bowed very respectfully. 'We are, Madam.'

"The Queen became very excited. 'Then you have letters for me?'

"'We have, Your Majesty.'

"'Speak not a word of them to anyone,' she told them, and after they departed, she cautioned me not to mention the matter to anyone. There was much that I wanted to know, but she refused to satisfy my curiosity and became very angry with me; so I did not persist."

Kristina had to find excuses to meet the two priests in private, but intrigue stimulated her inventive powers and she managed to see them daily. The strain on the two priests was considerable; not only were they placing their own lives in constant jeopardy, but Kristina was no eager, anxious novice — she was a skeptical, hard-headed logician who accepted nothing at face value and argued vigorously.

Father Casati wrote later that she had fought about everything. She disputed their definition of the distinction between good and evil, she questioned the immortality of the soul, and she drove them to the brink of despair by demanding that they prove the existence of God. After weeks of discussion, the two men were exhausted and ready to return to Italy. At Kristina's insistence, they made no attempt to convert her, but dealt with her exclusively on an intellectual level. One day, however, she began to probe the mystical element of Catholicism, and when the audience ended, she told them, "Perhaps I am nearer to becoming a convert to your faith than you suppose."

After a few more meetings, she broached a hypothetical question. If she were admitted into the Church, would the Pope grant her a special dispensation to take part in the ritual of receiving the Lord's Supper once each year, as prescribed in the Lutheran rites? His Holiness, she was told, could not and would not lend himself to any such deception. She argued that she could keep her throne only if she participated in such rites. The priests told her that she would have to make her choice.

"The die is cast," she replied, according to Father Casati's report. "I must resign my crown."

V: 1654–1655
THE CONVERT

Kristina's conversion to Catholicism was sincere, humble, and spiritual. She sought rest, a place of refuge, and she believed with all her heart that she had found it in Catholicism. She did not discover until later that she could not escape from herself, that her own nature was unchanged, and that she would remain a restless, dissatisfied woman. She had many faults, as she herself knew, but she was never hypocritical, and when she made up her mind to renounce her throne, her country, and her faith, she was convinced that what she was doing was right. Her conversion was one of the most hotly disputed events of the seventeenth century, and only the passage of three hundred years makes it possible to say that her decision regarding her soul was no one's business but her own.

She became extremely cautious, knowing that she would be expelled from Sweden without a copper if her countrymen suspected she proposed to give up the religion that had been the principal cause of the Thirty Years' War. So she sent Father Casati to Rome to prepare for her triumphal entry into the Eternal City. Father Malines remained in Stockholm to accompany her, but made no further attempt to see her. The Queen went into seclusion for several days, then appeared before the council and made a brief announcement:

"I have spent three years thinking about a matter that you persuaded me to abandon. I will not be persuaded in that manner again. My good Cousin sits here with you, and we have agreed that he shall succeed me. That time has come. I have decided, for many reasons, to abdicate. My mind is made up, and I shall not change it. I am not, therefore, asking your opinion but only your assistance in settling matters and arranging for the secure and tranquil succession of the Prince."

Her vanity must have been hurt, for many years later she records in her *Memoirs* that the members of the council "hid neither their pleasure nor their relief."

The political climate had changed drastically in three years. In 1651, under almost identical circumstances, every effort had been made to persuade the temperamental young ruler to change her mind. Now, however, the men who were closely associated with her wanted to get rid of her as soon as they could, and Chancellor Oxenstjerna's reply to her announcement was as perfunctory as it was mild. "We do not know," he said, "that Your Majesty would lead a more peaceful life after abdicating, for the future is hidden from our eyes, nor are we satisfied that repose would be consistent with Your Majesty's duty. Cares and anxieties are common to mankind and they especially appertain to soverign rulers, whose duty it is to seek their pleasure, and find their happiness, in work."

Having made his little gesture, he adjourned the meeting for twenty-four hours, and the following day the council voted unanimously to accept the abdication. Had the members realized that Kristina planned to become a Catholic, it is probable that she would have been arrested and confined in a fortress; certainly no one in a position of authority would have allowed her to leave Sweden.

The intensity of feeling about religion in seventeenth-century Europe can best be explained in modern political and ideological terms. For the sake of illustration, let it be supposed that Josef Stalin had been succeeded as dictator of Communist Russia by his daughter, and that she ruled, sometimes wisely, sometimes foolishly, for ten years after his death. Then suppose that she suddenly resigned her post and appeared in West Berlin, claiming refuge and advocating Western concepts of freedom and democracy. Let it be further supposed that she then traveled to London and Washington, where she was received as a heroine. In this imaginary situation, the furor on both sides of the Iron Curtain would be indescribable.

Kristina faced precisely such a tumult, and knew it. Obviously, then, it was in her best interest to guard her intentions closely. But, being Kristina, that was impossible, and when the senate sent her a polite request, asking her to reconsider, she replied in terms that must have turned Father Malines' gray hair a pure white. "If you knew the secret reason, which for the present I must conceal," she said coyly, "then my conduct would appear less strange to you."

The Queen announced her decision to the council in March, but the details were not settled for two months, during which time she met regularly with the ministers, arguing, demanding, and driving the peers to distraction. Apparently it did not occur to Kristina that she could not eat her crown and have it, too. Her first stipulation was absurd: if her cousin left no direct heir, he must be succeeded by Grave Tott. Aside from the fact that Tott, a minor member of the nobility, had no claim to the throne, her request was an impertinence the council could not tolerate. Kristina was informed unequivocally that her concern with the Swedish succession would end with her retirement.

Hurt and bewildered by what she considered callous indifference to her legitimate interests, she retired to her suite and stayed there for three days and nights, sulking. The routine business of the government was disrupted, the Chancellor wondered whether she had changed her mind again, and Charles Gustavus nervously paced the corridors of the palace. The Queen finally appeared at a council meeting, announced that she accepted the ministers' decision regarding the succession, and then proceeded to make fresh demands that were unacceptable.

She insisted that she retain the sovereignty of a long list of towns and islands, and it seemed only natural to her that she should receive the revenues from these places, as she had in the past. The Chancellor, giving his colleagues no chance to intervene, refused flatly. Kristina, however, was prepared to bargain, and offered first one compromise, then another. A full week passed before she finally understood the principle that if she abdicated, she must do so completely, and that she could keep neither sovereignty nor income of any crown possession.

Again she retired to pout and brood, and this time it appeared as though the whole scheme would be abandoned. But matters had progressed too far to turn back; the people had become impatient, and Magnus de la Gardie was sent to Kristina with a message. Whether she wished to abdicate or not, she had announced her intention to do so, the council had accepted her resignation, and she no longer had a choice. It can be imagined that Magnus must have relished his part in the drama, and it may not be accidental that he, of all the country's nobles, should have been selected for the role.

"His manner was stern and unpleasant," Mathilde von Echner writes in her *Memoirs*. "He spoke to the Queen in a loud voice and he told her that if she delayed in signing the Ministers' contract of agreement, she would be expelled from the country. But he promised her a large income if she would deal reasonably with the Ministers, and he declared privately that in such instance she could arrange for any ceremony of abdication that pleased her."

Magnus apparently understood Kristina better than anyone else, for she responded at once to the idea of a ceremonial abdication, and from that day forward there were no delays. The Chancellor and the council signed an order granting the Queen a generous allowance, and the senate ratified the agreement. It was stipulated that Kristina was to receive payments semiannually for the rest of her life, and the nobles gallantly voted her the privilege of being addressed as "Your Majesty." Kristina expressed no gratitude; according to Mathilde, it had not crossed her mind that she would be any less a queen after she stepped down from the throne.

Marie-Eleonore complicated the arrangements for the abdication by coming to the palace at Stockholm, where she spent her first night weeping until daybreak. Kristina, accustomed to her mother's tears, paid little attention to them.

The first ceremony was held on May 31, 1654, in the chamber of the lower house of the Riksdag and was, in a sense, a rehearsal for the final act of renunciation which was to follow one week later. Kristina, attired in a cloth-of-silver gown, her hair carefully arranged, her face rouged and powdered, rode in an open carriage, escorted by the more attractive of her ladies, among them Mathilde and Ebba Sparre. She was wearing her father's iron crown, and she continued to wear it while she read a brief statement of abdication to the members of the Riksdag while standing before them on a dais.

An unexpected, unrehearsed incident made the occasion memorable. The leader of the peasant party, sometimes called Marshal of the Boors, shuffled forward to make a speech. According to Whitelocke, who was present, he was "a plain country fellow, in his clouted shoon and other habits answerable, and he spoke without any ceremony."

"O Lord God, Madam, what do you mean to do?" the distressed man asked. "It troubles us to hear you speak of forsaking those that love you as well as we do. Can you be better than you are? You are Queen of all these countries, and if you leave such a large kingdom, where will you get such another?

"Your father was an honest gentleman and a good king and very stirring in the world. We obeyed him and loved him as long as he lived. You are his own child, and have governed us very well, and we love you with all our hearts.

"The Prince is an honest gentleman, and when his time comes, we shall be ready to do our duties to him as we do to you. But as long as you live we are not willing to part with you. Therefore, I pray, Madam, do not part with us."

"He spake from the heart," Whitelocke declares, "and when he was done he waddled up to the Queen, and took her hand and shook it heartily. Out of his pocket he pulled a foul handkerchief, and wiped the tears from his eyes."

Others wept, too, but Kristina appeared unmoved.

The final ceremony took place at high noon on June 6, 1654. An honor guard consisting of troops from every royal regiment escorted Kristina's open carriage through the streets. A huge crowd watched her ride past, but no one spoke, no one moved, no one waved to her. Kristina does not mention her feelings in her *Memoirs*, but Mathilde, who was riding in another carriage, wept openly, as did several of the other ladies.

Kristina was dressed for the occasion in a simple, flowing gown of white silk, with a cloth-of-gold mantle thrown back over her shoulders. She wore her crown for the last time, and in her left hand she carried her father's scepter. In her right hand was an emblematic ball of pure gold. She dismounted from the carriage a quarter of a mile from the senate chamber, and, flanked by members of the honor guard, walked the rest of the way. Preceding her were the Grand Marshal of Sweden, carrying the sword of Gustavus Adolphus, and the Lord High Treasurer, who held a golden key on a pillow.

Charles Gustavus, who would become King within an hour, was waiting for Kristina on the steps, and when she saw him, she suffered an unpleasant surprise. She had worked out every detail of the ceremony herself and had specifically instructed the prince to wear the uniform of a general. But Charles Gustavus was demonstrating that he, too, appreciated the drama of a public appearance. There were many generals' uniforms on view in the procession, and had he obeyed Kristina's order, he would have been lost in the crowd. The Queen thought of herself as the principal figure in the pageant, but Charles Gustavus had other ideas. Her reign was ending, his was beginning, and he achieved a master stroke, underplaying his part so neatly that Kristina was furious.

He was dressed in unadorned black from head to foot, and even the plume in his hat had been dyed black. So he managed, without speaking, to convey the impression that to him the occasion was a day of mourning, whereas in reality it was the most triumphant he had ever enjoyed.

As he gave her his arm, Kristina said something to him in an undertone, but he pretended not to hear. Unfortunately, her words were inaudible to others, and as she does not mention her remark in her *Memoirs*, succeeding generations have been forced to speculate on what she said. The only safe assumption is that her comment was other than pleasant.

Charles Gustavus escorted her into the senate chamber, where the members of the council, the nobles, and the high-ranking members of the clergy were gathered. A prayer was offered, and then Count Oxenstjerna, whose life work was ended and who would die in less than three months, read the Act of Abdication. His face was gray, he paused frequently to fight for breath, and his hands trembled, but he managed to complete the task, and handed the document to the prince. Charles Gustavus signed it, and Kristina sealed the parchment with her father's ring.

The procession formed again, and Kristina, preceded by the Grand Marshal and the Lord High Treasurer, and followed by the future King and all of the nobles, walked alone back to the palace. The foreign envoys and members of the court were assembled in the throne room, and when the Queen entered the hall, a silk cover was removed from the throne. There were gasps of admiration and dismay as people stared at a chair of purest silver. It had been wrought for the occasion by a Stockholm silversmith at Kristina's personal request, and she had supplied the funds for the magnificent object from the royal treasury.

It was later charged that she planned to take the throne into exile with her, but it is unlikely that she contemplated such a wild idea. The weight of the chair made it so cumbersome that several floorboards had been broken when it was moved into place. The throne, however, did not survive Kristina's abdication. The following day, Oxenstjerna proposed that it be melted down, and the new King, a sensible man, agreed at once.

But nothing spoiled Kristina's final moment of glory, and she looked radiant as she seated herself on the dazzling throne. The captain of the household guard took his place behind her, and Charles Gustavus stood below her on the dais, to her left. The Chancellor tried to read the Act of Abdication again, but the effort was too great for him, so the royal chamberlain took the document and read it in his stead.

Count Brahé, who had opposed the abdication, had been assigned the unpleasant task of removing the crown from her head. As he approached her, he raised his arms but let them fall to his sides again, helplessly. Color rose in his face, he wavered unsteadily on his feet, and as a murmur ran through the crowd, Charles Gustavus took a tentative step toward him. But Kristina refused to yield the limelight. This was one of the most dramatic moments of her life, and she intended to savor it to the full. She waited until the nobleman recovered his poise and breath, and when the company looked at her again, she slowly reached up, removed the crown, and handed it to Count Brahé.

Other nobles approached the throne, one by one, and she gave each of them an item of royal regalia. The scepter, golden ball, and signet ring of Gustavus Adolphus were placed on a table, and beside them were laid the sword and key. Then, at last, Kristina stood and unfastened her cloth-of-gold mantle. It was carried to another table and was cut into small squares, which were distributed to all present as a remembrance of the occasion. As nearly as can be ascertained, the idea of giving souvenirs to the guests was her own idea.

Her farewell speech was dull and anticlimactic. She said that, living in difficult times, she had tried to do her duty, she felt no qualms of conscience, and she graciously complimented her cousin, on whom her income would depend. She was confident, she told her listeners, that he would be a wise, strong king, a worthy successor to Gustavus Adolphus.

A series of other addresses followed, even more banal. Kristina was congratulated on the great qualities she had shown, and every speaker also took care to lavish praise on Charles Gustavus. Before the guests departed, Kristina's last order was read: she had granted a general amnesty to large numbers of political prisoners and to criminals who had been convicted of minor crimes.

The witnesses withdrew, and Kristina remained behind with her cousin and several members of their suites. Charles Gustavus planned to be crowned that afternoon in a quiet, private ceremony, and he was disappointed when Kristina told him she would not attend. She would be busy packing for her journey, she said, as she planned to leave for a health resort in the country for the mineral baths; her health, she intimated, had been undermined by the strain of recent months.

It was beginning to rain, and there were reports that a storm was sweeping in from the sea, so Charles Gustavus courteously invited her to remain in the city for a time. Her reply, reported by several sources, was emphatic: "How can you wish me to stay? How can you expect me to see another enjoy the power which was so lately mine?"

According to one report, which has survived the centuries, the new King asked her to marry him and become his consort, explaining that she would be able to retain her rank and dignity but be relieved of all burden of responsibility. Kristina's alleged reply was curt. Had she wished to marry, she would not have abdicated first. The authenticity of the story is questionable, but the mood is certainly in keeping with her character.

She retired to her apartment, ate a light meal, and while her ladies packed her personal belongings, she wrote two letters. Oddly, she seemed to be paving the way for a visit to France, although she had made secret plans to visit Rome. One letter, to the powerful Prince de Condé, struck a defiant note. "I will confess to you," she said, "that the leisure which I have so intensely desired has been bought at a high price, but I shall never regret having paid that price for it and shall never blacken an action for which I am very pleased with myself, by any base repentance."

The other, addressed to the members of the French Academy of Letters, was calculated flattery: "I have always had the highest esteem for you, because I have always had the highest esteem for virtue; and I doubt not that you will show me as much friendship in the solitude of my private life as you exhibited toward me when I was on the throne of my native land. My love of literature, which I shall now be able to cultivate at my ease and leisure, leads me to hope that you will sometimes communicate your works to me, works always worthy of your high reputation and written in the language which will generally, henceforth, be mine."

The storm became worse, and Charles Gustavus, now wearing the crown, came to Kristina's apartment and urged her to remain until the weather improved. She insisted that she would leave at sundown, however, and again declared that her weak health made it imperative that she seek medical treatment immediately. Whitelocke paid her a farewell visit, and she told him she intended to go to Uppsala; to others she gave contradictory stories. She was behaving cleverly, cautiously — and with good reason. Her enemies were active.

A group of nobles led by Magnus de la Gardie took the position that her pension was being paid by Swedish taxpayers, and that, as she would be doing nothing to earn the money, she should not be allowed to spend it abroad. The other danger was far more serious; some of the more important clergymen had heard rumors of her impending conversion to Catholicism and wanted to detain her in Sweden for the sacred cause of Protestantism. However, she was determined to leave, regardless of the perils, and she set out at dusk, accompanied by Mathilde — the only lady in waiting willing to go into exile with her — three secretaries, four lackeys, and a number of coachmen and grooms. There were thirty wagons filled with baggage in her retinue, and the party was escorted by a troop of royal household cavalry, augmented by detachments from other units.

The commander of the escort, a Captain P. Bergmann, has left his own account of the departure in the form of a report to the commander of the royal guard. The Queen, he said, insisted on halting at a small inn outside the city, and there was joined by a grave, middle-aged Italian gentleman. The officer thought Kristina was keeping a rendezvous with a lover, but he was mistaken. Mathilde explains in her *Diary* that Father Malines had been waiting at the inn since morning. Obviously, abdication had not diminished Kristina's passion for intrigue.

Captain Bergmann had been given no specific instructions by the woman who had been his sovereign, but after the "Italian gentleman" joined her and Mathilde in her coach, she sent word to the officer, who was riding with the vanguard, that she wanted him to take the road to the Danish border. Bergmann obeyed without question; he had been told to treat Kristina as though she were still a reigning monarch, and apparently it did not cross his mind that she was fleeing, that there were men who were following her in the hope of catching her and making her their prisoner if she tried to leave the country.

According to a romantic and dramatic story that has remained alive for more than three centuries, Kristina's pursuers closed in on her, but she eluded them by cutting her hair, changing into male attire, and escaping over the border alone. The account gained wide circulation and was accepted at face value in various Catholic countries, but there appears to have been no foundation for it. Bergmann's augmented troop, which had been ordered to take the Queen to safety, was capable of handling any misguided patriots who may have wanted to halt her, and the captain's report mentions no untoward incident. Mathilde is silent on the supposed histrionics, and so is Kristina herself.

The facts, as reported by both women and by Father Malines, sound authentic. The escort turned back at the border, and Kristina rode into Denmark. As there was no drama in the act, she made her own. "Free, at last," she declared, "and out of a country which I hope never to see again."

She directed her coachman to drive to a small tavern across the border, and there she ordered Mathilde to cut her hair short. The faithful lady in waiting protested, but the Queen was adamant, and after she had been shorn, she changed into the clothes of a youth. It pleased her enormously whenever she was mistaken for a boy on the rest of her journey.

If Kristina was happy to leave Sweden, her compatriots were even more delighted. Now, at last, the nation could become solvent again. The financial figures tell their own story: under Gustavus Adolphus, who lived as he died, a king, and who denied his family neither necessary pomp nor the luxury due their station, the royal household had spent less than three per cent of the total revenue of the country. Of that sum, the greater part was paid in wages to members of the guard and to servants. At the time Kristina abdicated, the royal household was spending twenty per cent of the national revenue, which had risen considerably since her father's reign.

She had lavished gifts on friends, and her collections of books, statues, paintings, cameos, foreign furniture, miniatures, and jewels had cost the nation vast sums of money. It has been estimated that odd items of bric-a-brac, ranging from enameled clocks to ingenious music boxes, had drained the treasury of three hundred thousand gold crowns.

Her greatest extravagance had been her abuse of the royal right to create new peers. She had granted titles to approximately five hundred men, and had either sold or mortgaged more than one and one-half million gold double-crowns in order to give each the land that a peer required. She gave pensions as lavishly as she granted titles, and one of her last acts was to sign an order directing the government to pay a generous pension for life to the tailor who had made the masculine clothing she now wore.

Perhaps her attitude toward property best illustrates her complex nature. She claimed that she disdained material possessions, that spiritual and aesthetic values meant everything to her, yet most of the thirty carts in her baggage train were piled high with precious books, paintings, and other items from her collection. These objects had been purchased with state funds, and, of course, belonged to Sweden, but she chose to regard them as her personal property and, less than a week before her abdication, had made a scene when Chancellor Oxenstjerna, in his last audience with her, tried to persuade her to leave the valuables in the castle at Uppsala and the palace at Stockholm.

In her mind, since she and Sweden had been one, anything she had purchased belonged exclusively to her. In later years she made life miserable for officials of the royal household, bombarding them with letters in which she insisted that certain books and statues be sent to her at once. And when her requests were either refused or ignored, she declared that she was the victim of a deliberate campaign of persecution.

Before Kristina's conversion was announced and the issue of her abdication became confused by the accusations and countercharges of the warring religious parties, the civilized world was stunned by her renunciation of the throne. The

Prince de Condé summed up the bewilderment of nobles everywhere when he asked, "Who is this lady who has so lightly abandoned the crown for which we others fight, pursuing it without attaining it throughout our lives?"

One of the more renowned scholars, Medonius, who had corresponded with her, rhapsodized idealistically: "Woe upon our Muses if we fail to transmit to posterity this unprecedented action on the part of an incomparable Queen, whose grandeur of mind surpasses all that history tells us about the heroes of antiquity!"

Father d'Auvrigny, a distinguished French Jesuit, was more cautious: "She resigned because she felt that her subjects were unworthy of her. The future will determine whether this judgment is true."

Bochart, who knew her and understood her better than most, expressed himself ambivalently. "I am so astonished at what I hear that I feel as if I were living in a dream. I cannot but approve Her Majesty's contempt for the glories of this world. But my heart bleeds when I think that she is voluntarily depriving herself of so many means of doing good, never to be recovered when once she has let go of them. She will regret what she has done a thousand times when it is too late and the damage is irremediable, if only because of the unfavorable comments which most people will make. For most people are only too glad of a pretext for barking at the heels of the great."

For the moment, Kristina paid no attention to the talk, and, behaving like an adolescent at the end of a long, hard school term, enjoyed herself enormously. She let it be known that she was "Count Donha," and she traveled at a leisurely pace through Denmark in this disguise, which fooled no one. The Queen of Denmark, whose curiosity was aroused, contributed to the musical-comedy atmosphere by making a rapid journey from Copenhagen to an inn at which one of Kristina's equerries had reserved a number of rooms. Wanting to see for herself what sort of woman would voluntarily give up a crown, the Queen of Denmark donned the dress, apron, and cap of a serving maid and waited on Kristina at dinner. Somehow, Kristina learned the real identity of her waitress and amused herself by making loud, uncomplimentary remarks about "Her Danish Majesty" throughout the meal.

On July 10, the party reached Hamburg, where they remained for three weeks. Kristina was the guest of a Jewish banker, who arranged to buy some of the treasures she had brought with her from Sweden. During her sojourn in the city she dressed as a woman. Crowds followed her wherever she went, and as she no longer was protected by a cordon of cavalrymen, she found them a nuisance. In order to protect her anonymity she wore a long, black wig, but then no one knew her and that irritated her, too, so on several occasions she tore the wig from her head and announced her identity in a loud voice.

Anti-Semitism was strong in Hamburg, and several ministers denounced the Queen from their pulpits for accepting the hospitality of a Jew. Kristina's public reply was sharp. "Our Lord, Jesus Christ, was Himself a Jew," she declared, "and throughout His life He consorted with Jews."

The leading Lutheran clergyman was so impressed by her retort that he invited her to attend services at his church and heaped praise on her in his sermon. When Kristina met him briefly after the service she presented him with a fine gold chain as a token of her regard, but a short time later he discovered a copy of Virgil hidden inside a prayerbook in her pew. She had reverted to her old habit of reading the classics in church, even on an occasion when she herself was the subject of the sermon.

The Landgrave of Hesse entertained her in style, but after spending a few days at his palace, Kristina resumed her leisurely journey, dressing again as a man, wearing high boots and a sword and carrying a carbine over her shoulder. Arriving at Munster, she spent two days at the Jesuits' College, where she teased the priests unmercifully on the subject of Jesuit morality, and, accusing them of Pauline cunning, declared that they tried to "appear in all lights to all men."

One of the more notorious incidents of her life occurred as she made her way via Amersfoort and Utrecht to Antwerp, and the story caused unpleasant repercussions for the rest of her life. Stopping overnight in the little town of Deventer, she ate dinner in the common room of the inn. Also present was a pretty young courtesan who, completely deceived by Kristina's disguise, flirted with her openly. The delighted Queen grinned, winked, and ogled in return, paying no attention to the scandalized protests of Mathilde, whom she finally ordered to leave the room, adding, "You women are all alike. A man shows you partiality for a time and you think you own him."

The other members of Kristina's party were shocked when she "pretended" to make love to the girl in public, and they were even more disturbed when the still unsuspecting courtesan and her swaggering "gallant" disappeared together. They spent the night alone in Kristina's bedchamber where, presumably, the courtesan learned her error.

At breakfast, Mathilde upbraided the Queen, and Kristina reports her reply in her *Memoirs*: "I said that I had been tolerably amused and that the girl received a heavier purse of silver than she had cause to wish. Both of us were satisfied, so no harm was done."

Kristina was killing time until she could announce her conversion to Catholicism, but Pope Innocent X was in no hurry. He wanted to reap the maximum benefit from the event, and the Vatican was making careful arrangements for a ceremony. However, when Kristina reached Utrecht, she learned that the Pope had died, and that, as a consequence, the ceremony would be delayed. Members of the College of Cardinals could not be convened overnight, and eight months were to pass until, after a heated election, Alexander VII was named to the papacy.

In the meantime, Kristina decided to settle somewhere, and as Antwerp was a center of learning and culture, she went there, rented a large house and cast off her disguise. She announced that she would receive visitors who wished to call on her, but trouble developed almost immediately. In Sweden she had shown a fine disregard for the nuances of etiquette, but now, sensitive to her new position, she demanded that she be treated with deference. Ironically, the first test came when one of the men she admired most in the world wanted to call on her.

Louis II de Bourbon, Prince de Condé, was one of the most renowned generals in Europe; although only five years older than Kristina, he was frequently called as great a warrior as Gustavus Adolphus and Prince Rupert. Kristina, whose reverence for successful generals was, for obvious reasons, even greater than her respect for scholars, had corresponded with Condé and had often expressed the desire to meet him. Now, through a stroke of circumstance, he was in the Low Countries, having fallen out of favor temporarily with the French regime. He had accepted command of the Spanish armies of the north, and as Antwerp was located in Spanish-owned territory, he was, for all practical purposes, the viceroy of the king of Spain.

A further, brief digression is necessary in order to set the stage for an incident as absurd as it was pathetic. The Prince's genius was recognized universally, and he had earned the name, "the Great Condé,'" to set him apart from his distinguished ancestors. He was a superb strategist, a brilliant tactician, and a keen student of military psychology, and he could generate great enthusiasm in his troops, who would follow him anywhere. But, as the French court had discovered to its sorrow, when he was not leading his soldiers into battle he was an exceptionally unpleasant man. Harsh, cold, and arrogant, he held a high opinion of himself and was quick to take offense when someone failed to share his exalted view.

Condé had been corresponding with Kristina since she was seventeen, so, shortly after his arrival in Antwerp from Brussels, he asked permission to call on her at her convenience. Whether the officer who brought the message started the fight over protocol or whether a member of Kristina's household began the harangue has never been learned; each side accused the other, and it is only known that a fierce argument followed. Kristina insisted that she would receive the Prince at the head of the staircase, which was located on the second floor of the mansion she had rented. Condé, outraged, declared that he would not visit her at all unless she descended to the ground floor to greet him.

Both sides held firm, and the battle ended in a stalemate. Condé spent ten days in Antwerp without calling on the Queen, but it was inevitable that they should see each other. One morning the Prince attended Mass at the cathedral, and as he and his retinue were leaving, his progress was blocked by Kristina and her entire party, who had been shopping. The two principals met on neutral ground, in the plaza facing the cathedral. It was noted by everyone who watched the pair that Kristina did not curtsy and that the Prince's bow was perfunctory. Nevertheless, they engaged in decorously animated conversation for a quarter of an hour.

Only one tidbit of their talk has been preserved. As they prepared to take leave of each other, Kristina was heard to say in a loud voice, "Cousin, who would have believed, ten years ago, that we were destined to meet like this?"

Another pair of royal visitors came to Antwerp for the express purpose of seeing Kristina, but made no attempt to meet her. Their case was somewhat different, however. Princess Elizabeth of England, sister of the late Charles I and aunt of the young Charles II who was learning bad habits in exile, brought her daughter, Elizabeth, from The Hague to attend the theater on an evening when it was known that Kristina would be at the performance.

It was said at the time that the ladies were afraid the imperious exile would not receive them as royalty and therefore they preferred to take no risks. That, however, is unlikely. It will be remembered that the younger Elizabeth had been the patroness of Descartes, and that she considered Kristina responsible for his death. So it is probable that the two Elizabeths wished to satisfy their curiosity, but did not wish to be subjected to the awkwardness of a personal confrontation.

Kristina passed the time by maintaining a steady correspondence with friends in Sweden, and she had no idea that all of her letters were being opened by the government. The new King and his council learned some things they had not known previously, and the letters that Kristina sent in a steady stream to Count Juan de Pimentelli, the Spanish

Ambassador to Stockholm, alarmed them. "They were filled with the strongest expressions which the most ardent passion could employ," the Dutch Ambassador informed his master, the Prince of Orange.

The Swedish ministers were astonished to learn that Juan de Pimentelli had been Kristina's lover for some months prior to her abdication, but they were not concerned with the caprices of her personal life. What disturbed them was the subject of her correspondence — her plan to become a Catholic convert. Desperate, they used desperate measures and sent young Grave Tott, the handsome nobleman who had been her previous favorite, to see her in Antwerp.

Tott carried documents identifying him as an official ambassador of Charles Gustavus' government, and his message was as direct as it was simple: Kristina's former subjects begged her to remain a Protestant and urged her to return to Sweden when she grew tired of her travels. She would be received warmly, the ministers said, and could choose any castle or palace in the land, other than the King's, as her permanent home.

Kristina received Tott amiably, spent a pleasant day listening to his pleas, smiled steadily, and said little. She refused to commit herself one way or the other, and Tott returned to Sweden knowing no more about her plans than when he had arrived in Antwerp.

He — and the world — soon discovered what her plans were. Pimentelli, a forty-eight-year-old bachelor, would meet her in Brussels, and she allowed it to become known that on her arrival there she planned to forswear the Luthern faith and embrace Catholicism. Her journey to this predominantly Catholic city became a royal procession — a portion of it was made on a barge decorated with streamers, and crowds of cheering citizens lined the banks of the canals. Soldiers saluted her, cannon boomed, and bonfires glowed. Late in the evening, Kristina entered Brussels through a triumphal arch that had been illuminated in her honor. When Pimentelli, who was impatiently waiting, hurriedly dismounted, ran to the arch and kissed her hand, the citizens roared their approval. The Maison du Roi, the royal palace located on the Grande Place in the center of the city, was made available to the Queen, and she moved into it with her retainers — and Pimentelli. At that time the palace, subsequently rebuilt on a more impressive scale after being bombarded in various wars, was tiny but ornate, and Kristina, who had spent all of her life in royal dwellings prior to her abdication, felt completely at home. She promptly sent for the rest of her belongings and gave up the rented house in Antwerp.

Brussels was the most sophisticated metropolis Kristina had ever seen. There was so much religious awareness and intellectual ferment, so much variety in entertainment, that the city was known as "the little Rome." Renowned university professors called on the Queen, she could attend the theater nightly, and as the citizens had learned the fine art of letting others live as they pleased, Kristina loved her sojourn there.

Before she could enjoy the pleasures of Brussels, however, there was a ceremony of the utmost gravity to be performed, and in the little chapel of the palace she privately "recanted her Protestant heresy" and embraced Catholicism. The news spread quickly through the city, church bells rang all day, and crowds appeared in front of the palace to cheer.

Kristina had an opportunity to bask in the unaccustomed sunshine of popular support and, with Pimentelli advising her, began to think seriously about her future. She came to the inevitable conclusion that she wanted to settle in Rome, "the capital of the world." The Pope was the only ruler to whom temporal monarchs bowed their heads, and she could not tolerate the idea of establishing a permanent residence in any community where, even as a guest, she would be forced to accept the authority of a king whom she regarded as her equal but not her superior. Accordingly, she wrote to the Vatican, asking for permission to establish her home in Rome. The reply had to await the election of a new Pope; in the interim, she contented herself with a variety of amusements.

A letter she wrote to her former lady in waiting, Ebba Sparre, mirrors her existence accurately during this period: "I am very well, and have been received with every honor, and get on exceedingly well with everyone except the Prince de Condé. I go nowhere except to the theater, and to the shops of this city, which frequently tempt me, their wares being exquisite.

"My principal occupations are to eat well, to sleep well, to study a little, to chat and to laugh, to entertain myself with French, Spanish, and Italian comedies, and to get through the time pleasantly.

"Above all, no more sermons for me! I have the profoundest contempt for all their preachers, holding, with Solomon, that one should eat, drink and be merry, and that all the rest is vanity."

Had Kristina displayed some measure of discretion in expressing her opinions of the faith in which she had been raised, she might have allayed some of the Protestant bitterness that was growing, as word of her conversion spread. But she had never been a polished diplomat, and her reckless candor did nothing to smooth the road along which she had dug so many holes. A Lutheran clergyman, writing to a colleague in Brandenburg, told a story that illustrates the Queen's impolitic bluntness perfectly. "Her Majesty," he wrote, "being asked whether she had no ministers of religion or preachers in her suite, replied that she had not. Since her departure from Sweden, she said, she had taken the opportunity of getting rid of all the people who were of no use to her."

The partisans of Catholicism were rejoicing prematurely, and they celebrated their victory so gleefully they failed to hear the faint but distinct warning note that was sounded when Kristina visited the Jesuits in the ancient Belgian capital of Louvain. The priests conducted her on a tour of the premises, and in their refectory showed her a series of panels on which portraits of various saints and heroes had been carved. Their admiration was sincere when they said they were reserving a place for her next to that occupied by a profile of Saint Brigitta of Sweden.

Kristina's reply was typical. "I would much prefer to find my name on a panel of philosophers," she said.

Her visit to the Low Countries was not marred by any unpleasantness other than the stubborn refusal of the Prince de Condé to bend his knee to her. Cardinal Mazarin of France sent a company of comedians from Paris to put on plays for her exclusive entertainment; also, she revived the joys of an old passion, the enlargement of her library. This pastime enabled the scholar Vossius, who had rejoined her, to steal her property again, and once more he made a considerable profit at her expense.

At last, word came from Rome that the College of Cardinals had succeeded in electing a new Pope, Fabio Chigi, who took the name Alexander VII. He was a scholar, a disciplinarian, an ascetic in his personal life, and a humble priest who disliked politics. A spiritual, austere man who wanted to rid the Church of its worldliness, he indicated at the beginning of his reign that he intended to place his reliance in the Jesuits. It was the misfortune of the Church that he lacked the strength to carry out many of the reforms he planned, and that he was often blocked by the cardinals of the Curia — the administrative heart of the Church — for these powerful princes had no intention of giving up their own prerogatives.

The new Pope, unlike some of his predecessors who loved the game of international diplomacy, took his religion seriously and considered the salvation of souls his first duty. So the communication he sent to Kristina through the Papal Legate in Brussels was as straightforward and blunt as some of her own letters. It would be impossible for one who had been converted to Catholicism *in private* to be received publicly by His Holiness and to be treated as a person of distinction. If Her Majesty wished to visit Rome, she must come as an open, avowed convert, and arrangements were being made for an appropriate ceremony at Innsbruck, in the Austrian Holy Roman Empire, if she wanted to avail herself of the opportunity being offered to her.

Alexander's communication stripped Kristina's situation to its essentials. The Swedish government had been unable to prove that she had abjured the Lutheran faith, so, in a sense, she had been able to enjoy something of a double life. She realized that if she took part in a public ceremony, her fellow countrymen would lose their tempers and patience. There was a very real danger that King Charles Gustavus and his council might reduce her pension or cut her off completely. But the Pope gave her no alternative; she had burned her bridges and was forced to take the risk. Whether she agreed willingly or reluctantly, whether she tried to find some third course that would expose her to less danger, or whether she faced battle eagerly is unknown. She does not mention the dilemma in her *Memoirs*, and apparently she confided in no one, for Mathilde says nothing in either her *Diary* or her *Memoirs*.

The Papal Legate, who sent a long report to the Vatican, a document which still reposes in the archives there, discussed many details connected with her travel plans and the ceremony itself, but his comment on the essence of the matter was terse. "Her Majesty," he said, "has accepted His Holiness' gracious offer."

On September 22, 1655, Kristina set out from Brussels for Innsbruck. According to the Papal Legate, who was stunned, and with good reason, there were two hundred and twenty-one persons in her retinue. Of this fantastic number, only Pimentelli paid his own expenses; the rest were Kristina's guests or retainers. A large number of Spanish, Belgian, Dutch, and Portuguese noblemen were delighted to make the journey, first to Austria and then to Rome, at the expense of a woman who apparently failed to grasp the fact that she no longer could demand any sum she wanted from the Swedish national treasury.

There were three monks in the party, three musicians to entertain the Queen at the end of each day's ride, and large numbers of coachmen, lackeys, grooms, and cooks. Significantly, aside from Kristina herself, Mathilde von Echner was the only lady who made the journey, although there were four other women: three serving maids to wait on the Queen, and one to help Mathilde.

No incidents of note marked the long ride. As was to be expected, nobles of the highest rank everywhere opened their castle doors to Kristina. Certainly she must have realized that many of them had fought in the Thirty Years' War against her father, but she is silent on the subject, confining herself to the statement that her hosts offered her warm hospitality on the road.

A special Papal Legate, Father Holsteinius, was waiting for her at Innsbruck. The Pope had shown wisdom in his choice of a representative, for the priest, a Canon of St. Peter's, was himself a convert from Lutheranism and chief librarian of the Vatican. Not only was his religious background similar to Kristina's, but he could discuss books, art, and philosophy, as well as theology, with her. Father Holsteinius wasted no time, and the ceremony was performed the day after Kristina arrived at Innsbruck.

The church was filled with dignitaries and her own followers. Kristina, wearing a dress of plain black silk, made her way to the altar. A long sheer scarf covered her blond hair, and her only jewelry was a large cross of diamonds which sparkled on her breast. She knelt and read the required repudiation of heretical opinions in a loud, firm voice. Then she recited the Nicene Creed, following it with a personal statement in which she declared her unalterable faith in the Real Presence, the doctrine of Purgatory, the right of the Church to interpret the Scriptures, its power to remit sins and grant indulgences, and all other articles of Catholic faith. She was also required to read an additional statement to the effect that she was unfamiliar with the fine points of Catholic doctrine, and that she recognized the Pope as the final authority in all matters pertaining to the Church and under no circumstances was she to contradict him.

It would appear that Alexander had made it his business to learn something about the character of the celebrated convert and was taking no chances. This theory gains strength from the fact that a special copy of her declaration was made for her and was signed by the municipal authorities of Innsbruck. Father Holsteinius presented the parchment to her solemnly, in the presence of a number of witnesses, who were required to swear they had seen her receive it. Such precautions were unusual, if not unique.

A Jesuit preached the sermon, using as an appropriate text: "Hearken, O daughter, and consider, and incline thine ear; forget also thine own people, and thy father's house."

Kristina was observed carefully during the sermon, and she neither played with her dogs nor read the classics surreptitiously. It is safe to assume that the sermon was the first she had listened to in years.

When she emerged from the church at the end of the service, she was cheered lustily by a huge throng. A military band played a lively air, and four batteries of cannon sent by the emperor from Vienna for the occasion fired a twenty-one gun salute. The Queen, enjoying a triumph that must have reminded her of her coronation, was radiant. That evening she acted as hostess to a large party of invited guests, and the evening was festive. Huge bonfires lighted the grounds of the villa she had rented, a company of Viennese actors performed a comedy, and a group of Italian singers enlivened the night with popular songs of the day.

Considering the solemnity of the occasion, the entertainment was shoddy, and even the young woman who made her own rules of conduct seemed to realize it. At one point, after the performance had ended, she was seen conferring hastily with one of her equerries, a former member of Pimentelli's staff who was temporarily in her service. The officer approached the Papal Legate and apologized, saying that if the ceremony had been delayed for a few days, it would have been possible to arrange a more appropriate entertainment.

In all probability, Kristina did not make one of the most shockingly caustic remarks ever attributed to her, although it was widely believed at the time that after the performance she told the Legate and a group of high-ranking Holy Roman nobles: "Gentlemen, it is most proper that you should entertain me with a comedy after I have entertained you with a farce."

Gottfried Leibniz, the eminent German philosopher-mathematician and student of human nature, who met her in later years, remarked solemnly that the speech, if true, exhibited a regrettable lack of decorum. He said he did not know whether or not Kristina had made the remark, but added that on the basis of his study of her character, he believed her capable of saying anything that came to her mind. The biographer, whose duty requires him to distinguish, where possible, between fact and legend, can only report that although the correspondence of the Queen's contemporaries mentions the comment repeatedly, there is no specific evidence to suggest that Kristina actually made it. It need only be added that in the light of her subsequent as well as her previous conduct, it is small wonder that people gossiped about her.

On December 3, the day after her conversion, Kristina took care to write a letter to Charles Gustavus, in which she told him what she had done and made a firm attempt to protect her pension. "Sir and Brother," she wrote, "I have arrived here in safety, and I have received the permission and orders of His Holiness to declare myself that which I long have been. It is a great happiness to me to obey him, and the glory of doing so is more to me than that of ruling over the dominions which now are yours. You ought to approve, seeing that though you think my choice of a religion a bad one, it is very advantageous to you and has in no way altered my affection for Sweden or my sentiments of friendship for yourself."

In the brief week that she remained in Innsbruck, Kristina wrote many other letters to former friends in Sweden, and in all of them her theme was the same: by embracing Catholicism she had removed the threat that she might change her mind and return to reclaim her throne at some future time, so Charles Gustavus had no cause to worry about the security of his crown. Clearly, she was her father's daughter, and was using the tactics he had made famous: fearing assault, she was attacking first.

On December 8, Kristina left Innsbruck for Rome, accompanied by a retinue so large that no one bothered to count the numbers of gallants who swarmed around her. Everywhere she received the acclaim due a conqueror. Mathilde notes in her *Diary*, "Never have I seen Her Majesty so happy. The whole Catholic world pays homage to her, and she is pleased to accept every honor."

When she reached the Italian states, the expressions of welcome became even more elaborate, the frenzy of the people increased, and the dukes who were responsible for her safety were forced to provide her with a strong guard to prevent enthusiastic crowds from crushing her. The Pope sent her a private message, asking her to travel slowly so she would not arrive before his arrangements for her reception were complete. As a gesture of his regard, he sent his own carriage for her, an unprecedented act.

There were triumphal arches everywhere, cities were illuminated in her honor, and bishops and nobles gave her banquets far more sumptuous than any she had ever attended when she had been known as the Minerva of the North. Bologna held a series of brilliant fetes, balls, and dinners, and the public took part in games for her entertainment. The small city of Ancola went wild, reproducing in miniature the seven hills of Rome; perhaps the most impressive part of the display was a river of red wine, representing the Tiber.

Two days before Christmas, the party arrived outside the walls of Rome, and Kristina was invited to stop for the night at a villa that had been vacated by its owners. She consented, but was too excited to sleep, so she spent part of the night planning what she would wear and the remainder preparing her wardrobe. Her staff was not permitted to rest either, and Mathilde tells us, "The Queen's restlessness drove everyone to distraction. She gave hundreds of orders, countermanded all of them and then became angry because they had not been obeyed. All of us were relieved when morning came."

Shortly after breakfast, a uniformed guard of honor was seen on the road, and a delegation of eight cardinals arrived to conduct the Queen into the city. Among the princes of the Church were Giulio Rospigliosi, the Secretary of State, who was destined to become the next Pope; de Medici, the most powerful member of the College; and Decio Azzolino, the clever young aristocrat who had been taken from the ranks of the lay nobility and given a red hat.

Cardinal Rospigliosi informed Kristina that the Pope planned to receive her in St. Peter's and that they would escort her there. She replied that she would be ready in a quarter of an hour, and the cardinals had no choice but to wait for her in the drawing room of the villa.

VI: 1656

OBEDIENT DAUGHTER OF THE POPE

Kristina, steeped in the literature and annals of Rome, was familiar with the Eternal City long before she set eyes on it, but the people who lined the streets were totally unprepared for Kristina. The cardinals who escorted her to the Cathedral were among the most brilliant men of their day; all were scholars, suave men of the world, and diplomats, but it is safe to assume that they were as startled as the citizens who watched the cavalcade. Rome, in all of its long history, had never seen anyone like Kristina of Sweden.

Instead of riding in the Pope's carriage, she rode a pure-white stallion. The mount's bridle was made of gold, the stirrups were gold, and the saddle and reins were covered with cloth of silver. But the woman who boldly sat astride the horse was even more dazzling. Although the day was chilly by Roman standards, it seemed warm to someone who had spent the first twenty-eight years of her life in Sweden, and Kristina wore an open-necked cloth-of-gold blouse that, on close examination, resembled a man's shirt. On her blond hair was a hat with a jeweled band and several ostrich plumes that swept high in an arc, then swooped down over the shoulder that she quietly favored. Completing her unorthodox dress, and even more shocking to the Romans — and presumably the cardinals — were her riding breeches, gorgeously embroidered with gold lace.

It had been arranged that she would receive the grace of confirmation from the Pope, and the great Church was filled as the Queen walked slowly to the high altar and knelt. Pope

Alexander appeared from his private entrance, and if he was shocked, he managed to hide his dismay. Laying his hands on her head, he administered the sacrament.

A banquet had been arranged at the Vatican in Kristina's honor. She sat at the Pope's right on a chair that had been made for the occasion — a chair that resembled a throne. A Jesuit preached the sermon before the meal began, and when he was finished, the Queen asked several thoughtful theological questions, all of which the Pope thoughtfully answered. An orchestra played sedate music, the banquet began, and the guests, waiting for His Holiness to lose his temper, listened eagerly to every word spoken at the head of the table.

Alexander, as Cardinal Chigi, had occasionally displayed a quiet sense of humor, but since his elevation he had frowned at levity. His manner had been cold at all times, and virtually everyone present expected him to rebuke Kristina severely. However, he chose to chastise her calmly, almost serenely.

"There are more spectacles in Heaven than on earth," he told her.

Kristina made the mistake of misjudging him and thought his gentle manner was a sign of weakness. Eventually she discovered her error.

In the days that followed the banquet, she spent most of her time seeing the sights of the city, as countless tourists have done through the ages. None ever had more distinguished guides. Cardinals competed with one another to show her churches and art galleries, museums and colleges. At a printing establishment, a few carefully selected words of flattery were printed in eight languages; at one of the theological seminaries, she received compliments in twenty-two tongues, among them Coptic, Armenian, Syriac, and Chaldean.

The leading members of the ancient, aristocratic families gave lavish entertainments for her; one, an "opera" performed on the grounds of the Barberini estate, was said to have cost more than forty thousand crowns. Hundreds of singers, dancers, and acrobats made up the cast; horses, bulls, camels, and elephants appeared on the stage.

Kristina rented an old palace from the Farnese family, and, fulfilling one of her most cherished dreams, formed a salon. The group met once each week, read poetry, discussed morality, and listened to a musical recitation. One or more cardinals invariably attended these gatherings. Cardinal Azzolino, an intense, ambitious man, was a frequent guest. Kristina was deliriously happy, but clouds soon began to appear in the flawless sky; the converted Minerva of the North was making enemies more rapidly than she was winning friends.

The Roman nobles, shrewd and clever, but informal in their relationships with each other, soon became uncomfortable in Kristina's presence. She was still defensive, as she had been in the Low Countries, and insisted on being treated with the deference due her rank. The nobles thought she was unnecessarily haughty, and soon she was receiving fewer invitations. Her sharp tongue was no asset either; she had not learned that while a crowned monarch may make a witty comment at someone else's expense with impunity, a woman who wants friends must demonstrate tact and warmth.

Kristina's social errors were minor, however. Her costliest blunder was a deliberate act that offended the Pope. A chamberlain came to the Queen's palace from the Vatican, and after informing her that His Holiness would receive her in private audience, stated that Alexander wished her to appear in feminine attire. The flowery compliments and adulation that had fed Kristina's vanity since her abdication had distorted her sense of values, and after the chamberlain departed, she flew into a rage. Alexander the Seventh might be Pope, she shouted, but he was only a man, and no man had the right to tell her what to wear. He might be the final authority in spiritual matters, but in temporal affairs she was her own mistress.

Her frenzy mounting, she sent two of her equerries into the streets to round up the most attractive strumpets they could find. She refused to tell anyone what she had in mind. Her staff was apprehensive, but she dismissed those who dared to approach her, and paced up and down the long gallery of the Farnese Palace for several hours, muttering to herself and glowering. Finally the equerries returned, shepherding a score or more of bewildered trollops. Kristina scanned the group quickly and discharged all but one, paying each of the girls she dismissed. Then to the wench she detained she offered an enormous sum for her costume and, in addition, recklessly allowed her to choose any gown she wanted from the royal wardrobe.

In the first year of his dictatorship, Julius Caesar had issued a decree ordering all prostitutes to wear saffron-colored gowns; and what had once been a law was now custom. The prostitutes themselves found it convenient to dress in saffron, as they could be identified more readily by potential clients, particularly the foreigners who came to the city from every nation on earth. The tradition was so firmly established that no women other than prostitutes ever appeared in public wearing orange-yellow. The higher-priced courtesans, more subtle than their less fortunate sisters, advertised their profession discreetly, usually by wearing a headdress or a sash of saffron, but those who roamed the city searching for customers, clad themselves from head to foot in the color.

Kristina's scheme was clear: she planned to wear the flimsy saffron gown she had purchased from the streetwalker, when she went to the Vatican for her private audience with the Pope. Various members of her staff tried to dissuade her — Mathilde even threatened to return to Sweden — but the Queen listened to no one and ordered her seamstress to make her a saffron scarf that she could drape on her head.

"Her Majesty laughed loudly, after the manner in which she enjoyed herself when hunting or riding," Mathilde writes in her *Diary*, "and she said it would be unbecoming to appear before the Pope with her head undressed. Women are required to cover their heads in the Pope's presence, and it was her jest to cover her hair with a shawl of the finest saffron silk."

The chamberlain who met Kristina at the entrance to the Vatican was shocked, but her manner was so imperious that he conducted her to the private quarters of the Pontiff, and Alexander received her. She tried to carry off her joke with an innocent air, pretending that she did not understand the significance of saffron, but the Pope was not deceived. Certainly he must have been disillusioned and bewildered by her vulgarity and childish defiance, for he had assumed that a woman willing to give up her throne to embrace Catholicism was a person of deep, abiding conviction, a dedicated lady who intended to devote her life to good works and set an example for the rest of the world.

There is no record of what was said at the audience, but it is clear that Kristina was chastised, for she sulked in her private suite at the Farnese Palace for three days after she returned to the drafty old building from her interview. If Alexander expected her to reform, he was disappointed; anyone acquainted with Kristina could have predicted that her behavior would become wilder and more outrageous.

When she appeared in public again, she used such coarse language that even the most sophisticated noblemen were uncomfortable. It was one of the pruderies of the times to drape nude statues when ladies were present, and Kristina, who had seen hundreds of such semiclothed works of art, now rebelled. She ripped the drapes aside herself, usually adding an off-color remark that embarrassed her host and offended her hostess. She attended church regularly, but reverted to her old habits, and even when she went to Mass at St. Peter's, she squirmed or lolled in her pew, giggled and whispered with her friends, and made it clear to everyone that the prayers and sermon bored her.

The most notorious incident of the period took place in February, and caused Alexander to lose his patience with her. It amused her to make a fool of Cardinal Colonna, an elderly member of the most patrician family in Rome. The Colonnas had been wealthy and powerful for the better part of two thousand years; it was said that they could trace their ancestry back to Romulus and Remus. Colonnas had been generals and governors, viceroys and diplomats, and since the advent of Christianity, two had been Popes. Prince Colonna, head of the clan, was the most prominent layman in Rome, and it was customary for at least one member of the family to wear the red hat. The previous cardinal, a devout and energetic man, had died unexpectedly several years before Kristina's arrival in Rome, and his place had been given to a foolish, elderly cousin of the ruling branch of the house, a courtier whose only qualification was that he would live only a short time and would vacate the place for one of the younger Colonnas not yet old enough to be made a prince of the Church.

Cardinal Colonna, who had never been a priest, understood the duties of his high station only vaguely, and as he became increasingly senile, he was gradually relieved of the few responsibilities the Vatican had given him. Kristina fascinated him, and he attended her salon regularly, wrote poetry that was little better than gibberish, and soon made himself a nuisance by appearing at the Farnese Palace daily, his hair powdered to make himself look more impressive. Kristina was urged by a number of prominent persons, including several cardinals and at least two members of the Colonna family, to discourage the old man's attentions. They could have saved their breath, for she flirted with him openly and often appeared with him in public. The climax came one night when the Cardinal, in full view of anyone who happened to be passing, stood in the street before the Farnese Palace, strumming a lute and serenading the Queen.

Pope Alexander reacted at once. Cardinal Colonna left Rome the following morning for one of his family's villas in the country, where he remained, more or less a prisoner. Kristina had succeeded in angering the Pope and making the most powerful clan in Rome her enemies.

The Pontiff, coldly paternal, sent Kristina a rosary with his compliments. Accompanying his gift was a brief message suggesting that in the future she should tell her beads instead of disturbing public worship with frivolous conversation. She dispatched an immediate reply to the Vatican: she had not become a Catholic, she told the Pope, for the purpose of telling beads. The gulf that separated them became wider.

In the meantime, the members of her suite were emboldened by her raucous conduct; the gentlemen threw off all restraint, and the servants behaved like vandals, too. A thick sheaf of complaints, reposing in the Vatican archives, reveals a part of the story. Several of the Queen's Italian, Spanish, and Belgian gentlemen tried to convert one of the apartments of the

Farnese Palace into a gambling casino, and two cardinals of the Curia had to intervene to put a halt to their activities. When Kristina visited various museums and palaces, it became necessary to assign guards to watch her followers, who stole valuable medals, coins, and other small art objects whenever they had the opportunity.

The Farnese family, who had rented their palace to the Queen, sent her a steady stream of complaints, and when she gave them no satisfaction, they took one case after another to the Vatican. Some of their charges are illuminating. One night, several gentlemen, finding the portion of the palace assigned to them unusually chilly, tore the doors off their hinges, chopped them up and fed them to the flames. The servants ripped gold lace off draperies, tapestries, and other hangings, and sold it; they also stole an unspecified number of expensive silver candlesticks, all of them family heirlooms, replacing them with cheap pewter holders.

Even Pimentelli, who had followed Kristina to Rome, was forced to lodge a formal complaint one day when his carriage was stolen as it waited in the palace courtyard while he called on her.

Perhaps the theft of the Spaniard's property was not accidental. Kristina was becoming involved in politics, and it dawned on her that Pimentelli had been relieved of his post in Sweden in order to serve the aims of his government. There was a fierce rivalry between the Spaniards and the French for positions of power and prestige at the Vatican, and as neither group realized that Kristina's relations with the Pope were becoming increasingly strained, both tried to use her for their own advancement.

The Spaniards, having acted as her patrons when she changed her religion, felt they had a proprietary interest in her.

Pimentelli was now assigned as the Spanish Ambassador to the Vatican, and a nobleman who had joined the Queen in Flanders, Antonio della Cueva, was her Grand Equerry. Both men had received orders from Madrid to discourage her friendship with the French and, if possible, to prevent her from forming strong attachments to any Italian faction. Pimentelli, a seasoned diplomat, went about the task quietly, but Della Cueva was less discreet.

The technique he employed was clumsy: when Kristina showed partiality to a French or Italian gentleman, Della Cueva spread an unpleasant rumor about the relationship, and the unfortunate nobleman was usually summoned to the Vatican for a lecture. One such session with an irate cardinal was enough to frighten away the majority of courtiers. Several, however, protested vehemently to the Vatican, and at last Kristina learned what was happening. She obtained no satisfaction from Pimentelli, who blandly denied the charges, but Della Cueva, who was neither clever nor bright, was less fortunate, and she attacked him violently.

Kristina wrote a long, agitated account of the scene herself, and her indignation knew no bounds. Della Cueva admitted that certain slanders had been perpetrated, but tried to blame his wife who, he said, was jealous of the Queen's beauty and wit. He urged Kristina to ignore the petty gossip of a woman, and he seemed anxious to end the discussion. But Kristina was neither fooled nor appeased. She gave the luckless Spaniard a "tongue lashing," to use her phrase; he charged later that she had cursed at him. Regardless of what was said, the scene was clearly an unpleasant one, and ended when Kristina declared she would gladly give Della Cueva permission to retire from her service and return to the Low Countries.

He retorted that nothing would please him more, and that he would like to resign immediately. Taking his personal belongings, he went immediately to the Spanish embassy. Kristina, aware that the quarrel had caused her to lose face, and knowing that a queen, even one who wore no crown, could not permit herself to become embroiled in heated arguments with inferiors, sent Della Cueva seven horses from her stables. He accepted the gift, but, still furious, he announced that she was "the woman of the lightest reputation in the world."

The matter should have ended there, but when Kristina's emotions were aroused she rarely displayed wisdom. She wrote a scathing letter to the King of Spain: "Only my regard for Your Majesty prevented me from causing an officer bearing your commission to be thrown from my presence by lackeys and beaten from my Palace with sticks."

She compounded the insult by having copies of the letter printed and distributed, and the uproar increased. The French gleefully took up her cause, the Spaniards claimed their national honor had been assaulted, and finally both nations appealed to the Pope. Alexander wearily summoned Kristina and made an attempt to instruct her in the basic principles of decorum. Unchastened, she retorted that although she submitted to him in all matters of conscience, she considered herself the sole guardian of her honor.

As a replacement for Della Cueva, she engaged the Marchese Giovanni Carlo Monaldeschi, an impoverished Italian nobleman who had acquired an unsavory reputation. Had Kristina bothered to make inquiries about him, she would have been told that he was a ruthless, dishonest schemer, a rogue who was denied admittance to the best houses of Rome. But during this period of disillusionment, she confided in no one and sought no advice. Monaldeschi was charming, and so she gave him an appointment. She showed an equally poor understanding of human nature when, to replace the Spaniards who had left her staff, she named two members of the minor Roman nobility: the Santinelli brothers, Ludovico and Francesco, hard-bitten soldiers of fortune, neither of whom was considered respectable.

Rome had welcomed the Queen warmly, but within a few short months, the patricians of the city turned away from her in impatient disgust. Kristina reveals in her *Memoirs* — and her account is corroborated by Mathilde in her *Diary* — that messengers no longer appeared at the Farnese Palace bearing invitations to banquets and festivals. Nor did the nobility call on her. Impoverished poets and dramatists continued to attend her weekly salon, principally because she supplied a royal feast for the occasion, but the more distinguished artists, like the noted sculptor and architect, Giovanni Bernini, who had been commissioned by the Pope to enlarge St. Peter's, made their excuses and kept their distance.

The Queen, making a valiant effort to regain her place in the Roman sun, invited sixty of the most prominent people in the city to a reception. Only Decio Cardinal Azzolino and two of his colleagues appeared. The three prelates, practicing the Christianity they preached, were willing and able to overlook Kristina's shortcomings. Her intellect never failed to astonish them, and they had discovered that she behaved calmly and rationally when treated firmly. But to everyone else, she was a crude boor, an overnight sensation who had gone into eclipse.

Financial worries made life even more difficult for her during this trying period. She had spent money extravagantly, and her funds were almost exhausted, but she relied on her forthcoming pension payment from Sweden to help maintain her household. The money did not materialize, and a letter she sent to her cousin remained unanswered. Fearing that she had been cut off because she had become a Catholic, she sent her private secretary, Elmo Davisson, himself a Swedish convert, to Stockholm. While she waited for his return, she continued to spend money prodigally, and when Davisson reappeared, he brought news that was neither as bad as she had feared nor as good as she had hoped.

King Charles Gustavus, the secretary told her, had no intention of punishing her by cutting off her allowance; he thought she was a fool, but he had too much on his mind to worry about her conscience. Sweden had gone to war with Poland, and the King needed all the funds he could raise for the campaign that would begin in the spring. As a token of his good will, he sent Kristina a purse containing approximately one-fourth of the money the Swedish government had promised to pay her. He would send more when he could, but in the meantime she, like her compatriots, would be forced to make sacrifices.

Kristina was desperate. She had hoped that the payment of her pension would enable her to leave Rome, where she felt she had been humiliated. Further, an outbreak of the plague increased her anxiety and spurred her desire to move elsewhere. In her frenzy, she concocted a plan and wrote hastily to Charles Gustavus, seeking his approval. France still owed Sweden large sums of money for services rendered during the Thirty Years' War, and Kristina contended that as she had been on the throne of Sweden when the war had ended, the debt could be paid to her. She would subtract her allowance, she said, and send the rest to Stockholm.

Charles Gustavus and his council, tired of the excuses and evasions in every letter they received from the French Finance Ministry, had virtually written off the French debt. Impractical as they felt Kristina's plan to be, they decided that there was something to be gained and nothing to be lost, and the King gave his consent.

Pope Alexander also agreed to her leaving Rome, perhaps a trifle too quickly. He saw an opportunity to be rid of a woman who had embarrassed him before the world, who had made a mockery of her conversion, and, instead of helping the cause of Catholicism, had done the Church untold harm. The French Ambassador was summoned to the Vatican, and an urgent letter was sent to Cardinal Mazarin, requesting him to invite the Queen to visit France. Not waiting for the reply he knew would be forthcoming, Alexander provided Kristina with four Papal galleys and their crews, free of charge.

Unwilling to admit that she lacked funds for the journey, Kristina reduced her staff from three hundred to sixty and quietly sold most of her horses and carriages. Had she been willing to leave most of the remaining sixty employees in Rome, she could have made the journey, but she still considered herself a queen, and the thought of traveling without her retinue was inconceivable. So she pawned some of her jewels and finally scraped up enough funds. Early in July, 1656, Pope Alexander sent her a parting gift of ten thousand crowns, and on July 19, Kristina sailed for France.

The faithful Mathilde von Echner accompanied her, as did Father Malines, who had been active in her conversion. All of the other faces were new: Monaldeschi and the Santinelli brothers were the most important; Captain Francesco Landini, the "captain of the royal guard," was an adventurer she had met only recently, and so was Count Annibale Thiene, whose title and family connections were obscure. Davisson, her secretary, was probably the only dependable person in the party, other than Mathilde and Father Malines. Virtually all of the servants had been newly employed, too. Their predecessors, some of whom had accompanied the Queen into exile from Sweden, had resigned because they had not received their wages regularly.

"It is good," Kristina told Mathilde, "to leave Rome. Now I feel free again."

"Our city will be more serene," said Pope Alexander, "now that our daughter is departing."

VII: 1656–1657

Kristina landed at Marseilles on August 29, 1656, and to most of the officials who came to greet her, she appeared a restless, bored woman. The Romans, asking no questions, were relieved to be rid of her, and the Swedes thought she had gone on a wild chase in search of golden goose eggs she could not collect. Only Cardinal Mazarin, who was awaiting her in Paris, knew her real purpose, and few historians have been willing to believe that he negotiated with her seriously.

Reporting only the facts, today's biographer must state that Kristina sent Mazarin a letter prior to her departure for France, suggesting that she be made queen of Naples.

There were several obstacles in her path, principal among them being the inconvenient reality that Mazarin could not give her the crown without a war, since the Neapolitan kingdom belonged to Spain. However, Kristina's dream was not as mad as it may seem at first glance. The Neapolitans were chafing under Spanish rule, and patriotic feeling was so intense that rebellions broke out every few months, even though large garrisons of Spanish troops were stationed in the city of Naples and in the surrounding countryside. Kristina's basic thinking on the subject was direct and simple. France, she argued, was Spain's enemy and could deal her foe a heavy blow without becoming directly involved herself. All Mazarin had to do was supply the necessary funds.

According to her reasoning, the Duke of Modena, an Italian general who was hungry for glory and hated the Spaniards, would be willing to raise and lead an army if someone gave him a war purse. Kristina had corresponded with him secretly, using the Santinelli brothers and Monaldeschi as intermediaries, and she was convinced that he was eager to undertake such a campaign. The people of Naples would join their liberators, she predicted, and the Spaniards would be driven into the Bay of Naples. She neglected to take one factor into account: she was the central figure in the conspiracy, and it never occurred to her that the Neapolitans might be somewhat less than elated to accept the Minerva of the North as their ruler.

The private talks with Mazarin were still in the future, however. In the meantime, Kristina enjoyed a tour through France that was as spectacular as her entry into Italy the previous year. Francois Louis-Joseph, sixth Duc de Guise, was sent to Marseilles to welcome the visitor on behalf of the young King, Louis XIV, Anne, the Queen-Mother, and Cardinal Mazarin. The duke was an excellent choice; an amiable courtier with impeccable manners, he greeted Kristina with a long, flattering speech. He escorted her on the journey north, and in every town there were celebrations, fireworks, and banquets. Aix, Montélimar, Avignon, Lyon, Mâcon, Dijon, and Auxerre demonstrated that the people of France could be as excited and generous as the citizens of Bologna.

At each stop the town magistrates came out through the gates to extend a welcome to a visiting monarch, and, because of Kristina's conversion, a priest preached a sermon. The clergyman who had been assigned the task at Montélimar made the error of delivering a discourse on the subject of "The Wrath to Come," and Kristina responded instantly and rudely.

She interrupted him again and again with sarcastic comments, and after the service was ended, she refused to receive him in private audience. The Duc de Guise wisely sent messengers ahead, and the subsequent sermons that Kristina heard were brief and flattering.

At last she reached Fontainebleau, where one of the most fascinating of French royal ladies was living in temporary disgrace. Anne Marie Louise d'Orléans, Duchesse de Montpensier — known throughout the civilized world as "La Grande Mademoiselle" — had been destined to become the bride of Louis XIV, but her own impetuous nature had betrayed her. In the uprising of 1652, when forces under the Prince de Condé fought loyal troops under Marshal Turenne in Paris, she had chosen the wrong side, Condé's. She had achieved a fame even greater than Kristina's by commanding the regiments at the Bastille herself. After she had given Condé and his staff an opportunity to escape, the cannon had been fired on Turenne's army at her personal command. When the brief rebellion had been smashed, she had been sent to Fontainebleau, where she lived comfortably and maintained her own court while waiting to be received in Paris again.

She was six months younger than Kristina and equally stubborn. In spite of her military exploits, she was extremely feminine in manner and dress, her personal deportment was exemplary, and her tastes were exquisite. She was eager to meet Kristina and confided to her intimates, "I am sure I shall die of laughter."

Kristina was anxious to meet La Grande Mademoiselle, too. "It will be difficult," she told Mathilde, "to speak civilly to one who is a friend of Condé."

The two famous ladies became friends immediately.

The Duchesse de Montpensier subsequently described the visit at some length in her letters.

> My principal impression upon meeting Her Majesty [she said] was that she was a very pretty boy, with a pale face, intense blue eyes, a nose of aquiline aggressiveness. She has a masculine habit, too, of sprawling in chairs and throwing her legs about over their arms and backs. She gives one the impression that she has behaved in this manner for so long a time that she does not act like a boy deliberately in order to shock those with whom she converses; rather, I deduce, the manners she has acquired have become a part of her being. Yet one must grow accustomed to her imperfect regard for decorum, for she frequently assumes postures which are scarcely decent.
>
> These imperfections are but slight when one considers the whole of her person. Her conversation, I found, was remarkable in manner as well as matter. She talked on many subjects, and whatever she had to say, she expressed herself agreeably. Sometimes she fell into profound reveries and heaved deep sighs. Then she recovered, like a person awakening with a start from a dream. In fact, she was a most extraordinary person.
>
> Her sympathy for my plight was tender. She offered to intercede on my behalf at the Court and expressed her willingness to patch up my quarrel with His Eminence, with whom she appears to be on excellent terms, albeit they have not met. I expressed my thanks to her, but explained that no person can persuade the Court that it has made an error in judging me.

Kristina expressed her opinions firmly, too, in a letter she wrote to Ebba Sparre.

> La Grande Mademoiselle is truly the daughter of Royalty [she said enthusiastically]. When she enters a room, all who are

present know instantly that a personage of consequence has arrived. Her inferiors are devoted to her, and she treats them with kindness, but she never permits herself to forget the differences in station that separate her from them, and her manner does not permit them to become unduly familiar with her.

I had expected to find an Amazon, and when first we met I thought I would not see that she who stood on the ramparts of the Bastille, defying the armed might of France, was all ribbons and furbelows. It is difficult for me to describe her person, other than to say that she is elegant and charming; she uses uncommonly great quantities of rouge and other elixirs to enhance her beauty, and she drowns herself in sweet-smelling scents even stronger that those with which the slatterns who frequent the student taverns at Uppsala drench themselves. But her use of these artificial aids to beauty, which I deplore in most women, do not detract from her appeal, so lively is her nature.

Her knowledge is greater than I had expected, and while she is no scholar, she is tolerably well acquainted with the works of Plato and Virgil, she can converse on the natural sciences and knows more than many men who are professors and put their students to sleep.

I told her plainly that she should be Queen of France and said that were I King, I would not hesitate to raise her to my side on the throne of France.

The members of both suites watched in amazement as the feminine young woman who had acted like a man and the masculine young woman whose behavior was feminine chatted together like old friends. Only one subject was avoided: each was aware of the other's opinion of the Prince de Condé, and neither mentioned him. Kristina's restraint is particularly notable because she so rarely exercised it.

On the first evening of the Queen's visit, a fireworks display was held in her honor, and the gentlemen in charge of the exhibition, wanting to make the occasion memorable, showed more vigor than delicacy. The explosions were so loud that Mademoiselle de Montpensier became frightened, thus giving Kristina a splendid opportunity to laugh at her fears. This brief exchange sparked a discussion of courage, and Kristina expressed astonishment that one who had smelled the smoke of cannon fire should flinch at mere fireworks. La Grande Mademoiselle confessed that she could display bravery only at moments of crisis, and Kristina admitted that it was the dream of her life to watch a real battle.

One other incident that occurred during the visit is illuminating. It was the habit of French ladies to greet each other on all occasions with kisses, and the custom irritated Kristina. "Why," she asked her hostess, "are these women so anxious to kiss me? I suppose it is because I look like a man."

Paris had made elaborate preparations for the arrival of the Queen, and Kristina, responding as an actor does to an enthusiastic audience, lived up to expectations. She was dressed from head to foot in scarlet — even her boots had been dyed to match her velvet suit — and she revealed later that she had designed her uniform herself. A magnificent black plume in her hat provided the only touch of contrasting color. She rode astride a huge, pure-white stallion whose trappings were of gold and silver; a brace of silver-handled pistols was visible in her belt, and she carried a slim, gold-plated cane which she raised repeatedly to salute the throng.

The Duc de Guise had spent enough time with her to form an estimate of her character, and at his request one thousand cavalrymen had been dispatched from a bivouac outside the city to act as her escort. A group of distinguished officials, headed by the governor of Paris, the provost of the merchants, and the grand masters of the guilds, rode to the ancient south gate to greet her. They dismounted, and the governor tried to deliver a welcoming speech, but the crowd that had gathered was cheering so loudly that he could not be heard.

Archers led the procession into the city, and the Duc de Guise, enjoying one of the most pleasant experiences of his insignificant life, rode at Kristina's left. According to the official estimate subsequently submitted to Cardinal Mazarin, more than a quarter of a million people lined the route. Never had Kristina seen such huge throngs, never had she tasted such a triumph. She was taken to Notre Dame, where a *Te Deum* was sung in her honor, and then she was conducted to the Louvre, where a luxurious apartment had been prepared for her. Great ladies were on hand to wait on her; deputations from the University, from the Academy, and from the City Parliament called on her. Never in her life had she been made to feel so important.

She continued to savor her triumphs in the days that followed. The Papal Nuncio was the first member of the diplomatic corps to pay his respects, and he was followed by all of the other ambassadors. The representatives of the guilds flocked to the Louvre, too, competing with one another in flowery speeches. She received the widow of the slain Charles I of England, Queen Henrietta Maria, in a private audience, and the splendors of the City of Light paled for a short time as Kristina listened to a harrowing tale of poverty. Henrietta Maria was so poor that when it became bitterly cold she could not even buy firewood to heat the old palace at St. Germain, which France had been allowing her to use. Although Kristina's own financial situation was precarious, she impulsively gave her sister-in-exile the ten thousand crowns that had been Pope Alexander's parting gift to her.

The intellectuals who were the real crowning glory of France were as eager to meet the great patroness of arts and letters as she was to see them, and Kristina devoted several evenings to receptions at which the majority of guests were philosophers and poets, scholars and dramatists. But adulation did not change Kristina's habits, as several anecdotes that shocked the court illustrate.

Ménage, who considered himself the greatest wit in Paris, wrote an account of one incident:

> M. Gilbert had recently completed work on a new comedy, some of the lines of which were more than a trifle bawdy. He read the play in Queen Kristina's presence, at the house of the Duc de Guise, and she enjoyed it immensely. The first person whose opinion about the piece she asked was M. Chapelain. As the world knows, Jean Chapelain is a poet of great distinction, and it was due to his efforts that the Academy was formed under the auspices of the late Cardinal Richelieu. He is elderly, and, as one who has enjoyed many honors, sedate. He said to the Queen what he thought, as indulgently as he could, but nevertheless let it be seen that he was not blind to the impropriety of certain passages.
>
> Then the Queen asked me what I thought. Having previously noted her delight, I replied, like a good courtier, that I considered it one of the best comedies that had ever been written. Her Majesty was pleased, very pleased, with my critique. "I am happy that you like it," she said. "One can trust your judgment. As for poor M. Chapelain, how limited his taste! I fear that in spite of his years and sex, he is at heart a maiden."

Mademoiselle de Montpensier, who heard all the gossip of Paris, although she was not allowed to visit the city, reports in her *Memoirs* several significant straws in the wind. Some members of the clergy were surprised, she says, when Queen Kristina chatted and laughed with several bishops, and she created a crisis one day when she announced that she wished to confess her sins, but haughtily refused to confess to a cleric of less stature than a bishop. The bishop of Amiens, who happened to be in the Louvre at the time, was hastily called, and Kristina disconcerted him by insisting on confessing in her own way. She refused to retire behind a screen and, instead, sat facing the bishop, looking him straight in the eyes as she confessed.

She caused another stir when she insisted on paying a visit to the most notorious woman in Christendom, the infamous courtesan, Ninon de Lanclos, who had achieved such ill fame that the Church had persuaded the state to lock her away in a convent so she would have time and opportunity to repent. All that is known of the visit is that Kristina spent the better part of an afternoon with Ninon. Neither wrote a word about their meeting, and the nuns who were present during the interview also maintained a discreet silence. According to some accounts written in later years, Kristina's firm intervention was responsible for Ninon's release from the convent, but there is no evidence to substantiate the story, which must consequently be consigned to the realm of charming legends.

In spite of her blunt and sometimes coarse manners, Kristina was popular with Parisians, principally because of her knowledge of all things French. When a nobleman was presented to her, he was astonished and delighted to discover that the Queen was familiar with his family history and had read various books about his distinguished ancestors. When she visited a church or a museum, she amazed the priests and curators who acted as her guides by displaying a remarkable familiarity with their treasures. She won the hearts of the people when she publicly challenged an assertion of the Dean of Notre Dame, who said that a certain precious gem was in the collection at the Cathedral. Kristina asserted that it was in the Sainte-Chapelle at Saint-Denis and backed her claim by offering to wager the enormous sum of five thousand crowns that she was right. The Dean, trapped, had to accept the bet, and the whole city laughed with the Queen when she won.

Men were enchanted, but, as usual, most feminine noses were out of joint. Kristina, up to her old tricks, "made herself very agreeable with gentlemen," in La Grande Mademoiselle's words, "but was haughty and silent when ladies were presented to her."

Françoise de Motteville, principal lady in waiting to France's Dowager Queen, Anne of Austria, whose *Memoirs* describe her mistress' life in the most minute detail, devotes many pages to Kristina. At this time, when the bloom was still fresh on the peach, she was favorably inclined to the capricious Minerva of the North. Young King Louis XIV, Mme de Motteville says, had heard so many stories about the visiting Amazon that he decided not to wait until she came to pay her official visit to his court at Compiègne, but to come to Paris. Quietly dressed in a dark suit, he arranged to have himself presented as a "nobleman of distinction"; apparently he thought he could fool the Queen and learn her opinion of him.

Kristina, however, was far too shrewd. She had studied numerous portraits and miniatures of the French royal family and she recognized Louis instantly. He was charmed and freely admitted his identity. Mme de Motteville concludes her story by saying, "The young King got on very well with the haughty, learned, and audacious lady, and they conversed with one another freely and with mutual satisfaction."

The King urged Kristina to come to Compiègne soon. She needed little urging; her business with Mazarin was pending, and she was anxious to see him. Her plans were so delicate that she decided to leave her retinue in Paris, and she traveled to Compiègne in a carriage alone. Although the court had steeled itself, French propriety was outraged when she had to borrow the services of a maid to help her dress for dinner. Even minor ladies in waiting, young women of comparatively little consequence, never traveled anywhere without their personal maids.

A ceremonial banquet was held on the night of Kristina's arrival, and Anne of Austria, who never took second place to anyone, graciously yielded and permitted the younger woman to enter the dining hall first. There had been great curiosity about the Queen who had captivated Paris, but the court was disappointed at the banquet. She looked, wrote Mme de Motteville, "like a dissolute gypsy who did not happen to be quite so dark in complexion as one would have expected…"

Later in the evening, Kristina lived up to her reputation, and her eccentric behavior satisfied everyone. She lapsed into daydreams in the midst of conversations, she hummed under her breath when the talk bored her, and from time to time she sighed heavily. The French, who considered manners of paramount importance, were titillated and duly shocked by her conversation, too. According to Mme de Motteville, "she discussed subjects concerning which reticence is more proper to her sex."

On the surface, at least, the moral tone of the court was rigidly high, and Mme de Motteville levels several sharp accusations at the unusual guest: "She took the name of God in vain and allowed herself no less license in her actions than in her thoughts and speech. She could not sit still, and, in the presence of the King, the Queen-Mother, and the entire Court, she threw up her legs onto chairs as high as the one on which she was sitting, making them much too conspicuous to the view."

The following evening, a group of Jesuits gave a dramatic reading in Latin for her edification and entertainment. Selections from various classics had been culled for her benefit, and, as few of the guests understood Latin, they were forced to sit blankly while Kristina enjoyed the readings. Her comment, which was heard by everyone present, startled the polite French. "Jesuits," she declared, "are as unfit to be actors as they are to be confessors."

Jules Cardinal Mazarin, the real ruler of France, postponed his meeting with Kristina for more than a week. In the meantime he watched her carefully, received reports on everything she said and did, but kept his opinions to himself. He held power because of his intellectual strength. An Italian by birth, related to the Colonna family of Rome whom Kristina had offended, he was cordially disliked by the French people, and experience had made him cautious. Anne of Austria obeyed his instructions in all things. He was hatching a plan to retain his control of the affairs of state when King Louis began to rule in his own right. Among the more prominent young ladies at the court were the Cardinal's nieces. The King was in love with one of them, and it was Mazarin's hope that they would marry, thus enabling him to keep his power.

Himself the pupil of the wily Cardinal Richelieu, his predecessor as prime minister, Mazarin never acted impulsively or rashly, and he waited until he had formed a firm conclusion about Kristina before sending word to her that he would be honored if she paid a visit to his office. She had been planning to go hunting with King Louis, but broke the engagement on short notice and hurried to the Cardinal's office. Had she been less arrogant, less sure of herself, she would have realized that she was as malleable as wax in Mazarin's clever hands.

He made allusions, intimated, and hinted deftly; he made remarks open to a variety of interpretations, and when Kristina jumped to erroneous, wishful conclusions, he made no attempt to contradict her. He was not opposed to the idea that she become Queen of Naples, he said, and considered her thinking on the matter sound. However, it was his practice to move slowly in matters involving important state policy, so he could not approve her plan at the present time. Nevertheless, he was not rejecting it and was giving her no reason to lose hope. Confusing the issue still further, he reminded her that he was a prince of the Church and could take no action without the specific consent of the Pope.

Kristina gained the distinct impression that Mazarin intended to consult the Pope, and that as soon as he complied with this technical formality, he would supply the funds necessary for the venture. Had she been less eager to deceive herself, she would have understood that he had no intention of writing the Pope, and that, if France should support a war and gain possession of Naples, he would place a more stable person on the throne.

Mazarin was more specific on the subject of the 1,150,000 crowns that France owed Sweden. He was sad to tell her that tax revenues had failed to come up to expectations, prices were rising, and although the court appeared to enjoy every luxury, the finances of France were strained. Therefore, he could not pay the debt immediately. However, he hoped that at the first possible opportunity — perhaps within the next few months, if all went well — to make a token payment. In that event, she could certainly expect to receive the money as the legal representative of her cousin, Charles Gustavus, and she deserved every consideration because she was the former monarch.

In the meantime, the Cardinal said, she should return to Rome.

There were times when Kristina appeared to be incredibly obtuse; never in her long, varied career was she deafer to a direct hint than at this moment. Blithely ignoring Mazarin's request, she remained at Compiègne, and a letter she wrote to Cardinal Azzolino reflects her dazed state of mind. Anne of Austria, she declared, had beautiful hands, and furthermore she refused to believe the nasty rumors she had heard about the Queen Dowager and Mazarin; they simply could not be true.

She hinted in the letter that all was going well for her, and then she went on to discuss a matter that was none of her business — the romance between King Louis and Mazarin's niece, Marie de Mancini. Louis, she said, was shy, a boy who would die of love without daring to touch the tip of a lady's finger. But Marie, she added harshly, "is a past mistress of all the arts of Roman coquettes." However, it was her opinion that Mazarin was too wise to permit such an unsuitable match.

"He knows very well that marriage is the sovereign remedy for love," she wrote, "and that the nuptial bed is generally its tomb. I don't think, therefore, that he will put his fortune to so dangerous a test, for that might suffice to ruin him. His Eminence has held power for so long that he can smell potential disaster in the air from afar.

"This love is only calf love, there is no genuine passion in it. Of passion I believe Louis to be incapable. To marry him would be to make him hate those who had taken advantage of his impressionable youth, and you can imagine how such a revulsion in his feelings might bring about Mazarin's disgrace. But Mazarin is too clever to take such a risk."

Had Kristina been satisfied to play the role of a seer, she might have saved herself considerable trouble. But she decided to act as a matchmaker, probably because she wanted to place Mazarin under obligation to her. Not only was her judgment of character mistaken — her estimate of Louis was a colossal blunder — but she should have realized that in such a delicate affair, outside interference would not be tolerated. To complicate the situation still more, let it be recalled that she had promised to intercede on behalf of La Grande Mademoiselle.

"You should marry for love," she whispered loudly to the young King one afternoon, and the echoes of her remark were heard in every corner of the huge palace.

The following day she walked out onto a balcony where Louis and Marie were flirting happily. "Marry!" she told them stridently. "Rely on me to help you. I should enjoy being your confidante."

Mazarin and Anne of Austria knew how to act ruthlessly when it was necessary, and in this instance, speed was essential. The gala entertainments ended abruptly, and Kristina left Compiègne the following morning. Nothing in her own correspondence or her other writings indicates that she felt she had been thrown out of France. On the contrary, she was convinced that she and Mazarin had made a "secret treaty" and that the Cardinal intended to support her plan to become the ruler of Naples.

Mademoiselle de Montpensier takes a somewhat different view in her *Memoirs*. Perhaps she exaggerates. Certainly she had every right to be bitter, for Kristina had not only failed to live up to her word, but had actually encouraged La Grande

Mademoiselle's rival. It is impossible to blow away the mists of time, but Mademoiselle de Montpensier's remarks are, to say the least, explicit: "The Swedish Amazon went off in a hired carriage provided by the King, who also provided money with which to pay the post boys. There was no splendor; she had neither a bed, nor silver plate, nor any other indication of her royal rank. Her miserable retinue, considerably reduced in number, met her near the border, and she crossed into the Italian peninsula over the Mont Cenis Pass, while all France sighed in relief and said, 'Good riddance.'"

Kristina remained in Italy for a short time, arriving in October, 1656, and returning to France in July, 1657. During that period, her Neapolitan scheme became an obsession with her, and she devoted most of her time and energy to it. The plague was still raging in Rome, making it impossible for her to go there, although the Pope and the cardinals of the Curia refused to leave the city. She paid a short visit to Turin, but finding the court atmosphere chilly, she moved on to Pesaro, where she rented a palace for a relatively small sum of money. Her retinue had indeed been reduced, so her first act was to enlarge it. Once a queen, always a queen, she declared, and proved it, at least to her own satisfaction, by engaging a number of ladies- and gentlemen-in-waiting, hiring a company of Swiss guards, and sending emissaries to scour the area for handsome young boys who could be trained as pages.

Her dignity restored, Kristina plunged into a furious round of activities — giving balls, organizing amateur theatricals, and attending picnics. But she thought of very little except the scheme to conquer Naples, and she wrote Cardinal Mazarin several times each week, asking for the financial support that she considered her due. His replies were vague and unsatisfactory, so she sent Monaldeschi to Paris to conduct negotiations on her behalf. She gave him instructions to obtain the more than one million crowns that France owed Sweden and to urge the Cardinal to abide by the terms of his "treaty" and make specific plans for the invasion of Naples. The Marchese returned to Pesaro empty-handed, and the vague assurances of financial and political support that he brought with him, all of them verbal, were cold comfort to a woman who needed money and dreamed of fresh glory.

Kristina, reducing her sights for the time being, dispatched the Santinelli brothers to Paris with a letter to Mazarin saying she would accept a token payment of two hundred thousand crowns. (She told the Santinellis privately that if the Cardinal remained obdurate, she would take one hundred thousand.) The busy Mazarin tried to ignore the Queen's persistent emissaries, but Kristina continued to inundate him with letters, each more reproachful than the last, so he tried to silence her by making her a gift of fifteen thousand crowns.

Kristina was insulted. The sum was so paltry that it was no more than an act of charity, and, having received a partial payment of her allowance from Sweden, she decided to return to France herself. No one else was clever enough or wise enough to deal with Mazarin. She found it hard to believe that he was avoiding her; there had been a misunderstanding; she would clear it up in person, obtain his firm support, and launch her grand adventure.

She set out at once, accompanied by her entire suite. Immediately prior to her departure, she wrote to Azzolino and he, suspecting that she had become involved in a love affair, sent an inquiry to the Papal Vice-Legate, Giovanni Lascaris, who had been stationed at her court to keep an eye on her. Father Lascaris' reply was unequivocal: "The Queen loves no one in this world. She only loves her whims and caprices, and she lacks the powers to execute them."

Azzolino, who had gleaned something of her scheme to invade Naples, discussed the situation privately with several of his colleagues. It is probable that he also talked to the Pope about the problem, and that Alexander decided it would be a mockery of his dignity to intervene personally to halt the wild venture. Apparently he was disinclined to take the idea seriously, but Azzolino, who understood Kristina's nature and realized that she might further embarrass the Church if she became sufficiently aroused, sent her a strong letter that finally reached her at Avignon.

"I urge you," he wrote, "to abandon your plans for the present. The time is not ripe for their execution, and many of your friends here believe you will do yourself more harm than good by trying to fulfill them at this time. I have been informed on excellent authority," he continued, making an obvious reference to the Pope, "that you will be welcome in Rome if you will return quietly to Pesaro and resume your life there. The plague dwindles here, and your friends await the day when they can greet Your Majesty again."

Kristina respected Azzolino, but she stubbornly ignored his advice.

The French did not want her, and Gui Patin, historian of the court, expressed the opinion of Mazarin and Queen Anne when he wrote, "The Queen of Sweden comes here because Paris is the refuge of all wanderers. Her pretended conversion serves her as an excuse and a pretext for playing the pilgrim and journeying all over the world in search of excitement."

Mazarin made strenuous efforts to halt Kristina's progress, sending messengers to Avignon, Lyon, and Nevers. His letters were anything but subtle; he hinted broadly that she was not welcome. Complicated affairs of state made it difficult for him to devote his best efforts to her project, he wrote, so he suggested that they postpone their meeting until he could devote more time to the matter.

Thick-skinned, headstrong, and undismayed, Kristina gave no thought to Mazarin's convenience, and she continued to ride north through France. The Cardinal and Anne were such firm believers in the institution of monarchy that they felt they could not ask Kristina to leave the country without damaging the popularity of young Louis XIV, who had yet to prove himself and win the affection of his subjects. So they decided to make the best of a bad situation, and, as La Grande Mademoiselle's exile had ended at last, the palace at Fontainebleau was unoccupied.

Fontainebleau was sufficiently far from Paris to prevent the Queen from pestering Mazarin for a time, so the palace was placed at her disposal, and the Cardinal sent her a firm letter informing her that he hoped she would enjoy herself there until such time as he could confer with her. Anne, who pretended to be ignorant of all affairs of state, prepared to pay a courtesy visit to the persistent Queen so as to maintain a polite façade, and King Louis was requested to make a similar, brief journey.

Kristina settled down at Fontainebleau as though she owned the place. She had convinced herself that her plan would soon materialize, and she felt positive she would sit on the throne of Naples before Christmas. "Her Majesty," Mathilde said in her *Diary*, "talks of nothing but driving the Spaniards from her new kingdom and spends all of her waking hours preparing for that great day."

We learn from Mathilde and from Kristina's letters to Azzolino that the preparations were thorough, no detail being overlooked. The political and military aspects would be handled by subordinates; Kristina's sole concern was the personal effect she would create as she rode in triumph through the streets of her new capital. She ordered splendid uniforms for her Swiss guards, bought new livery for her serving men, and spent long hours with dressmakers, working out every detail of the gowns she and her ladies would wear on the glorious day.

Never had she savored such an intoxicating daydream.

VIII: 1657
MURDER

Just as the King was about to start out for Fontainebleau to see the Queen of Sweden [Gui Patin wrote], he received news which prevented him from doing so; news to the effect that she had caused her First Equerry, who was an Italian, to be put to death by another Italian, on account of certain rascalities and deceptions practiced on her, and on account of certain forged letters which the Equerry had shown her and which caused her the greater offense because even her honor was compromised in them.

The name of the assassin is Santinelli, and the name of the man assassinated is Monaldeschi.

As soon as he was dead, she had the wretched man's body conveyed to the Mathurin convent, where it was buried.

They say that she was herself in the gallery, close to the apartment in which the assassination took place. It is a very tragic affair; it also gives the impression of being a very black and scoundrelly affair. The poor fellow evidently had some suspicion of what was about to happen, for he was wearing a coat of mail, which made it very hard to dispatch him.

The Queen of Sweden, told of this, replied that in the circumstances it would be necessary to cut his throat, which they duly did.

I have heard that the Queen of Sweden has written to the King, saying that this is the proper way to treat officers who betray their sovereigns or are lacking in respect and loyalty toward them. Nevertheless, everyone whom I meet puts an unfavorable construction on the proceeding. People talk of nothing else, and all consider it an act of evil omen.

The facts, as Patin reported them, were surprisingly accurate. His reference to Kristina's "honor" hints that her motive was that of a scorned mistress, but his other observations come closer to the mark. The execution was deliberate, cold-blooded, and premeditated in every sense. Kristina, believing that Monaldeschi had been a traitor to her cause, had ordered his death. Her communication to Louis, which has not survived, is a precise indication of her state of mind. Living in an age when monarchs claimed they ruled by divine right, and unable to grasp the basic fact that she had given up certain privileges when she abdicated, she had ordered her equerry put to death on grounds that were, in her own mind, morally and legally right.

What she failed to realize was that the civilized world would not share her opinion and would be horrified by her calm assumption that she had the power of life and death over others. The murder was interpreted in the same way everywhere: people promptly assumed that Monaldeschi had been the Queen's lover, that he had been unfaithful, and that when she had discovered his infidelity, she had ordered him killed to obtain vengeance.

Certainly, the affair was the most celebrated murder of the century, and although Kristina eventually made her position clear to a few men of high station, the erroneous popular assumption followed her to her grave. In brief, when Monaldeschi's throat was cut, she lost her own reputation and never recovered it.

Apparently the rulers of Europe and those standing near their thrones understood the situation from the first, but even they were repelled by the barbarism of the act. Mme de Motteville, discussing the crime at length in her *Memoirs*, referred repeatedly to Kristina's vicious cruelty, and wrote that

Monaldeschi was "a man of no consequence who had committed the error of offending her."

She continued: "After her abominably cruel action she sat quietly in her room, chatting calmly as if nothing in particular had happened. Our Very Christian Queen-Mother, who had so many enemies, always overwhelmed them with marks of kindness instead of the punishment they deserved. She was inexpressibly shocked by the pagan act. The King and his brother blamed the proceeding, and His Eminence, who had no cruelty in his nature, was amazed at it. In fact, the entire Court was horrified by the ugly act of vengeance, and those who had praised the Queen were ashamed of their eulogies, though they did not fail to ridicule her unhappy victim for neglecting to defend himself. At the very least he should have carried a dagger and he should have used it."

La Grande Mademoiselle, who loved scandal of any sort and was never reluctant to walk where crowned heads feared to tread, hurried to Fontainebleau. After spending the better part of a day with Kristina and hearing the whole story, Mademoiselle de Montpensier came to the emphatic conclusion that her first impressions had been false. Kristina, she felt, was a savage. Writing in some detail, she said: "The Queen had told Monaldeschi her complaints against him and given him to understand that it was all one to her whether she had him beheaded in Sweden or executed in the Fontainebleau gallery. Santinelli had some difficulty in killing him, as he was wearing a coat of mail. He had to strike several times, with the result that the gallery ran with blood, and the stains can still be seen, in spite of vigorous attempts to wash them out.

"The general view taken of the proceeding was very unfavorable, and strong remarks were passed on her audacity in committing the killing in the King's Palace. Her claim is that she was doing justice, and that a sovereign's power of life and death over his subjects remains with the sovereign, wherever he might be. It is difficult for one who is untutored in the finer points of law to judge whether this opinion be true. But this kind of death is very cruel for anyone — and especially for a woman — to inflict."

Sweden was stunned by the news, and groups in both houses of the Riksdag initiated a movement to cut off the Queen's allowance permanently.

When word of the murder reached the Vatican, Pope Alexander canceled all of his appointments and spent the day alone in his private chapel, praying.

Mathilde von Echner, loyal to her mistress, states flatly in her *Memoirs*, "Monaldeschi was a traitor and deserved to die."

The situation that led up to the murder has been clarified only in part by scholarly detectives who have sought to shed light on the case over the course of more than three hundred years. There is no doubt that Monaldeschi admitted he had been forging letters, but there is still some question as to what he forged. He confessed, it is true, but the exact nature of the confession has never been revealed. It has also been established that he had a quarrel of long standing with Francesco Santinelli, and that he made a strenuous effort to blame Santinelli for what he himself had done. But what was it that he did?

Kristina, in her long explanation and justification of the murder, at no time states the precise charges. Nor was Santinelli blameless in his own relations with the Queen; his own faithlessness to her cause and her person should have sent him to prison for the rest of his life. Santinelli was an opportunistic thief. Kristina, using the better part of the allowance she had received from Sweden, sent him to Rome to redeem her jewels. He returned to Fontainebleau without the jewels, and it subsequently developed that he had redeemed them, pawned them again, and kept the money. In addition, he submitted a padded account of expenses to the Queen and she, trusting him, asked no questions and paid his reckoning in full.

Monaldeschi was aware of his colleague's dishonesty, and had he gone to Kristina with what he knew, Santinelli certainly would have been discharged. But the Marchese had fish of his own to fry. Afraid that his own lack of loyalty had been discovered, he made a clumsy attempt to shift the blame by forging letters to which he signed Santinelli's name and then offering them to the Queen as "evidence" of the assistant equerry's perfidy.

One of the unsolved mysteries of the whole case is the nature of the act of treason that was committed. Kristina sent several letters to Cardinal Azzolino and discussed various aspects of the unsavory matter, some of them petty, in great detail, but she did not spell out the crime that caused her to have Monaldeschi executed. Years later, in her *Memoirs*, she recalled long passages of purported dialogue, but here again she skirted the edge of the situation and avoided essentials.

Although concrete proof is lacking, it has long been assumed that Monaldeschi was in the pay of the Spaniards and was reporting Kristina's activities to Madrid. Thus, Spain was aware of her scheme to drive the viceroy out of Naples and seize the throne for herself. This theory is probably correct, and it may even be deduced from allusions in correspondence between the Vatican and the Papal Nuncio in Madrid that Monaldeschi cleverly magnified the threat, deliberately leading the Spaniards to believe that Cardinal Mazarin favored the Queen's plan. If this semieducated guess is correct, the Marchese presumably received higher fees from Madrid than he would have been paid if the Spanish government had realized that France had no intention of supporting the wild idea.

In any event, Kristina, whose passion for intrigue was undiminished, trapped Monaldeschi and caused him to "sign his own death warrant." Or so she says in her *Memoirs*, citing a melodramatic and most unlikely exchange. She declares that she had learned that Monaldeschi was guilty, but that he had no reason to believe she suspected him when she summoned him to the library at Fontainebleau and showed him the "proof of treachery," which he examined gravely.

The Marchese supposedly became indignant. "It is quite clear, Madam, that Your Majesty has been betrayed, and the traitor must be either the absentee known to Your Majesty and me, or else it must be myself. The treachery can emanate from no third quarter. Your Majesty will soon know which of us is guilty, and I trust that Your Majesty will not pardon the offender."

"What punishment do you consider to be due to a man who betrays me in that style?"

"Your Majesty should show him no mercy, but should instantly put him to death. I am quite prepared to be either executioner or victim; it is an act of justice."

"Very well. Remember what you have said. I promise you, for my part, that I will not forgive him."

Whatever exchange may have taken place, Monaldeschi was sufficiently apprehensive to wear armor.

An impartial eyewitness has preserved the actual story of the murder and the events that preceded it. The prior of the monastery near the palace of Fontainebleau, Father le Bel (Christian name unknown), was subsequently requested to submit a full report in writing to Cardinal Mazarin, and that document is the only authentic account of what happened.

Father le Bel writes that one of the Queen's grooms of the chamber appeared unexpectedly at the monastery, the Community of the Maturins, and asked if he would come to the palace on a private matter. He agreed, of course, and Kristina received him alone in the *Galerie des Cerfs*. She opened the interview by asking whether she could depend on Father le Bel to respect her confidence, and he promised that she could, saying that in all confidential matters he was as one blind and deaf. Kristina then gave him a packet of papers, which was sealed in three places. When she asked him to return it, she said, she wanted him to give it to her in the presence of such witnesses as she chose to summon.

Here, obviously, were the documents that "proved" Monaldeschi's "treason." Kristina herself refers to them repeatedly, but no trace of them can be found today, and it is probable that she destroyed them herself or that they were burned under her supervision.

The prior, who had no idea of the importance of the papers, thought he was merely humoring a woman who appeared distressed, and he kept the packet in a safe place. Several days later, at one o'clock in the afternoon, he was called to Fontainebleau again, where Kristina was waiting for him in the ornate *Galerie des Cerfs*. The first inkling of trouble came when the groom of the chamber slammed the door behind the priest with unnecessary violence.

Apprehensive, although he did not know why, he approached the Queen, who was standing at the far end of the gallery conversing with Monaldeschi and another attendant, while several retainers remained some paces behind the trio. "She called to me in a loud voice, 'Give me the packet, Father. I want to read it.' I did as she had bidden and sought to take my leave, thinking my part in the strange affair concluded, but

Her Majesty insisted, still speaking in a loud voice, that she wished me to remain."

Kristina broke the seals with her own hand, opened the package and, showing the documents to Monaldeschi, demanded an explanation. Father le Bel writes that Monaldeschi was very confused, and after offering various excuses in an undertone, finally admitted that the handwriting was his.

"Oh, the traitor, cried the Queen, and he threw himself at her feet, imploring her forgiveness, while the other members of the suite drew their swords. I said that I refused to be a party to violence, and Her Majesty assured me that she was guided in all things by reason. My fears were allayed."

Monaldeschi begged Kristina to listen to his explanation, and she seemed agreeable. He spoke to her earnestly for more than an hour, and her attitude, the prior writes, "was one of great patience and moderation, and she gave no sign that she was displeased by his importunity."

However, after an hour had passed, she turned to the priest and said, "Observe, Father! You are my witness that I am making no undue haste but am giving this traitor more time than he has the right to ask for from a person whom he has wronged, to justify himself, if he can do so."

Monaldeschi continued to address her, speaking in an undertone, but finally she gestured sharply, terminating the conversation, and said to the priest solemnly, "Father, I now leave this man in your hands. Comfort his soul and make him ready for death."

Father le Bel was totally unprepared for the dramatic declaration. He stresses in his report to the Cardinal that he had expected Kristina to forgive the man and he himself had been thinking about his dinner. But he realized that Kristina was in earnest, and he became an active participant in the drama. His own conscience made it imperative that he intervene, he declared, and he implored the Queen to be merciful. She refused, at great length, and apparently was somewhat less than coherent. "He is a worse criminal than those who are condemned to be broken on the wheel!" she exclaimed dramatically. "I trusted him, and he betrayed my trust. His own conscience should be his executioner."

She swept out of the gallery, and three men, all armed with swords, approached Monaldeschi. He pleaded with them, and as all seemed reluctant to carry out the Queen's orders, one of them followed her, only to return with the crisp message: "No, Marchese, you are to die. Think of God and of your soul."

Monaldeschi appealed to Father le Bel, who hurried out of the gallery. "I found the Queen in her apartment," he writes, "with a serene and unmoved countenance. I threw myself at her feet, and with tears streaming from my eyes and a voice shaken with sobs, implored her, by the Wounds and Passion of the Saviour, to have pity on the Marquis. She assured me that she was very sorry she could not grant my request and spoke to me of the blackness of the miserable wretch's perfidy and of the cruelty of his intentions toward herself, adding that he must not look for pardon or pity, and that many who had been broken on the wheel deserved their fate less than he did."

The desperate prior used other arguments. The Queen was not in her own palace, and the King, whose hospitality she was enjoying, might not approve. The act might be a just one — the priest did not set himself up as an authority in such matters, but emphasized that the forms of the law had to be obeyed by all. If she lodged a complaint, he said, her host would not grudge her satisfaction and her reputation would not be sullied.

But Kristina answered every point firmly. She was neither a prisoner nor an exile in France, she was a sovereign ruler, supreme over her own subjects, and had no need to ask any man's leave to do justice, least of all when she held the proofs of a traitor's guilt in her hand.

"I saw," Father le Bel writes, "that the Queen was frightened. I asked her what she feared, and she said that if she failed to execute the traitor, he would kill her."

Her final words were loud and firm. "No, Father, I cannot permit myself to listen to you. Never fear, I shall tell the King all about it. Go back to the man and see to his soul. My conscience will not let me do what you ask."

The prior wanted to leave the palace at once and summon help, but two of Kristina's retainers were waiting for him outside her apartment and forcibly conducted him back to the gallery. Realizing there was no hope, he asked Monaldeschi to confess his sins.

> The confession was made, punctuated with agonizing shrieks of terror. Then the Queen's Almoner entered the Gallery, and to him also, Monaldeschi addressed his piteous plea. There was a conference between them, but the chief executioner cut it short, saying: "Marquis, ask God's forgiveness. Your death cannot be delayed any longer. Have you finished your confession?"
>
> And he pushed him, without waiting for an answer, against the Gallery wall and stabbed at his stomach. Monaldeschi caught at the sword with his hand and cut his fingers. Then he was slashed in the face, and then the executioners went in and finished their work, which was a slow business, because of the coat of mail he wore.
>
> And then the Queen, having been assured that the Marquis was really dead, expressed her regret at having been obliged to execute him, but said that justice required her to punish him

for his crime and his treason, and that she prayed God to forgive him. She told me to take him away carefully and bury him and added that she wished several Masses said for his soul. Later she sent one hundred livres by two of her men to the Monastery to arrange for prayers for the repose of the said Marquis' soul.

Cardinal Azzolino, whose correspondence with Kristina had been informal and friendly, sent her a curt note. "The murder of the Marchese," he said flatly, "has much displeased His Holiness and all the Court of Rome. Should you journey here in the near future, I fear you would find but cold welcome."

The reaction in other cities was even more vehement. Students rioted in Paris; Cromwell's government lodged a formal protest with the Swedish Ambassador; and in Stockholm, King Charles Gustavus, not allowing himself to forget that Kristina was his cousin and that attacks on her, if unchecked, might weaken his own position, announced publicly that although he deplored her act of violence, he was a man of honor and would continue to pay her semiannual allowance. His ministers approved the statement, and no one seemed to be bothered by the knowledge that, to date, only a small portion of the promised subsidy had actually been paid.

No one was more embarrassed than Cardinal Mazarin. Queen Anne, who was outraged by the crime, made his life miserable by demanding that Kristina be expelled from France, but Mazarin wanted less talk, not more. He had allowed Kristina to entertain her Neapolitan dream because of the nuisance value the scheme had in his own dealings with Spain, and he was afraid that if the scandal spread, relations with Madrid might become seriously complicated. So he sent the Queen's old friend, the Comte de Chanut, now a deputy foreign minister, to Fontainebleau. Chanut brought her a simple request: the problem would be solved if she issued a brief statement saying she was the victim of a whispering campaign and that Monaldeschi had died as a result of a courtiers' brawl.

Kristina refused and wrote a letter to Mazarin that minced no words:

My Cousin, — M. de Chanut who is, I believe, one of the best friends I have, will assure you that I have received your communication with respect, and if he has not frightened me, as he expected to do, that was not for lack of terrifying eloquence. To tell you the truth, we Northerners are somewhat ferocious and not easily alarmed.

You will excuse me, therefore, if his errand to me has not had all the success that you could have wished, and I beg you to believe that I will willingly do anything to please you except showing myself afraid of you. You are aware that any man who has passed the age of thirty has ceased to be afraid of bogeys; and I, for my part, find it much easier to cut people's throats than to be frightened by them.

As to what I did to Monaldeschi, I assure you that if I had not already done it, I would do it tonight, before going to bed. I have no reason to regret my action, but every reason to be delighted with it.

Those are my sentiments. I hope they meet with your approval; but if they do not I shall nevertheless entertain them, always remaining your very affectionate friend, Kristina Maria Alexandra, *Regina*.

Her tone, which was undiplomatic and discourteous, made her sound like an angry woman whistling in the dark. But she meant every word, as she demonstrated in a brief covering note that she wrote to Chanut. "I send you the letter which I have written to the Cardinal. I have nothing to add to it beyond begging you to assure him, as a message from me, that

I will gladly do anything in my power for him and the King except showing fear and repenting, or disavowing any of my actions. I know of no one who is great enough, or powerful enough, to compel me to conceal my sentiments or disown my actions. I am not telling you this as a secret confined to a friend, but as a sentiment which all the world is welcome to know and which I have no intention of disguising as long as I live."

Knowing that neither communication would be publicized, she hit on the novel idea of writing to Santinelli, who was still living at Fontainebleau as a member of her staff, and she took care to send copies to various acquaintances in Paris and Rome. She began by assuring Santinelli that she had never believed Monaldeschi's aspersions on his character. "You have proved your unswerving loyalty to me and I believe in your fidelity," she declared, still unaware that he was robbing her regularly and systematically.

The rest of the letter is a defiant statement of her position. "In the end, Monaldeschi died, confessing his infamy and admitting your innocence, protesting that he had invented the whole fantastic story in order to ruin you.

"Take note of his example and pray God that He may never let you lose either your intelligence or your honor. Always behave like a gentleman and never do anything unworthy of that character.

"You need not trouble to justify my action to anyone.

"I do not propose to render an account of it to anyone but God, Who would have punished me if I had pardoned the traitor his abominable delinquency. Let that suffice for you.

"My conscience assures me that I acted in accordance with the precepts of Divine Justice and that I could not act, and ought not to have acted, otherwise.

"Keep yourself in a good temper, and I will do my best to procure for you the consolation on which your heart is set."

That "consolation" was a dukedom that he wanted, and Kristina persuaded some who had believed that the crime was political, not one of passionate revenge, that they were mistaken when she wrote to her cousin, to King Louis, and to Pope Alexander, telling each of them that a duchy should be granted to her loyal retainer. There is no record that the recipients of these astonishing communications even replied to her request.

Cardinal Mazarin, still trying to keep the lid on the bubbling pot, sent Chanut back to Fontainebleau with a verbal message: King Louis's calendar was crowded, and the Cardinal himself was exceptionally busy, so neither would be able to find time to receive the Queen within the near future. Therefore, he suggested she might prefer to return to Italy.

Kristina dug in her heels and stayed at Fontainebleau. The French court retaliated by pretending she did not exist. Members of the nobility avoided her, the scholars and artists she invited to visit her did not reply to her letters, and she spent the long autumn and the better part of the winter at Fontainebleau, which was cold, damp, and lonely. The snubs aroused in Kristina a fierce determination to achieve a triumph that would cause all of Europe to hail her again. Realizing that she had to abandon her Neapolitan scheme for the moment, she concocted another one even wilder.

She would become immortal, she reasoned, if she could persuade England to return to the Church.

Blandly ignoring history, the strong anti-Catholic feeling in England, and the personality of the dour Puritan, Oliver Cromwell, she sent an emissary to London with a private message to Cromwell, proposing that she be invited to cross the Channel on a visit of state. The title of Lord Protector had just been declared hereditary, so she envisaged a neat plan that would create and bind a permanent alliance between England, France, and the Vatican. The idea was as basic as it was startling: she suggested that Cromwell divorce his wife and marry one of Mazarin's nieces. She wanted nothing for herself, her emissary declared, not mentioning that she was hoping Mazarin would be so overcome with gratitude that he would act immediately to win her the crown of Naples.

There is no record of Cromwell's reaction to the novel suggestion, but he must have been dumfounded. Aside from the fact that he had been happily married for many years and that he was opposed to divorce in principle, marriage to one of the Mancini girls, who were approximately his son's age, would have been political suicide. The Lord Protector brushed aside the nonsensical notion and refused to consider inviting Kristina to England. The daughter of Gustavus Adolphus was regarded by the British people as a renegade, Cromwell himself hated women who interfered in affairs of state, and the recent scandal had shocked the Roundheads. Kristina's messenger returned to Fontainebleau empty-handed.

Kristina knew she could not go unbidden to London, but, refusing to admit defeat, decided that nothing stood in the way of a journey to Paris. Traveling there with her entourage, she arrived unexpectedly at the Louvre on the coldest day of the winter.

Mazarin tried desperately to cope with an impossible situation. Anne of Austria had hysterics and threatened to leave the city at once, but the Cardinal, who was trying to mend his relations with Spain, persuaded her not to act hastily. The word was passed around that Kristina was to be received with chilly reserve, and she was given a small, dark apartment at the palace. She accepted it in grim silence and made no complaint when the members of her entourage were treated with even less respect.

"I was forced to accept a serving maid's room," Mathilde von Echner writes in her *Memoirs*, "but Her Majesty's pride was inspiring and wishing to emulate her, I made no protest."

Kristina went to see young King Louis dance in a ballet, and held her head high when no one spoke to her at the supper that followed. She attended several masked balls given by high-ranking nobles, even though she had not been invited, and rode to their houses in public carriages that she herself hailed on the street. No one danced with her at any of these affairs, but she doggedly continued to attend them. She also took advantage of a standing offer she had received on her previous visit to Paris and went to a meeting of the French Academy. The members treated her courteously, and after reading several of their unpublished papers, they discussed the dictionary they were compiling.

They invited her to study it, and called one item in particular to her attention. It was a definition of a rather unusual type of practical joke, one which diverts the perpetrator at the expense of his victim. Kristina was not always thick-skinned, of course, and in this instance, understood the subtle Gallic slur at once. According to some accounts, she blushed; other reports say she laughed too loudly. In any event, she finally knew she had lost the battle and she went to Mazarin, ready to admit defeat. She would leave Paris and return to Rome if he would give her sufficient money to travel in style.

The strings of the Cardinal's purse, which had always been knotted tightly, were suddenly pulled open. Kristina was given twenty-five thousand crowns to spend as she pleased. The money was a gift; there was only the single condition that she depart at once.

No one said farewell to her, and on the morning she left Paris, the palace was strangely empty. King Louis was indisposed, Anne of Austria slept late, and Mazarin, who had told Kristina he would speak to her about the Neapolitan business before she departed, was unavailable. She tried to save face by leaving a member of her staff behind as her "ambassador," but the gesture was feeble, and she rode unimpeded, south to Toulon, stopping en route in cities that had once hailed her but now resolutely ignored her.

Bitter and lonely, she sailed to Livorno. The murder of Monaldeschi had reaped its harvest.

IX: 1658–1667

THE WANDERER

Kristina knew she could not realize her dream, but she persisted to the last in maintaining the fiction that she would soon sit on the throne of Naples. She met the Duke of Modena after landing at Livorno and signed an agreement with him that was meaningless, as both of them realized. The Duke promised to begin military operations as soon as the Queen gave him four hundred thousand crowns in gold, but he had heard, as had everyone of consequence, that Sweden was slow in paying her subsidy. And Kristina herself was aware of the fact that never in her life had she been so poor.

What she did not know was that Francesco Santinelli was continuing to take advantage of her carelessness in financial matters and that the scoundrel was becoming wealthy at her expense. Accustomed to extravagance and still incapable of understanding the value of money, she happily allowed him to handle her affairs. Some of his tricks were so bold that only an incredibly naïve person could have been fooled by them, but Kristina had never learned how to guard her purse. Santinelli "borrowed" various pieces of clothing from her wardrobe for "theatrical entertainments and pageants," then quickly pawned them. When he took her ermine cloak, a magnificent garment embroidered with gold crowns, no pawnbroker would accept it from him, believing he had stolen it, so he made out a paper transferring its ownership to himself and persuaded the Queen to sign the document without reading it.

He stole silver plate, jewels, and paintings from her collection; he persuaded her to dismiss her Swiss guards, then calmly disposed of their uniforms and lied to her about the proceeds; and, taking full advantage of his new position as First Equerry, he insisted that the cooks, dressmakers, and other members of the staff who made purchases, submit their bills to him. When they did, he padded them and pocketed the difference. He hurried ahead of Kristina to Rome to rent a house for her — the Farnese family being reluctant to let her return to their palace — and he succeeded in complicating an already delicate situation by making love to the grand-niece of the Pope, who did not consider him an eligible suitor.

When Kristina arrived in Rome, late in the winter of 1657–58, she found the atmosphere strained and the people aloof. She might have imagined herself back in Paris, except that several of the cardinals, Azzolino in particular, understood her better than she knew herself, and befriended her. They admired her intellect, and although they deplored her talent for creating trouble, they believed she was misguided rather than wicked and they made a strenuous effort to set her on the right path. When Pope Alexander expressed his reluctance to see her, Azzolino convinced him that the Protestants would use the incident to discredit the Church. Like Mazarin, Azzolino believed that the gossip about Kristina would die if men in high places observed the ordinary amenities and received her without fanfare. He was successful with the Pope, and the Queen was invited to a private audience at the Vatican.

Azzolino, who was destined to become Kristina's closest friend and protector, was a remarkable man. A member of an ancient Roman house, he had never been a priest, but had been given a cardinal's red hat for political reasons. Before becoming a prince of the Church, he had been a scholar of note and a patron of the arts, and he never lost his enthusiasm for intellectual achievements; this passion gave him a common interest with Kristina, and as he was a compassionate student of human nature, he made strenuous efforts to rearrange her disordered life.

Many years passed before he succeeded, and as Kristina's reputation was certainly less than immaculate, it was inevitable that gossips should link their names romantically. There is no evidence to suggest that Azzolino failed to keep the vows he took when he became a cleric, however, or that he ever allowed himself to forget that he was a man of honor. The correspondence of various seventeenth-century notables assumes that he was Kristina's lover — and she might have been delighted to add a cardinal to her list of conquests — but Azzolino, who was ambitious and wanted to become the Vatican Secretary of State, if not Pope, was too clever and far too austere to become involved in an illicit romance with the most notorious lady of the age. It is true that Kristina gradually learned to lean heavily on him for help and advice, and during periods of depression there can be no doubt that she imagined herself in love with him.

Some of her messages to him read like a young girl pining for an idol, but all of Azzolino's letters to her are courteous, dignified, and correct. "Her Majesty's temperament," he wrote to Pope Alexander in 1665, "is vigorous, and her enthusiasms are spontaneous. She possesses an intellect that causes us to err by treating her as a mature woman. We are inclined to forget that her nature is unstable, and are, as a consequence, unpleasantly surprised when her conduct disturbs us. I have learned that when she is treated firmly, as a tutor treats a pupil, she becomes docile, decorous, and meek. Her talents and energies, which are considerable, could be utilized for the benefit of the Church if we could find the proper channels in which to direct them."

There is no doubt that Azzolino practiced what he preached, and in 1658 he made strenuous efforts to help Kristina. The Pope was still annoyed with her, more because of Santinelli's attentions to his niece than because of the murder of Monaldeschi. The age was one in which the lives of rogues were regarded as cheap, and no men of power, either spiritual or temporal, seem to have been unduly upset by the death of the equerry. Most of the gossip about the unfortunate incident was kept alive by literary men and scholars.

Azzolino knew that the Pope would not forgive Kristina until she got rid of Santinelli, which she refused to do, so he invented a diplomatic mission that would take the equerry to Vienna and keep him there for some months. Alexander, relieved, promptly summoned the Queen to the Vatican and gave her his blessing.

That Santinelli was a thief, the Cardinal had learned by accident: A bishop visiting the Queen one day was surprised to hear her express sympathy for Azzolino. She hoped he would soon recover from his financial difficulties, she said, and she wished she could do more to help him. Azzolino, when he received this report from the bishop, was astonished. Probing delicately, he learned that Santinelli had told Kristina he had loaned considerable sums to the Cardinal, but had warned her to say nothing for fear of hurting His Eminence's sensitive feelings.

Carefully biding his time, Azzolino waited until Santinelli had departed for Vienna, then sent for all of his account books. Ludovico Santinelli, loyal to his brother and aware of the discrepancies in the ledgers, tried to block the inquiry, but subsided when Cardinal Azzolino threatened to have him imprisoned as a practitioner of black magic. Ludovico fled to Milan, and Azzolino made a thorough study of the books.

Kristina was reluctant to believe that her trusted equerry had been cheating her, but the evidence against him was overwhelming. Finally, even she lost her temper with the thief and determined to prosecute him, but his brother had warned him that his activities had been discovered, so Santinelli traveled to Switzerland and stayed there, hiding from the long arm of Roman authority.

Azzolino, who had gained Kristina's complete confidence, discharged almost all of her staff after learning that most of them had been parties to the conspiracy and had been paid for their treachery. Seeing no reason why a queen-in-exile should live like a reigning monarch, the Cardinal reduced the size of the household staff drastically, and replaced petty thieves with honest, responsible men and women. These people became her permanent retainers, and the majority remained with her the rest of their lives. Some were still serving her when she herself finally died in 1689.

But Azzolino was a mere human, not a sorcerer; he could not produce funds out of the air to maintain Kristina's household. King Charles Gustavus continued to send her only a portion of her allowance, and so she was unable to redeem the valuables Santinelli had pawned. She was living in the Farnese Palace again, thanks to the new dignity she had achieved with Azzolino's help, and she sent to Antwerp for many of the paintings and other art treasures she had stored there at the time of her abdication. The Cardinal persuaded her to sell some of them in order to obtain gold, and in a letter that subsequently became famous, he told her, "If you would be treated with the respect due a Queen, you must live an exemplary life; and it ill becomes Majesty to allow her plate and her very clothes to lie in the vaults of the pawnbrokers."

Kristina obeyed him meekly and managed to redeem most of her belongings. Unfortunately, Azzolino could not keep constant watch on her; his work in the Curia was demanding, and when his back was turned, Kristina could not resist temptation. Wanting larger quantities of cash than she had in her strongbox, she pawned some of her diamonds.

Azzolino was annoyed, as were several other cardinals who were trying to help her attain respectability. She tried to appease them by donating three thousand crowns to help raise a regiment of troops to fight in what was being called the Last Crusade, a proposed holy war against the Turks.

Once again she was demonstrating her almost infallible instinct for sponsoring hopeless causes. The crusade never moved out of the talking stage, for the Ottoman Empire was powerful, wealthy, and vigorous, and the nations of Europe were too busy bickering with one another to show any genuine enthusiasm for a holy war. Kristina's three thousand crowns vanished, but she refused to learn her lesson. The idea of a crusade appealed to her, and, allowing her vivid imagination to control her reason, she tried to interest others in the project. Azzolino and his fellow cardinals were pleased that she was devoting her energies to a scheme that was harmless, so they made no attempt to interfere.

The Venetian Ambassador became a regular caller at the Farnese Palace, and Kristina spent long hours with him, discussing the details of the crusade. But the Venetian Republic was the only nation that was eager to declare war against the Infidel. Venice depended on commerce for her prosperity — her ships were being attacked and captured by pirates from North Africa who were operating with the semiofficial sanction of Constantinople — and the Venetians had sound reasons for wanting to wage a war that would smash the power of the Turk.

Negotiations with other rulers produced such a feeble response, however, that Kristina, still restless, began to explore other avenues of excitement. Blithely ignoring the fact that her income depended on her cousin and that Charles Gustavus was embroiled in a dispute with the Holy Roman Emperor in Vienna, she wrote to the Austrians, proposing an alliance. If the Emperor would come to terms with her, she said, she would give him Pomerania, but as it was not her domain and she had no right to dispose of it in any way, she failed to mention how she intended to keep her promise. At the same time she was obviously afraid that Azzolino — and perhaps the Pope himself — would chastise her for meddling in affairs that were none of her business, so she told the Emperor, "If you will work with me, I will do something that will be of great benefit to the Church."

In general, her life remained relatively calm until early spring of 1660, when she received word that King Charles Gustavus had died and that his sickly four-year-old son, Charles XI, had been raised to the throne. There was every reason to believe that the five Regents, among them her cousin's widow, would not honor the commitment to pay her pension, so Kristina decided to go to Sweden in person to protect her interests.

Accompanied by a small staff, she left Rome on July 20, 1660, and, after a rapid journey by way of Rimini, Verona, Trieste, Augsburg, and Nuremberg, arrived in Hamburg on August 18. As usual, her motives were not merely those that appeared on the surface. It was far easier for Kristina to act the role of a dedicated missionary than to lead a truly religious life, and the letters she sent to Cardinal Azzolino indicate her determination to transform Sweden into a Catholic country.

She planned to achieve her end in a direct way: as she had made Charles Gustavus her heir, she thought it only fitting that she, in turn, should be named heir to little Charles XI.

The idea was absurd. The Regents certainly had no intention of handing over power to a capricious woman who had proved her instability by abandoning her crown and homeland. And the clergy, suspecting her ultimate aim, were strongly opposed to her. Lutheran ministers, whom she had mocked when she had played with her dogs or read classics during Sabbath services, preached strong sermons, warning the people not to be fooled and urging them to reject the former monarch who had repudiated them.

Kristina was confident that she would succeed, though, and apparently her desire for freedom meant less to her now than wealth, power, and importance, for Mathilde von Echner writes in her *Diary* on August 16, 1660, "Her Majesty's spirits continue to rise each day, and she speaks of little except the joys of returning to the land of her birth."

At some point on her journey, Kristina decided to mention her ambitions openly, and she wrote to various Swedish nobles, all of whom she addressed as "Cousin," telling them she thought that if she were made the legal heir to the throne, a difficult problem would be solved for Sweden, and she would have no more financial worries, as her allowance would be paid regularly.

A record of one of the meetings of the Regents is illuminating. Count Brahé read the letter he had received, and then expressed himself firmly. "I believe she should be sent to Jaelland," he said, referring to a large island off the southern coast of the Swedish mainland, where a fortress was located. "She should be conducted there by a man of honor and determination."

Magnus de la Gardie, uncle of the child King, asked cautiously, "Would not that be rather like taking her prisoner?"

"It would," Brahé said. "That is exactly what I mean, and I think it would be the very best thing that could happen to her. It would save the nation much embarrassment."

The Regents were tempted to accept the suggestion, but everyone was reluctant to place the daughter of the great Gustavus Adolphus under arrest, so it was finally decided to send an officer of high rank with a letter telling her that she would not be welcome in Sweden. The officer intercepted her in Denmark, and she sent him home with a tactful but unyielding reply, addressed to Brahé:

"My Cousin, — I esteem you so highly that I cannot possibly feel offended by any sentiments which you express; and you use such flattering language in your communication that I regret extremely to find myself placed in circumstances in which it is incompatible with my honor to follow your advice.

"It is necessary for me to come to Sweden, and I think it is necessary also for Sweden. So I will come."

A full meeting of the council was called, and the Regents recommended that an augmented troop of cavalry be sent to the border to prevent her from entering the country. If necessary, the Regents said, the soldiers should use force to dissuade the former monarch. The council accepted the suggestion without a dissenting vote, and a colonel was placed in command of the expedition.

Unfortunately for the council, the commander of the troop and his deputy were veterans of Gustavus Adolphus' legion, and when Kristina informed them that no power on earth was strong enough to deter her, they could not bring themselves to drive an unarmed woman, the daughter of the King they had loved, across the frontier into Denmark. Kristina calmly continued her journey, escorted by the confused cavalrymen.

When she arrived in Stockholm, the Regents had to swallow their anger and, realizing that there would be a loud protest from the Catholic nations if they mistreated the Queen, received her with as much pleasantness as they could muster. Little King Charles conducted her to her suite, the same apartment she had occupied when she had been the country's ruler, and the court waited tensely for an explosion. Kristina, true to form, reacted immediately. She summoned the principal housekeeper and the royal chamberlain while her belongings were being unpacked and ordered them to convert one room into a chapel where, she said, she planned to attend Mass daily.

The following day she decided to drive through the city in an open carriage "in order to see sights familiar to me all of my life."

The Regents, continuing to make the best of a thoroughly unpleasant situation, ordered a twenty-one gun salute fired in her honor, but Kristina was not satisfied and complained because she did not receive a salute of one hundred and one guns. The common people, remembering that she had been their champion during the early years of her reign, gathered in the streets to cheer her. She made the mistake of interpreting their gesture as a sign they wanted her restored to the throne, and when she returned to the palace, she announced that she planned to seek legal assistance in drafting a document that would rescind her abdication.

She faced a stone wall; even men who had been her friends, joined hands to prevent her from seizing the throne. Both chambers of the Riksdag held emergency meetings and condemned her proposal. Charles Gustavus' widow retired to her apartment with her son, declaring that she would not leave the suite until Kristina was sent away, and a strong guard was placed around the boy King for fear that one of Kristina's followers might murder him. The murder of Monaldeschi was fresh in the minds of the Regents, and everyone was hysterical.

The Lutheran clergy were Kristina's most determined foes, and after waiting so long to avenge the humiliations they had suffered before and after her abdication, they attacked her unmercifully. Strong sermons were delivered every Sunday from every pulpit, and their theme was the same: "She who was our Queen has become a foreigner, so drive her out."

The assaults became increasingly bitter when Kristina, never one to run away from a fight, appeared regularly in public, wearing a cross and telling everyone she saw that she attended Mass every morning. The clergy stepped up the pace of its attack, and Archbishop Lenaeus, who had officiated at Kristina's coronation, outlined official policy in a firm statement delivered in the Storkyrka. Lutherans, he said, were well aware of the Catholic doctrine that faith need not be kept with heretics. Furthermore, Kristina had displayed gross contempt for the faith of her fathers by changing the last of her given names from Augusta to Alexandra. Therefore, Lutherans were under no obligation to keep faith with her.

Later that same day, at the palace, Kristina and Lenaeus confronted each other, and their encounter was reported in a score of journals and diaries. "We know very well what the Pope wants," the Archbishop said. "We know his zeal for our souls."

"I know the Pope better than you do," Kristina replied, "and I am quite sure he would not give four crowns for the souls of all of you."

Lenaeus ignored her withering scorn, at least for the sake of the record, and asked the question that so many people in

Sweden had raised: "Why did you desert the true Lutheran faith?"

"Because I was disgusted with your long and idiotic sermons," the undiplomatic Queen retorted.

The more sophisticated enjoyed a laugh at the Archbishop's expense, but Kristina had won only a minor skirmish. The bishop of Åbo added fuel to the controversy by writing letters to a number of high-placed persons, stating that he had seen Kristina weep, and that she had admitted to him that she was sorry she had changed her religion.

This was the last straw, and Kristina wrote a blistering letter, addressed to little Charles XI and delivered to the Regents, demanding that the Bishop be punished for his lying effrontery. The letter concluded on a note that sounded ominous to all who recalled the murder of Monaldeschi. "Should I, despite my expectations, be so unfortunate as to fail to obtain true satisfaction through Your Majesty's intervention, I trust that Your Majesty will not be surprised if I should myself take steps to bring down upon this Bishop's head a punishment adequate to the enormity of his crime and the intolerable dishonor which he has tried to inflict upon me."

The Regents were stunned, the nobles shocked, and the clergy alarmed. An armed guard was assigned to protect the Bishop. Kristina's chapel was dismantled and her priests were ordered to leave the country within twenty-four hours. Her own movements were restricted, members of her entourage were ordered to remain at the palace, and even Mathilde von Echner, who had managed to retain many friendships in Sweden, was placed under the watchful eyes of sentries.

Public opinion had solidified, and the Regents, who had been waiting for the Queen to go too far, now felt strong enough to send her a letter which they took care to have copied and distributed throughout the country. "When we reflect upon the last will and testament of the Great Gustavus," they declared, "we find it sets forth in very explicit terms that anyone who departs from our doctrine and embraces Popery shall lose all his rights and possessions in the Kingdom of Sweden. We are willing, however, that Her Majesty shall continue to enjoy the revenues granted to her, not in virtue of the agreement entered into at the time of her abdication, which she has contravened and flouted in many ways, but simply and solely in view of the signal merits of her ancestors."

Magnus de la Gardie delivered the letter, and Mathilde states in her *Diary*: "He took pains to address Her Majesty rudely, and suggested that she might suffer the fate she had planned for the Bishop of Åbo if she failed to leave the country at once. She protested that she had meant no personal harm to the Bishop, but Magnus refused to hear her explanation, and taking his leave of her while she was still speaking, closed the door behind him with great force."

Kristina became panic-stricken, and, giving in to her fears, sent a note to the lord treasurer, scribbled in her own hand. "For Heaven's sake, send me my money that I may be able to make haste and leave this country, where they persecute me so cruelly. I assure you that if only I could get my money, I would not stay here an hour longer; and I would rather perish in poverty elsewhere than live in Sweden, subject to daily insults.

"If you have any affection for me, arrange things in such a way that I may be able to start at the earliest possible moment, for I give you my word of honor that I shall not tarry a single instant after my affairs are settled."

The Regents promptly paid the current installment of her subsidy, and she departed the following day, accompanied by a strong cavalry and infantry escort under strict orders to see her across the border.

Frustrated and humiliated, Kristina returned to Hamburg, where she relieved her feelings by leading a dissipated life. Some of her orgies, similar to the one described in the opening chapter, made her thoroughly unpopular, and she was finally warned that she would be asked to leave the city unless she behaved more discreetly. The Pope, disturbed by the bitter feelings she had aroused in Sweden, sent word to her through Cardinal Azzolino that he did not want her to return to Rome for the present, so she modified her behavior. She had no choice, for she was not welcome in France; the Protestant Dutch closed their border to her; the Spaniards wanted no part of someone who had intrigued against them and announced publicly that if she traveled to Brussels or Antwerp, the gates of both cities would be closed in her face. Charles II, who had just been restored to the throne of England, was less crude but equally firm, and sent her a message through an emissary, saying that the climate of England was unsuitable for a visit.

Kristina settled down, gave no more parties and lived soberly. Private orgies had never appealed to her — she had demonstrated throughout her life that she indulged in outrageous conduct only to shock people — so it was no hardship for her to act like a lady. However, she could not curb her restless energy and she threw herself into a variety of projects. Perhaps the silliest of them was her search, conducted exclusively by correspondence, for the mythical "philosopher's stone." According to legend, it contained the key to all wisdom, and Kristina, a product of a superstitious age, apparently believed in the existence of the stone. Her experiences with Monaldeschi and Santinelli had rubbed away the bloom of her ingenuousness, however, and she replied cautiously and with cunning when various charlatans wrote to her that they could obtain the stone for her, provided she was willing to pay a fortune for it. She answered these letters by demanding proof, and her correspondents, unable to pierce the armor of her intelligence, gave up their attempts to fleece her.

She revived her interest in the Last Crusade, and in an outburst of enthusiasm, pledged to the cause vast sums of money that she did not and would not possess. She conceived the idea of writing to every Catholic ruler, urging that he support the project, and she inundated the monarchs of Christendom with propaganda. Her campaign reached a climax when she wrote a letter that she considered exceptionally persuasive, and decided to send it to various princes and dukes as well as kings. Her secretary copied the document ninety-eight times. In return for his hard work, Kristina received a few polite, evasive replies. She concluded that ignorance was responsible for royalty's lack of zeal, so she sent the secretary on a tour of European capitals, and made his life miserable by writing him long, detailed instructions at every stop on his journey. When he finally returned to Hamburg, reporting failure, she decided to forget the idea.

Azzolino, to whom she wrote regularly, made every effort to encourage her, but he had no faith in her schemes. "The Queen," he said in a note to a fellow cardinal, "is unable to distinguish between the useful and the frivolous and exhausts her energies on both. Also, I fear, she is very apt to take things up and drop them again before they are half finished."

Time dragged in Hamburg, and Kristina awoke one morning with a fresh idea that, Mathilde says in her *Diary*, "Her Majesty believed to have been inspired." The project was startling, simple, and unique: she would open a campaign to obtain special concessions for Catholic worshipers in Protestant countries. The secretary was busy again, and the Queen wrote long letters to every Protestant ruler. Most of these monarchs did not bother to reply, and the few who were sufficiently courteous to write to her, declared that if she hoped to win such concessions, equivalent rights must be granted to Protestant worshipers in Catholic countries. Kristina was abashed. Admitting that she had not thought in such terms, she dropped the plan.

A messenger arrived from Stockholm with the semiannual payment of her subsidy and, as usual, she received only a portion of what she had been promised. She sent an indignant letter to Azzolino, hoping he would sympathize with her, but he replied sensibly that she could do nothing except trim her expenses, and he advised her to dispense with the services of those members of her household who contributed neither to her comfort nor her stature. Since she believed that loyal service should be rewarded, she sent a letter to Louis XIV, proposing that various of her ladies and gentlemen be granted titles; also, she suggested that members of her entourage with military experience be given high ranks in the French army, and she expressed her certainty that the staff at the Louvre would be more efficient if places were found for various chambermaids and valets who had been working for her. The reply, sent by a secretary, was brief: His Majesty declined the offer.

The Queen's financial embarrassment aroused her interest in alchemy, and after she had read everything she could find on the subject of the transformation of base metals into gold, she opened a correspondence with a scoundrel called Nils Borri, who advertised himself as an alchemist. Perhaps it is not to Kristina's discredit that Borri succeeded in fooling her, for he was a clever rogue who subsequently persuaded the King of

Denmark to build him an expensive laboratory. In any event, Borri proposed that he journey to Hamburg, and Kristina assented. She turned over several rooms to him and spent most of her time helping him conduct experiments. Borri ate heartily, drank large quantities of wine, and made himself at home, but Kristina refused to pay him the bonus he demanded, until he succeeded in making gold for her. She was learning, at last, that all men were not what they seemed.

Borri remained in Hamburg for a month, and when he failed to live up to his claims, Kristina quarreled with him, then dismissed him. In order to protect his own reputation, he announced that he had refused to tell the Queen his secrets because she was a depraved woman. Her past had caught up with her and she could do nothing to defend herself against the slander.

An unexpected windfall made life somewhat more tolerable. The Swedish Regents were discovering that it was unpleasant to have their former Queen waiting nearby, ready to visit them in person if they ignored her. Hamburg was too close to Sweden for their peace of mind, and everything Kristina did was duly reported to the people of her native land. Hoping that she would go south again, they sent her a large subsidy which included some of the money they owed her, and she became solvent again. When she wrote the good news to Cardinal Azzolino, he replied promptly, insisting that she send him the funds. As a lure, he suggested that she purchase her own home, and he made the bait more tempting by saying that one of Rome's finer estates, the Riario Palace, could be purchased for a reasonable sum and that he would make it habitable for her.

The prospect of owning her own home after years of wandering was so strong that she could not resist, so she gave most of the money to Azzolino's messenger, a monsignor. Only after he had taken her gold, did the priest reveal to her that the Pope had not forgiven her and that she could not yet return to Rome. She accepted the ultimatum dispiritedly, but soon thereafter she found an opportunity to restore herself to His Holiness' good graces.

A scholar who called himself Lambecius fled to Hamburg from Paris and, having met Kristina when she had visited France, appealed to her for help. Lambecius was a Protestant, a philosopher of distinction, and a poet; unfortunately, he was also a poor judge of people, and had married a girl half his age who subsequently revealed to him that she was a trollop and had no intention of giving up her profession. The distracted man had not been able to keep order in his classes, and had made the grave error of speaking too freely and carelessly on the subject of religion. His colleagues had charged him with being an advocate of atheism — a serious offense — and he had fled the country when he learned that he would be arrested by King Louis's agents.

Kristina, moved by his tale of distress, gave him refuge, and offered him intellectual and spiritual comfort. In her relations with Lambecius, she displayed a compassion and sensitivity that often had been lacking in her dealings with others, and he gradually recovered his health. Kristina, sensing a chance to win a convert, introduced him to Catholicism, and he became a student of the faith. His wife, learning that he was the guest of the Queen of Sweden, came to Hamburg, and the scholar hid in his room while Kristina dealt with the woman. The courtesan was no match for the indignant Minerva of the North, and although there is no record of what Kristina said to her, the young woman left after an interview of no more than half an hour.

Lambecius embraced Catholicism and, with Kristina paying his expenses, traveled to Rome. He impressed several members of the Curia, was presented to the Pope, and quickly demonstrated that he was a sincere convert as well as a distinguished scholar. Alexander gave him the post of chief Papal librarian at Vienna, a position which Lambecius held for the rest of his life. He was grateful to Kristina, remained her friend, and frequently wrote epigrams and poems in Latin, praising her lavishly.

At last she had done something constructive, so Pope Alexander ended the ban against her and she left Hamburg after little more than a year in the city. A delegation of cardinals met her on the road as she approached Rome and took her direct to the Pope, who received her in a public audience. From her appearance, Alexander must have realized instantly that she was the same flamboyant, stubbornly independent woman he had punished, but there were many foreign ambassadors present in the throne room, so he received her calmly and refrained from lecturing her on the true meaning of repentance. As the Venetian Ambassador reported to his government:

> Her Majesty's hair was tied up with ribbons of various colors, arranged at random, and was sprinkled with the dust of travel instead of powder. A veil, loosely attached to the back of her head, hung over her shoulder and was gathered up under her arm in the manner of a cavalier's cape. She wore the clothes of a man and a skirt so transparent that one could see her riding breeches beneath it; that skirt constituting her sole article of specifically feminine attire.
>
> The Queen greeted His Holiness humbly, and did not speak until he had addressed her. Although her dress was unorthodox, her manner indicated that she was penitent, and His Holiness seemed inclined to forgive her the unfortunate

episode in Sweden, which caused so much bitterness in that country against the Church. After His Holiness withdrew from his Throne Room, however, the Queen's manner changed and she spoke in a loud, challenging voice. Cardinal de Medici was distressed, and left the room, as did several others.

The Pope wisely made no attempt to chastise Kristina for her demonstration of defiance. He, too, was learning that she could not accept discipline without rebelling, and that something in her nature forced her to misbehave when she felt she was being restrained.

The Riario Palace was ready for her, and she took possession of it in late January, 1663. There were relatively few sleeping chambers in the building, but there was a large museum, an enormous library, and a long gallery where she could display her works of art. She was delighted with the place. Her collection of books astonished the scholars who saw it, and she was flattered when a visiting Jesuit stated that she owned the largest and best private library in the city. Portraits painted by a score of masters were hung in the gallery, the most prominent place being given to a painting of her father, on horseback. One hundred and thirty pieces of magnificent tapestry were hung in various rooms, the cases in the museum were filled with valuable objects, and guests were so dazzled that they talked of nothing else after making a tour of the palace. Even the Pope's curiosity was aroused, and he paid Kristina the honor of calling on her and seeing the treasures for himself.

The Queen could thank Azzolino for the change in her fortunes. Not only had he spent her money carefully, but he had invested a portion of what she had sent him and had earned a handsome profit for her. All of her belongings had been retrieved from the pawnbrokers, and she could hold her head high again, at least until the next payment was due from Stockholm.

All that was lacking was a court, and Kristina made a number of appointments, but Azzolino, who still controlled the bulk of her money, insisted on approving each appointment in advance. There were twenty gentlemen in waiting, among them an Italian duke, a general who had fought against Gustavus Adolphus, and a dashing but impoverished young Englishman, Sir Robert Dudley. The only lady in the house other than Kristina herself was Mathilde, who felt that her reputation was being compromised and wanted to resign.

"Her Majesty was willing to permit my retirement and promised me a pension," she writes in her *Memoirs*. "But His Eminence, Cardinal Azzolino, persuaded me to remain, saying that if I departed, Her Majesty would live in a house surrounded by men and chambermaids. The Queen cared not at all what was said about her, but the Cardinal was concerned for the sake of his Church, saying there had been more than enough gossip about her. I was indifferent to the plight of the Roman Church, but Her Majesty was still dear to me, so I consented, with misgivings, and had my belongings unpacked."

Mathilde knew her mistress, and her fears were justified. The members of Roman society, following the Pope's example, were ready to forget past slights and make a fresh start, but Kristina went out of her way to treat them rudely. When ladies called, she kept them standing, offered them no refreshments, and, refusing to listen to their small talk, yawned in their faces. She made no attempt to conciliate the noblemen either, and the Venetian Ambassador reports a story that seems to have been typical. A nobleman "of ancient lineage but only moderate talents" tried to sympathize with Kristina and rather clumsily declared that her life must be dull and lonely.

Her retort withered him. "I would rather spend three days alone than half an hour in your company," she said.

Members of the nobility avoided her again, but scholars and authors, scientists and artists came to the palace frequently, and she generously allowed them to use her library. She discussed intellectual matters with them, and still pursuing the interest she had developed in Hamburg, continued to seek the philosopher's stone, even though the Church specifically forbade such a search. She corresponded with professional and amateur alchemists in almost every nation of Europe, had a laboratory installed on the top floor of the palace and worked there secretly, trying to change base metals into gold.

A trivial diplomatic affair occupied the Queen's attention for more than two weeks. The new French Ambassador to the Vatican, the Duc de Créqui, who had not met her in France, was curious about her and wanted to call. Fearing he might otherwise be snubbed, he sent her a letter asking with what ceremony she would receive him. Questions of protocol were dear to Kristina and she bickered amiably with the duke, exchanging as many as three or four letters each day with him. The matter was finally settled to the satisfaction of both parties: if cardinals were present, the ambassador would be offered an armchair, but if no cardinals were present, he would sit on a stool.

The duke, elated by this nonsense, became a frequent caller, and soon had good cause to learn that the Queen did not give her friendship lightly, nor did she fail to support her friends in times of emergency...

Some members of the Pope's Corsican guard and a squad of French troops attached to the ambassador's legation became involved in a brawl — the cause of the fight was known neither at the time nor later, although it was suggested that the

Duc de Créqui himself was involved. According to one story, he had been enjoying an affair with the wife of an officer of the Corsican guard and the enraged husband was trying to obtain revenge. In any event, the fight took place near the embassy, and the French, outnumbered more than two to one, retreated into the building. The Corsicans caught the ambassador, pummeled him, and would have killed him had several of his followers not intervened. Men on both sides were injured, and a French page was shot on the front steps of the legation. The case became the sensation of Rome overnight, and although Kristina was not involved in any way she made it a personal affair.

She said she wished to act as a mediator, and even though neither side accepted her services, she sent several strong letters to the Pope and members of the Curia, condemning the Corsicans and demanding the execution of all members of the guard who had participated in the attack. Her bloodthirsty attitude was reflected in a note that she sent to Cardinal Azzolino.

"When all is over," she said, "the Pope will understand that I have rendered him an important service in this matter. Try, once more, to persuade him to give the Ambassador satisfaction, for I foresee that there will be grave trouble if he fails to do so. Some of the Corsicans, if not all of them, must be sacrificed. If the guilty cannot be discovered, then the innocent must be punished, in order to make it clear that they are not being shielded, and that you are having recourse to no tricks in order to protect them. My proposal may strike you as shocking, but great evils require extreme remedies."

Pope Alexander failed to appreciate the Queen's unusual concept of justice, and both the Vatican and the French government, embarrassed by the unfortunate affair, wanted nothing more said on the subject. But Kristina kept the issue alive, and each day sent new demands to the Pope and to various cardinals. She was De Créqui's self-appointed champion, and she would not rest until Corsican blood flowed. Azzolino tried to silence her, and the duke made desperate attempts to persuade her that while he appreciated her loyalty he wanted no more help. The determined Kristina replied by requesting a public audience with the Pope to discuss the subject.

Alexander avoided her, and what had been a nasty but minor incident threatened to disturb the relations between France and the Church. King Louis finally ended the tragicomedy by sending Kristina a letter, in which he assured her that she had performed a valuable service by calling the case to the attention of the world. Now, he said, secret considerations of state made it necessary to drop the subject, and he added that he knew he could count on the discretion of his dear sister, the Queen of Sweden. Kristina, flattered by his confidential tone, subsided.

Financial worries caused her to forget the troubles of the French ambassador and concentrate on her own affairs. The Swedish government owed her more than fifty thousand gold crowns, and she was running into debt again. Stonemasons, butchers, and even members of her own household were beginning to complain, and Roman gossips repeated the remark that although there were forty-five horses in the Queen's stable, she was unable to pay for her own table wine.

Azzolino came to Kristina's rescue and offered to send to Sweden a member of his own household, an expert in finance and law, to straighten out matters. Kristina agreed, but entertained faint hope that the mission would be successful. However, she conferred privately with the man before he departed and charged him with an additional, secret mission.

She was still smarting over the treatment she had been accorded when she had visited Sweden in 1660 and she wanted permission to journey there again. She had no desire to live there, but she wanted to salve her vanity.

Actually, although she had a magnificent home, she was bored. At heart she was still a wanderer.

Azzolino's envoy enjoyed unexpected success. He brought Kristina all the money the Swedish government owed her, and told her that when he had brought up the question of her making another visit to the country, the Regents had appointed a secret commission to consider the matter. It had finally been decided that she could return, provided she obeyed certain stringent conditions.

The first was the most important: wherever else she might claim the privileges of extraterritoriality, she could not claim them in Sweden. The Regents were reminding her, forcibly, that Sweden was a Protestant country and intended to remain Protestant. Under no circumstances could she set up a Catholic chapel during a visit, and she was forbidden to bring a priest with her; in fact, she could not attend Mass, even in the chapel of a Catholic ambassador. She could not visit Stockholm except when the Riksdag was in session, and if she should decide to make such a journey, her entourage must be composed exclusively of Swedish Lutherans.

Pope Alexander could have told the Regents they were asking for trouble by setting such stern conditions, and had Chancellor Oxenstjerna been alive, there is no doubt the message would have been modified. Naturally, Kristina reacted at once. She wrote a letter to Azzolino, informing him that she intended to visit her native land, but stating, "I do not plan to obey the stupid rules regarding my conduct that have been established for this visit."

She listed several reasons for her attitude. In the first place, she declared, the provisions were unofficial. She had received them informally, and therefore did not consider them binding. Furthermore, she had many friends in Sweden who would be outraged when they learned that their former monarch was being subjected to petty humiliations, and she stated that the daughter of Gustavus Adolphus refused to bow to threats. The Regents had challenged her, and she accepted the gage of battle.

So, after spending three years in Germany and Italy, she raced north again, going first to Hamburg. She was accompanied by a suite of thirty-five persons, but arrived in Hamburg with only half that number, for she had traveled with such speed that many of her retainers had been unable to keep up the pace. The courts of Europe buzzed with the story, which happened to be true, that her rush had been so great that she had spent most of her nights sleeping on straw in humble country inns.

No one, including the apprehensive Regents in Stockholm, knew why she was in such a hurry, and they had no intention of admitting her to the country until they learned her reasons. Sudden delays blocked her progress after she reached Hamburg. A courier brought word from Stockholm to the effect that the rulers of the country agreed in principle to her visit, but wanted to settle all details. They requested a letter from the Queen, promising she would not be accompanied by priests nor would say Mass in Sweden. She refused, and the issue was deadlocked. Magnus de la Gardie, now Chancellor, realized that the challenge to her right to worship as she pleased infuriated her, so for the moment he let that question drop.

After another delay, the Regents wrote that they would not refuse the Queen entry into the country, but required her to wait three months until the Riksdag held its next meeting. Kristina fumed, but there was nothing she could do except wait. Her one alternative was to return to Rome, but she stubbornly refused to admit defeat. When three months had passed and the meeting of the Riksdag was postponed without explanation, it became clear to her that Magnus and his colleagues were playing a game with her, using every delaying tactic they could until she got tired of waiting.

A letter she wrote to Azzolino during this period exposes her frayed nerves, but also indicates her grim determination to have her own way. "I suffer almost daily from severe headaches and I find life in Hamburg tiresome, but the end justifies the means, and I will not be denied the right to visit the land of my birth."

Swedish agents investigated Kristina thoroughly. They secretly read most of her correspondence, planted spies in her household, and carefully watched every move she made. Finally they were satisfied that she was not engaging in a new intrigue to seize the throne, so there was no valid reason of state to keep her out of the country. Nevertheless, as all responsible men knew, she possessed unique talents and could stir up unexpected storms in tranquil waters. So Magnus resorted to another stratagem, one that was as subtly clever as it was cruel. The payment of Kristina's allowance was due, and she sent an agent to Stockholm to collect it for her. The Regents gave him the full amount, and then Magnus borrowed the better part of it from the man, who was in no position to refuse the most powerful official in the country.

The apprehensive agent tarried in Sweden and wrote Kristina a letter in which he said that he had been powerless to refuse the request from one who was the Chancellor, the principal Regent, and uncle of the little King. Kristina lost her temper, of course. She understood the significance of Magnus' trick; the transaction had crippled her, making it far more difficult for her to travel. She sent the agent a furious reply, ordering him either to recover the money or repay her out of his own pocket. She concluded on an ominous note: "You may thank God and the kindness of my heart that I do not inflict on you a more severe punishment, which you well deserve."

The frightened wretch undoubtedly remembered the fate of Monaldeschi, and, having no funds of his own, made a futile attempt to see Magnus. A secretary told him that the Chancellor was too busy to receive him again, and the agent, realizing he had been duped, fled from Stockholm and disappeared. There is no record of his fate; it is known only that neither then nor at any future time did he return to Rome.

Kristina now began to suffer from a number of ailments. Headaches tortured her, a surgeon was called in to remove an infected tooth, and she spent two weeks in bed, unable to rid herself of a raging fever. She became melancholy, spent her days brooding, and even suspected that Magnus was plotting to assassinate her. She pined for Rome and the comforts of her own palace, but her pride would not let her admit defeat, and she wrote daily letters to Azzolino, whom she called her only friend.

A quotation from one of the letters illustrates her nervousness. "No one has ever dared accuse me of timidity, but nevertheless I deem it wise to take precautions. The passion for power inspires strange proceedings, and those who hate me make no secret of their feelings. In Sweden, as elsewhere, they know how to use the dagger and the bowl; and, to tell you the truth, I believe they are making their preparations to employ both, in order to finish me for all time. My presence is more embarrassing to them than you think, and although I perceive your intention to calm me with your assurances, you waste ink and time. The affection that the people of Sweden feel toward me, great though it is, affords me no protection, for if I were less loved I should have less to fear."

She poured out her heart in her letters, discussing every conceivable subject: her personal business affairs, international diplomacy, spiritual matters. The Cardinal, whose work in the Curia occupied his mind and energies, could not reply to each letter, but he wrote when he could, gave her advice that he hoped would encourage her, and in an attempt to revive her drooping spirits, repeated cheerful anecdotes and bits of light gossip. Kristina did not appreciate his kindness, however, and occasionally unleashed her temper on him in bursts of jealous sarcasm.

"You edify me very much," she says caustically in one letter, "by the moral and theological lessons which you draw from all the accidents of life, and I do not doubt that all your thoughts were, as usual, of God, when you went to the French Ambassador's to see the theatricals, and that the two ladies who recited there, and are the delight of Rome, merely annoyed you by catching your eye. I suppose you set to work, like the Lord Jesus, to convert them. A virtue so scrupulous as yours would not have braved such a spectacle for any other purpose."

Azzolino lost neither his poise nor his sense of perspective, and replied serenely, which enraged Kristina all the more. "In reply to your sermon," she wrote, "I will merely tell you that I know very well what I owe to God, to you, and to myself, and will try to discharge the debt."

Eventually the Cardinal's patience won him a reward of sorts, and Kristina stopped lashing out at him. But she remained inconsistent in her thinking and in her approach to any topic that interested her. Certainly there are strong indications that she had not yet become a devout Catholic, although she showed a strong interest in political matters that dealt with religion. In one letter she said, "We hear from Holland that the King of England and his Parliament have declared themselves Catholics, and that the King and the House of Lords are disputing with the House of Commons, which is still obstinately heretical. I would give my life to find that this report is true, but I dare not believe it, though we know that God can work miracles, and one must not doubt either His goodness or His power."

These sentiments are pious, even humble, but later in the same communication she expresses contradictory feelings. After informing him that she has heard that a priest named Father Zucchi has been preaching against her in Rome, she asks Azzolino to send her copies of his sermons. "That," she says, demonstrating the temperament the Lutheran clergy of Sweden knew all too well, "will save me the trouble of going to church when I am back at Rome."

In still another letter her mood is also ironic: "Please tell Father Fozio from me that he is wasting his time in praying God to make me a saint, for I shall never be virtuous enough to become one, or wicked enough to make hypocritical pretenses."

The illness of Pope Alexander distracted her for a short time, and she wrote to Azzolino asking whether he might be elected to the office. He replied, briefly and bluntly, that he did not consider himself eligible, that he felt he was neither sufficiently pious nor experienced. His tone was stern and uncompromising, and Kristina became penitent.

"You know that I am quite disinterested for my own sake," she wrote. Then, apparently realizing this sounded glib, she went to pains to explain. "If I did consider my own interest, I should adopt another tone, but as God has given me the grace to resign so much for His service, I should be happy if, by the sacrifice of my life blood, I could help God and the Church for a single day. You, who have been my Confessor and know the secrets of my heart, must know that this is my most intense desire."

Magnus de la Gardie and the other Swedish Regents continued to postpone the meeting of the Riksdag, but Kristina waited tenaciously in Hamburg, trying desperately to pass the time. She caught a head cold that caused her eyes to run and made reading difficult for her, and she asked Azzolino, "If I give up reading, what on earth am I to do? This is a frightful country; everything that I see in it irritates and bores me. Elsewhere it only takes four and twenty hours to make up a day and a night; here a single hour lasts four and twenty days, while the days, which at Rome were only of a moment's duration, here seem to spread themselves over centuries.

"Occasionally I play at chess or cards with members of my Court," she added lugubriously, "but as I cannot afford to lose money and do not wish to embarrass other people by winning from them, we do not play for money, but only for amusement."

The German nobles, who had avoided her somewhat nervously, began to call on her again when she behaved decorously and created no fresh scandals. But they irritated her, too, and in one letter to Azzolino she described an inane conversation with a countess, who had confided to the Queen that since her eyesight was weak and her ability to read limited, she had spent the past ten years glancing repeatedly through only one book, a distillation of the philosophy of Aristotle.

Kristina's mood showed evidence of desperation as she added,

> I report this talk in order to show you what these Germans are like, when one is so unlucky as to meet one of them who knows four words of Latin — a knowledge which only makes them bigger idiots than Nature has already made them. Imagine the pleasure I derive from such absurd conversations!
>
> I am afraid the influence of these stupid people will affect me, for I see it affecting some of the Italians and I sadly fear it is contagious. If that should happen, you must prepare yourself to be bored, as I doubt not that you are already, by the perusal of this letter, which does not deserve to be forgiven for the foolish nonsense contained in it.
>
> But, having commenced, I will speak my thoughts. My nights are the worst time, and I can tolerate the presence of no one. I have hurt the feelings of my patient Mathilde by dismissing her from my presence, and I spend long hours alone, pacing up and down my room, which is very cold. It is also very true that I pass nights in weeping for my sorrows. But I beg you to tell no one that I am despondent, and, as you are devoted to God, I know that you will keep my secret.

Azzolino urged her to forget her visit to Sweden and return to Rome, but she paid no attention to his pleas and ignored similar advice from several other cardinals. Perhaps she was at the breaking point, but a rumor from Stockholm to the effect that she would soon give up her quest, strengthened her determination to see the matter through to the end. Defiance ignited a spark in her again, and she decided to give a fancy-dress ball. She remembered her last party, which had created such a furor, so she announced that this affair would be more sedate, and she signified her good intentions by asking the guests to wear the clothing and armor of the Middle Ages.

The Germans decided that she had earned a reward, and members of the nobility appeared in large numbers, the ladies wearing towering headdresses and stiffly brocaded gowns, the men weighed down by heavy suits of armor taken from the museums in their drafty castles and manor houses. It was now early April, in 1667, and the weather was sufficiently warm for the party to be held in the open, so the tennis courts were converted into a theater for the performance of a ballet. Kristina allowed nothing to spoil the decorum. The gentlemen drew lots for their partners and for their places at the tables, and as everyone participated in the game, there were no quarrels about rank and protocol.

The banquet lasted four hours, and even though Kristina had been obliged to pawn several paintings, she told Azzolino in a letter she did not regret the expense. The ballet was a huge success and was followed by a lottery. The gentleman in waiting who presided over the silver bowl from which lots were drawn, made certain that Kristina won the grand prize for ladies — a bolt of expensive cloth of silver — but she rebuked him and offered the material to the sixteen-year-old daughter of a German baron.

An orchestra was summoned and the guests invited to dance, the gentlemen first retiring to change from their armor into more suitable attire. The gaiety continued until dawn, and the party was an unqualified success. Kristina enjoyed herself, but her costume and demeanor were modest, and she gave the company no reason to gossip about her. According to Mathilde, in her *Memoirs,* "The spectators declared that Her

Majesty looked and acted like a goddess who had descended from heaven."

So Kristina enjoyed a few brief hours of triumph, but she paid heavily for them. She was so exhausted that after the last guests had departed, she stumbled and fell, and when the members of her household staff could not persuade her to eat or drink they called in one of the city's most prominent physicians, who had attended the ball and had not yet gone to bed. He returned to the palace and bled his patient, extracting a half-pint of blood. Kristina slept most of the day, shortly before sundown ate a light meal, then drifted off to sleep again.

Two days later she received word that the Swedish Riksdag was in session; the last obstacle to her visit had been removed.

Magnus de la Gardie and his fellow Regents knew their regime enjoyed only moderate public support, and consequently they were afraid that the public, whose memory was short, might rally behind Kristina if she made a bid for power. To circumvent this danger, they decided to hold no public receptions in her honor. Magnus, who understood her better than most, believed it would be wise to flatter her, entertain her sumptuously but privately — and get rid of her at the first opportunity. His tactics were approved, but a sense of uneasiness persisted, chiefly because no one knew why the Queen was so determined to visit Stockholm.

After her arrival there, Kristina added to the confusion by telling several stories, all of them conflicting. To some who questioned her she announced that she had returned for the sole purpose of settling her financial affairs, and would retire to Rome as soon as possible. To others she said that she had been wounded by the refusal of men who had been her subjects to let her practice her religion and that she intended to remain until they reversed their order and permitted her to attend Mass. Compounding the bewilderment, to still others she indicated that she contemplated remaining in Sweden for the rest of her life.

Perhaps she herself did not know what she wanted or precisely why she had made the journey. Certainly her attitude on the subject of sending Catholic missionaries into the country was inconsistent and vague. A Roman bishop wrote her a letter suggesting that she use her influence to permit Jesuits to enter Sweden, and she replied firmly, "Your suggestion is not practical. It would be equivalent to sending the Jesuits to their deaths; and as for converting the Swedish Lutherans, that is a sheer impossibility."

A few days later she quoted a statement of Turenne's which most Swedes had not heard, "I am a Catholic, but my sword is Protestant." The remark was received favorably, and she made no attempt to correct those who thought it was original.

But only twenty-four hours after she wrote to the bishop, she sent a letter expressing the opposite view to Cardinal Azzolino. "They have recently published here a most shocking edict against the Catholics," she said. "And yet I undertake to predict that if the new Pope would spend as much every year on missionary enterprises in these countries as Cardinal Chigi spends on his dogs and horses, miracles would be worked in spite of all the obstacles put in the way of the missionaries. The Regents would not take so many or such severe precautions if they did not know how necessary it is for them to obstruct the progress which our religion would be sure to make in Sweden, if pains were taken to spread it."

There can be no doubt that Kristina was a sick woman when she left Hamburg, and her condition showed no improvement when she arrived in Stockholm. She complained in all of her correspondence that she had never felt worse in her life, and she repeatedly described her symptoms: nausea and thirst, shooting pains, and insomnia. Her skin was sallow, and in later centuries, physicians have thought it likely that she was suffering from malaria. Whatever the cause of her ailment, it made her lightheaded, and she was even less consistent than usual.

One day she wrote to Azzolino, "How good it is to be home again. I had not realized how much I missed my native countryside until I saw it again, and I am content to spend the rest of my days here. I will permit no person and no mean manipulation of popular support to send me into exile again."

A few days later she sent him another letter, which voiced doubts. "I have risked both my life and my liberty by coming to Sweden. But that is nothing to me. I care so little for my life in the state to which I am reduced that I do not in the least mind losing it. There remains nothing in life for me to regret."

The following week her tune changed again. "I shall stay only a short time at Stockholm. If death does not prevent me, I shall begin my journey to Rome at the end of a month at the latest, and if I can conclude my business in less time, I shall not remain for a month."

Her illness persisted, but even when she began to recover, she still remained melancholy. "I do not think that my life will be a long one," she wrote the long-suffering Azzolino. "If only I had paid my debts, I should die happy."

She could not complain about her reception, and she was singularly silent on the subject. Magnus had arranged a greeting worthy of a reigning monarch. The guns of the Swedish navy fired salvo after salvo in salute, a committee of nobles waited to receive her, and Magnus' brother, Pontus de la Gardie, was present on behalf of the Regents. A regiment of infantrymen presented arms, seven hundred cavalrymen raised their sabers, and three bands played rousing military airs. Pontus escorted her to a huge carriage, and as it was raining, she could not complain that she was being hidden under the roof of a closed coach.

A large private house had been made ready for her use, and on the night of her arrival a sumptuous banquet was held. All of the Regents attended the affair, and Kristina was served on a dais, sitting on a carved oak chair that resembled a throne. Magnus, missing no details, had even provided a canopy over the chair. The Queen's private bedchamber was splendidly furnished, too, and even Mathilde was impressed by the bed-of-state, which was hung with gold-embroidered green velvet. Everyone was respectful, and the guests took care to observe every rule of protocol and etiquette.

Kristina was exhausted, and when she remained in bed for the next two weeks, she was attended by the finest physicians in the country. Every effort was made to insure the correctness of her reception, but trouble developed as soon as she began to recover.

A rumor had spread that there were at least a score of Jesuits in her suite. The report was false, and the Regents knew it. Their spies in the household had told them there was only one priest in the entourage; he, foolishly, had allowed Kristina to persuade him to dress in layman's clothes and to act the part of her secretary. However, the Regents wanted no unpleasant incident that might cause international complications. They were prepared to look the other way, and hoped that the Queen would behave with discretion. The matter was discussed at some length at a council meeting, and Magnus declared, "It is Her Majesty's right to worship as she pleases, and I hope that she will obey the law and do so privately. If we dismiss her priest, we will be accused of persecuting her, and I wish to maintain good relations with all nations at present. We are at peace, France is our ally and we are on good terms with the King of England, who is a Catholic in secret. We will take no action against Her Majesty."

Kristina felt compelled to assert herself, however. Unwilling to accept a quiet compromise, she took drastic steps as soon as she felt strong again. She ordered the priest to say Mass in the great hall of the house, and when he obeyed, the whole city knew of the incident. Some nobles demanded that she be expelled from the country at once, but the Regents bided their time. She was spinning a strong rope, Magnus said, and he refused to act until she hanged herself with it.

The Queen felt she had won a victory, and was hungry for others. She expressed a desire to tour the country, and, accompanied by an entourage of one hundred and forty persons, left Stockholm on May 18. She traveled at a leisurely pace, and was received everywhere with great courtesy. At each stop a banquet was given in her honor, the dining hall was decorated, and she sat beneath a magnificent canopy of state. Each day the priest, following her instructions, said Mass, and each day she took fewer pains to keep the service secret. The nobles accompanying the party were infuriated, and the climax was reached a week after Kristina left Stockholm. Arriving in the town of Jönköping, where she had once owned a castle, she openly invited the Crown's disfavor when she asked the Swedish members of the entourage, the local dignitaries, and even the two Lutheran ministers to attend Mass.

Pontus de la Gardie, who represented the Regents, sent a full report to Stockholm, and the courier returned with a flat order: Pontus was instructed to tell Kristina that the presence of a priest in Sweden could not be tolerated. The law of the land stated that no priests were permitted to conduct services on Swedish soil. Foreign embassies were considered to be on the soil of the nations they represented; therefore, priests could conduct services on the premises of Catholic legations, but nowhere else.

Kristina understood the law, and even though Pontus explained the order to her in gentle, diplomatic terms, she became violently angry. She had known what would happen, of course, and had deliberately courted trouble, but that did not matter. The law, she said, did not apply to her because she was a queen and was, therefore, a law unto herself. And she added that she no more expected it to be enforced against her than laws prohibiting trespassing were enforced against the personal friends of the landlord.

Pontus, who was a gentleman, listened to her tirade in embarrassed silence, and after she exhausted herself, he persuaded her to write a letter to the King. Charles XI was a minor who never saw the mail addressed to him, of course, and the communication was opened by the Regents, who were neither surprised nor shocked by the contents. They were unhappy, as they had tried to avoid a dispute, but all of them knew Kristina, and her rage was typical of the temper she had displayed so often in the past.

She declared that she was "much surprised," that she "had never expected to be treated in such a manner," and that "such civility as I have received in Sweden is only my due." Her temper soaring, she added, "The annoyance to which I am now exposed dispenses me from the necessity of expressing any thanks. Plainly, I am not wanted here by those who are jealous of my popularity. So I shall show, by leaving the country, that I am not one who will sacrifice my religious convictions for the sake of material advantages."

The letter ended on an extremely discourteous note. "I should have departed this very evening if Count Pontus had not urgently entreated me to wait to hear again from Your Majesty and see whether Your Majesty has not sufficient regard for me to alter your decision. Failing that, I shall no longer be able to receive any courtesies from you, but shall instantly take my departure. At the same time, in order to remind you what you are and what I am, I beg you to believe that you are not the sort of person from whom people in my position take orders. I am your sister and aunt, and it is you who owe homage to me; I owe none to you."

Obviously, she was going out of her way to challenge the men who were the custodians of the crown she had abandoned, and she seemed determined to flaunt her challenge to them before the world, for she made several copies of the letter, sent two to Rome and one to the Marquis de Pomponne, the French Ambassador in Stockholm. However, she continued her leisurely journey, and three days later made plans to entertain her suite at a banquet which she planned with meticulous care. The scene was the fortress at Norrköping, and it was not accidental that the place had been one of her father's favorite garrisons.

Before the banquet began, a messenger arrived with the Regents' reply. They said they were sorry, but could grant no exceptions to the law, particularly as Kristina was making a test case of the issue. Her priest was ordered to leave the country immediately. Nevertheless, the Regents added, making a conciliatory gesture, they had no desire to cause Her Majesty undue hardship or inconvenience, and had conferred with the Marquis de Pomponne, who would gladly permit her to attend Mass openly at his legation.

They refrained from adding that Pomponne, a clever diplomat who would later become the French secretary of state for foreign affairs, was playing a careful game himself. He had just learned that Sweden, Holland, and England were planning to sign a treaty of alliance, and as it was reasonable to assume that the three nations would oppose the expansionist policies of Louis XIV, he was making a special effort to win the friendship and gratitude of the Swedish rulers before they committed themselves to a course of action harmful to his own monarch's interests.

Kristina failed to appreciate the Marquis's thoughtfulness or the Regents' tact. She lost her temper again, and her comments were reported by at least half a dozen people. She herself proudly recalls them in her *Memoirs*: "What! I to wait upon Pomponne! If he made that proposal to me himself, I would have him driven away with sticks! Yes, I would do that even in his own King's presence!"

She would accept no further hospitality from the Swedish government, she added, her temper rising, and, dismissing the delegation from Stockholm, refused to ride in the royal coach that had been transporting her around the country. She canceled the banquet, sent two members of her own staff to hire ordinary commercial carriages, and paced up and down, cursing in several languages.

Pontus, who had been instructed to keep up appearances and avoid antagonizing the new Pope, Clement IX, who had not yet established his policies, was in an uncomfortable spot. He urged Kristina to let him accompany her to the border, but she refused, haughtily. He had been studying her ever since she had arrived in the country, so he tried a different approach. If she traveled alone, he said, the governors of fortresses, some of whom were her enemies, might seize the excuse to detain her by force and lock her in their dungeons.

His threat changed her mind. "The free exercise of my religion means more to me than all the crowns in the world," she said, and graciously invited Pontus to share the delicious meal that had been prepared. At the table she facetiously offered toasts to the boy King and the Regents, and Pontus carefully toasted her in return. She became furious when she was kept waiting for her horses, and although a crowd had gathered outside the fortress, she made a spectacle of herself, pacing up and down, striking out blindly with her riding crop, and cursing in such a loud voice that women who had come to catch a glimpse of her returned to their homes in dismay.

Pontus conducted himself admirably under these extraordinary circumstances. The officers and gentlemen of the Swedish court who had been assigned to make the tour were still in the town, and although they resented Kristina bitterly, De la Gardie forced them to conduct themselves in a dignified manner. He insisted that they fulfill the obligation they had undertaken, so they accompanied the Queen to the border, pretending that nothing unusual had happened.

Kristina, always determined to speak the last word, halted the procession several miles short of the frontier, and, temporarily commandeering a small public tavern, ordered her priest to say Mass. The cleric protested, but she refused to listen, so in the end he obeyed her. As she later recalled in her *Memoirs*, "I wanted to show that I was not afraid of doing so."

Pontus wisely closed his eyes to the incident, restrained several impetuous officers who wanted to arrest both Kristina and the priest, and when the Queen emerged from the tavern and returned to her carriage, he resumed the journey, acting as though nothing out-of-the-ordinary had happened. His composure gave Kristina the opportunity to recover some shreds of her own lost dignity, and when she reached the border, she finally remembered to behave like a queen.

Thanking Pontus for his courtesy and attentions, she gave him a sapphire and ruby locket and presented suitable gifts to the other Swedish officers and gentlemen. Then she made a farewell speech in which she managed to recover at least a portion of the queenly role she had abandoned. She sent a public message to Charles XI, saying, "I am too proud to complain of His Majesty's treatment of me, and I am too deeply attached to my country to seek to avenge myself. Sweden, I will never see you again, and my heart will always be heavy. My beloved home, farewell!"

Kristina was radiant as she crossed the frontier. The quarrel with the Regents had restored her spirits, her health was excellent, and she had enjoyed herself enormously. The fact that her visit had accomplished nothing did not bother her.

Others were less fortunate. Pontus de la Gardie collapsed when he reached Stockholm and was confined to his bed for a week. The members of Kristina's entourage were exhausted, too, and Mathilde notes in her *Diary*, "They did not dare permit themselves to sleep, even when they had the chance, for fear they would not awaken in time to resume the journey when the Queen commanded. As for the chambermaids, their appearance was disgraceful. They were so sunburned, travel-stained and dirty that they hardly dared to show themselves. I was tired, too, and wondered whether I had not spent enough of my time in Her Majesty's company. I was tempted to make the journey back to Stockholm and remain there, but the Queen dissuaded me; she was going to make a wonderful new beginning in life, she said, and she promised that I would share her glory with her. She spoke mysteriously, and at first I thought she was using a ruse to detain me, but I have at last concluded that her enthusiasm is genuine, so I will stay, at least for a time."

Kristina sent word ahead that she was returning to Hamburg, and that weary city braced itself.

X: 1667–1668
THE POLKA

Kristina wrote and spoke constantly of her longing for Rome, and said she would be miserable until she returned there. But she went to Hamburg again and took up residence in the gloomy rented palace. Her reasons are difficult to understand and analyze. The only logical explanation is that a banker who lived in Hamburg and who had been handling some of her complicated financial affairs for a number of years required her presence. Certainly she hated the city and described it in scathing terms in her correspondence. Frequently it was "this accursed place" or "a stinking desert," and in one letter to a cardinal of the Curia she declared vehemently, "The Cossacks of Russia or any other primitive people you might like to name are less barbarous than the Germans." Even her Italian mules, she wrote plaintively, were disgusted with the German mules.

She did her best to fill the empty days by reading, playing chess, and spending much of her time in the laboratory with a new alchemist she had found. She was alarmed, however, when Azzolino informed her in a brief note that the alchemist had been excommunicated, so she discharged the man immediately. There were other distractions to take her mind off the failure of her journey to Sweden, but her pride was still one of her worst enemies. Her cousin, the sister of the Elector of Brandenburg, paid a brief visit to Hamburg and wanted to call on her, but was wary. Would Kristina receive her as an equal and offer her a chair? If so, would it be an armchair?

The reply was uncompromising. Kristina said she could not make such a concession to anyone. She offered armchairs only to fellow monarchs; if she weakened, minor members of various royal houses would give her no peace. However, her cousin was a determined woman and when she persisted, Kristina finally promised not to insult her guest by remaining seated in her presence. So the German princess paid a call, and the two ladies spent an entire afternoon together, chatting for almost four hours — standing the entire time.

The election of Pope Clement IX delighted Kristina. As Cardinal Rospigliosi, he had been one of her good friends in Rome and had treated her with consideration when the aristocrats of the city had gone out of their way to snub her. He was a cultured man, interested in literature and education, and had written the librettos of several operas, one of which had been dedicated to Kristina and played in her honor at the Barberini Palace. The new Pope's first act was to name Cardinal Azzolino Secretary of State, and Mathilde von Echner thought the Queen would hurry to Rome. Instead, she tarried in Hamburg and created an incident that tarnished her already badly soiled reputation.

She celebrated the election of Clement by giving an extravagant fete to which she invited all of the citizens of the city. Wine flowed in the fountains, the palace was illuminated and, blithely ignoring the fact that most of her guests were Protestants, she erected a huge sign in the garden. Beneath an oversized replica of the three-tiered Papal crown was the Latin inscription: *Clemens IX Pont. Max. Vivat.*

The people became drunk on the wine and, resenting the sign, tore it down. Unruly elements gained the upper hand, and a riot erupted. Stones were thrown through the windows of the palace, and the Queen's ungrateful guests demanded that she be evicted from the city. Kristina lost her temper, ordered her gentlemen to arm themselves, and commanded them to fire on the throng.

"I no sooner gave the order," she wrote in her *Memoirs*, "than it was executed, with excellent results. A number of persons were killed on the spot, and several others were wounded. Then we sallied and gave them such a fright that they all ran away."

At last she had participated in a battle, and could now think of herself as a heroine whose exploit would dim the luster of Mademoiselle de Montpensier's bellicose antics in Paris.

While the damage to the palace was being repaired, Kristina took temporary refuge in the house of the Swedish Resident, and the following day, accompanied by the gentlemen of her suite, she went out for a stroll — a deliberate act of provocation. "Although rage and terror were visibly imprinted on the countenances of the people," she wrote happily, "no one dared to raise a hand against me."

She sent dramatic accounts of the unfortunate affair to everyone she knew. Her letter on the subject to Azzolino is a typical exaggeration. "God," she said fervently, "has preserved us by a miracle. With the help of a dozen men, I withstood eight thousand — I might even say the whole city of Hamburg. The city has received a snub which it will not forget, and I flatter myself that I have worthily maintained the Pope's honor and my own."

Azzolino disappointed her by replying sharply that the Pope was dismayed and that he himself was angry. Her conduct was giving Catholicism a bad name everywhere and many of the faithful were becoming so disgusted that they might abandon the Church and embrace Protestantism unless she desisted.

Kristina sulked for almost a week and then wrote him that she was thinking of returning to Sweden again in order to put her financial affairs there in final order. The Regents, she said, would permit her to enter the country provided she took no priest with her, but she asserted that she did not know what to do and would not make up her mind until the Pope and Azzolino could confer and give her their advice.

Clement and his Secretary of State had other matters they deemed more important, and Kristina's letter went unanswered.

She refused to let the subject rest, however. Feeling very sorry for herself, she wrote to Azzolino again. "The uncertainty of life alarms me, and I am afraid to take the risk of dying without confessing. Suppose I should die in Sweden, without a priest near me, would God forgive me, and should I be able to forgive myself for having faced this peril for the sake of temporal interests which truly are not worth the anxiety which this thought causes me? It is true that I am in good health and strong and vigorous, but might not my health fail me at any moment? A fever, a pleurisy, or any other of the many accidents to which I am liable, may easily carry off the most robust in four and twenty hours."

Azzolino replied through one of his secretaries, a monsignor, who sent the Queen His Eminence's soothing reassurances that she would live for many years.

Kristina changed her tune again, and in her next letter complained that her health was frail and that the German doctors who were treating her did not know their business. "I would rather take advice from my horse than from them," she said acidly. "They are beasts and ignoramuses. They kill their patients with a phlegm and gravity which is worse than death itself. They know nothing whatever about my constitution or my way of life and expect me to die whenever I am bled. I will survive their bleeding, but Nature is my enemy. This accursed climate spares no one. The mortality here is terrible, but the fear of death shall never prevent me from doing my duty."

The Cardinal sent her a diplomatic note, expressing the hope that she would recover quickly. Kristina, irritated because her histrionic poses had failed to alarm the Vatican, renewed her threat to make another journey to Stockholm. "I intend to secure the permanence of my revenues, but I refuse to be intimidated by attempts to deprive me of spiritual consolation.

"I shall take my priest with me as far as I can, and if they require me to send him away, I shall have no choice and shall obey them and go on to Stockholm without a priest. The circumstances are not what they were on the last occasion, and I wish to show them that the pretext is not good enough to stop me if I choose to come."

Apparently unable to admit to herself that she was annoyed because Clement and Azzolino refused to take her seriously, she used the Swedish Regents as whipping boys. "Magnus de la Gardie and the venal creatures who comprise his clique hate me. All the ruling faction in Sweden fears me and detests me; all their subjects love me and desire to have me among them. Now you can understand what are, and must be, my hopes and fears.

"I am feared and hated only because I am loved, and my glory and my fortune are the source of all my apprehensions. Time will teach you all these truths. I, for my part, do not intend to speak to you of them again."

Cardinal Azzolino, showing a remarkable degree of restraint, wrote that while she, the Queen, would know whether her presence was required in Sweden, he was unfamiliar with the details of the situation. He pointed out that her last visit had ended unpleasantly and had not benefited her in any way. Neither had it advanced the cause of the Church, which was his principal concern. Nevertheless, she would have to make her own decision.

Mathilde sums up her mistress' reactions to this communication in a few words. "Her Majesty is convinced that Pope Clement and Cardinal Azzolino are indifferent to her fate," she observed in her *Diary*. "She believes they have used her badly and want no more to do with her. She has become very melancholic."

Kristina brooded for a few days and then, unable to control herself any longer, wrote a sharp letter to Azzolino. "I assure you that I do not value my life so much that I hesitate to risk it on this occasion. I have lost everything which could make life agreeable to me, and, after that loss, I feel neither able nor anxious to take any trouble to protect it. In short, the day of my death will be the happiest day of my life, because it will be the last."

This adolescent self-pity did not calm her, so she launched a direct attack in a postscript. "I will tell you, for your consolation, that the time of my return to Rome is not so close as your silence on this subject hints that you fear. Your felicity will not be troubled by my presence for any length of time, and if I can, as I hope, overcome the power which attaches me to Rome, I propose to seek out a corner of the world where poverty is not a disgrace, as it is at Rome, and where I shall at least have the consolation of escaping your everlasting reproaches on the subject."

Azzolino had not reproached her, but, knowing her, he ordered a private investigation of her affairs, and when he discovered that she was spending money on a frighteningly lavish scale, he and Pope Clement reached the inevitable conclusion that she was setting a bad example. The whole world watched her escapades — which were magnified by

Protestant clergymen — and it was imperative that she behave with decorum. The Cardinal wrote to her that she was spending money beyond her means, and she became furious.

"I shall say nothing to you about my debts," she replied. "I will only point out that debts are often incurred by people much wealthier than I am and that I have the means of paying my debts and intend to pay them when I can. I respect you too much to argue the point further, and can only beg you not to scold me again. I am beset by troubles, and it does not please me to be treated like a wicked child."

Kristina's only real troubles were financial; she certainly did not plan to pay another visit to Sweden. In spite of her voluminous correspondence with Azzolino on the subject, she wrote nothing to the Regents in Stockholm. She was merely passing the time by making idle threats, feeling annoyed when the Cardinal saw through them, and in general was marking time until she found a new interest.

A relative, John Casimir, supplied that interest by giving up the throne of Poland, and his abdication created a far greater political stir than had Kristina's abandonment of the Swedish crown. Casimir was as odd in his way as Kristina was in hers, and for years he had behaved erratically and unpredictably. The last legitimate male representative of the royal Polish house of Wasa, he had been a Jesuit priest, had risen to the rank of cardinal, then had become heir to the throne of his ancestors. The Church had released him from his vows, he had become King of Poland and had married, but had preferred the company of light ladies to the joys of the marital couch, and his wife had died without giving him an heir.

Like Kristina, John had become tired of carrying the burdens of state and had informed various people that he planned to retire. Louis XIV, hoping to secure the crown for a French nobleman, had quietly offered him estates that would bring him an annual revenue of fifty thousand crowns, and Casimir had told the Papal Nuncio in Warsaw that he was tempted to accept, as the income would enable him to live the life of a gallant. This news had been transmitted to the Vatican, and Azzolino reacted vigorously.

According to ancient Polish law, the vacant throne would be filled by means of an election. Various factions traditionally brought pressure to bear on the nobles who were the electors, and bribes and threats were common. As the French had already indicated that they planned to enter the arena, the Vatican was disturbed. Louis was beginning to show his independence, and Pope Clement agreed with his Secretary of State that it would be wise to support someone other than a French candidate. The Church was forced to keep another factor in mind, too: Casimir had been a priest before he had become a king, and if he behaved wildly after his abdication, he would give the Protestants too much ammunition to fire at Catholicism.

So Azzolino offered him an estate in the Papal States, where Casimir would live under the secular as well as the spiritual authority of the Church. In that way, Clement and the Cardinal reasoned, it would be possible to control the erratic monarch's activities. The offer was transmitted to Casimir, who accepted it on three conditions. He wanted to live near a monastery where he could retire to pray when he wished; he insisted that the estate be wooded and filled with game, as he loved hunting; and he demanded the right to entertain any women it pleased him to invite to his house, regardless of their reputation.

Azzolino promptly withdrew the invitation. Casimir was told he would have to live and practice his religion elsewhere than in the Papal States — the Vatican made it clear that it was washing its hands of him. Poland was anxious to be rid of him, and John obligingly gave a farewell banquet at which all of the guests were prostitutes. Then he melted down his crown, had it made into coins, and departed. The throne was vacant, and the race began.

The second son of the Tsar of Russia threw his fur-trimmed hat in the ring, and the rulers of the German states named the Duke of Neuburg as their candidate. Friends of the Prince de Condé entered him, partly to relieve King Louis of the embarrassment of dealing with a man who hated to take orders from anyone, and the French, feeling their chances would be better if they did not pin all their hopes on such a controversial figure, also supported Prince Charles of Lorraine. A fifth candidate, who had conferred with no one, sought no help, and asked no one's advice, suddenly thrust herself forward.

Kristina announced her aim by sending a letter to the Papal Nuncio in Warsaw, in which she stated: "Seeing that Her Majesty surpasses all the other candidates in nobility of birth and perhaps also from the point of personal merit, she considers that she can offer herself as a candidate without giving offense, and ought to tempt fortune, in order to ascertain the will of God."

She assumed that the Nuncio would support her and she outlined the arguments she expected him to use in persuading the electors to vote for her. "Tell them," she said, "that Her Majesty would never have quitted the throne of Sweden if Sweden had been a Catholic country or if there had been any reasonable prospect of it becoming one; that it would be unjust to prefer some stranger, less worthy of occupying the throne of her ancestors, and that it is distinctly in the interest of Poland to choose her because, as Her Majesty is too old to marry, has no inclination to do so, she would, in consequence, leave no heirs. Therefore the electors' freedom of choice would be unimpeded at her death, and at that time they would be able to transfer their favor to any other royal house that they might prefer."

She also enclosed a private postscript, promising the Nuncio a cardinal's hat if he supported her candidacy.

The Vatican was surprised and embarrassed, as Kristina stirred waters already thick with mud. As she was the most prominent convert of the age, it would seem odd if the Church failed to support her. And Azzolino was in a particularly uncomfortable position, for it was common knowledge that he was the Queen's closest adviser, and if he abandoned her, the Holy See would be accused of being a fair-weather friend. Clement and Azzolino worked out their tactics accordingly.

The Cardinal sat down and wrote a public letter recommending Kristina, but not having seen her communication to the Nuncio in Warsaw, he made an unfortunate error. She was still a young woman, he stated, and if she ascended to the throne, she would marry, bear children, and found a new dynasty.

The rest of his testimonial was on firmer ground, although his defense of Monaldeschi's murder was brief and glib. He denied the charge that she had been a pensioner of the Pope, and, of course, was telling the truth. He was at his best when he described her as a tireless Amazon. "She can sit her horse all day long, and all night, too, if necessary, dispensing with sleep, comfort, and food," he said. "Her courage and her martial spirit are so great that she only needs an opportunity to dazzle the world with them."

Kristina thanked him for his intervention, in a curious letter which indicated that some inner compulsion had forced her to enter the race, but that she did not really want the crown.

Rarely was her ambivalence more marked. "I am pleased to perceive your zeal in this Polish business, and I thank you a thousand times for it," she began. "I send you copies of the letters I have written to the Nuncio, and with them copies of letters to acquaintances in Warsaw. You will see how I meet the difficulties with regard to my sex and my marriage; I do not agree with all that you have said about me, but I readily submit my arguments to your correction."

Doubts crept into the next paragraph. "I do not know how I ought to wish the matter to turn out. More than a thousand times I have regretted having touched it, and I fear I might become inconsolable if I should succeed. I reflect that, if I should succeed, I shall have to leave Rome forever and pass the rest of my life among a barbarous people of whose language and customs I am ignorant; the reflection distresses me terribly, and my only comfort lies in the hope that the negotiation may be broken off."

Her chances of obtaining the crown were remote, although she did not know it. Pope Clement sent a letter to the Nuncio, commending Kristina as "this heroine, equally remarkable for her piety, her wisdom, and her virile courage." Azzolino sent her a copy, but neglected to inform her that the Nuncio had received strict instructions from the Secretariat not to use the Pope's recommendation unless it seemed certain that she would win.

In her innocence, Kristina believed the Vatican was supporting her fully, and she wrote again to Azzolino. "The Pope is too good to me. I cannot say how much I am obliged to him. To me, personally, my success is a matter of indifference, but it will be a delight to me to owe such an obligation to His Holiness. I value his favor much more than I value the crown. Please tell him so."

For a time it appeared as though Kristina might win. The Polish nobles, knowing comparatively little about her, were inclined to believe that a woman would be easier to control than a man, who might become a tyrant. They entered into detailed negotiations with her, and, true to form, as usual she was her own worst enemy. The electors sought her promise to marry anyone they might select as her husband, but she outsmarted herself and merely pledged that she would not marry without their consent.

She became an object of ridicule, and a crude joke permanently ruined her chances. A sixth candidate had entered the field — Prince Johann of Austria — and one of the electors said that he and Kristina should marry. They would be a perfect match, the man declared, because both were ineligible to rule, Kristina because she was a woman and Johann because he was illegitimate. Kristina was humiliated when she heard the story, but she could do nothing to defend herself. She knew that she would not be elected, and so was not surprised when a seventh candidate was elevated to the throne. Prince Michel Wiesnowiecki wept when he was chosen by his compatriots, and Kristina declared publicly that she understood how he felt.

Nevertheless, she was depressed, chiefly because she hated to be beaten in any competition. She retired to the privacy of her suite for several days, then announced that she planned to leave for Rome as soon as she could put her affairs in order.

She sold a diamond and emerald bracelet in order to discharge her more pressing debts, sent a letter to the Regents in Stockholm demanding that they pay her subsidy in full and, not waiting for a reply, began to pack. Her mood changed again, and her last letter to Azzolino indicates that she did not take her defeat in Warsaw seriously. "A few days after you receive this letter, I will greet you in person and present myself at His Holiness' apartment in the hope that he will give me his blessing. You cannot imagine how great is my joy at the prospect of returning to Rome, my home, the only true home I have ever known, or shall know, on this earth.

"At last I am leaving this dreary place, with all the joy of a soul escaping from purgatory, and I can only hope that my stay here will be allowed to count for a part of my sojourn in purgatory."

One mystery remains, which has never been clarified. When she had left Sweden hastily and returned to Hamburg, the members of her entourage expected that she would remain in the city she hated for only a short time. Instead, she stayed for the better part of a year; and no record even hints at what detained her there. A good friend had become Pope, her closest friend and mentor was now Papal Secretary of State, and there was every reason for her to believe that she would receive a warmer welcome at the Vatican than had ever been accorded to her during the reign of the Pope's predecessor. Yet she lingered in Hamburg, attending to "business matters."

According to one theory, which has never been substantiated, Clement was afraid her presence might embarrass him. According to another, Azzolino told her that he was too busy to see her, and deliberately kept her at a distance. But there is no proof to verify either thesis. If a messenger from Rome brought her the news that she was not welcome there, she would have mentioned the subject in her correspondence or, later, in her *Memoirs*. However, she is silent, and so is Mathilde.

All that is known is the simple fact: after retreating in haste from Sweden, Kristina made a nuisance of herself in Hamburg, tried in vain to become queen of Poland, and finally set out again on the road to Rome.

XI: 1668–1669
THE DREAM THAT CAME TRUE

Kristina had learned that any man who wore the three-tiered crown and sat on the throne at St. Peter's under the soaring canopy designed and built by the architect, Giovanni Bernini, was set apart from other mortals. As a cardinal, Rospigliosi had composed the librettos for operas and had been interested in all things cultural, but now that he had become Clement IX, Kristina assumed that he was undoubtedly preoccupied with Church business. So she paved her way by sending him a letter immediately before her departure from Hamburg, dispatching it by special courier. She composed it carefully and told him what she thought he would like to hear.

"My Swedish contracts," she said exuberantly, "are signed, sealed and delivered. The Riksdag has granted me liberty for the exercise of my religion and has ordered full satisfaction to be given to all of my claims, judging that they are just and reasonable.

"I leave for Rome in a vainglorious spirit, having adjusted everything in such a manner as to give Your Holiness great satisfaction. Everything is settled in Sweden. The Regents have granted all that I have asked, and more. It is my belief that, in future, the precedent that has been established in my case will spread, and all Catholics will be granted complete freedom to practice their faith in that Lutheran land. Surely this example will be noted by other Protestant nations, and the practice will spread. Sweden, after living in darkness, has seen the light of Immortal Truth, and I rejoice."

Had her assertions been true, the Pope would have had good reason to be pleased. Unfortunately, however, the claim was a lie from beginning to end. Cardinal Azzolino knew that her visit to Sweden had ended in failure, that her relations with the Regents were strained and that, thanks to her intransigency, anti-Catholic feeling was stronger than it had been in many years. Her own situation was precarious, too. The Regents had forbidden her to return to Sweden, and the Riksdag had added teeth to the order: if she crossed the frontier again for any reason at any time, her allowance would be cut off permanently.

Cardinal Azzolino was in full possession of the facts, as were other members of the Curia, and it is inconceivable that the Secretary of State would have been negligent and failed to keep the Pope informed. Therefore, neither Clement nor Azzolino was fooled by the silly boast. But they understood Kristina, and Clement wisely planned to use her great energies and her superior intellect for the benefit of the Church. "His Holiness," a monsignor on the staff of the Secretary of State wrote to a colleague in Milan, "received His Eminence, our Cardinal, last night, and they conferred at great length on the subject of the Queen of Sweden. Her caprice has upset the decorum of His Holiness' court too often in the past, and His Holiness will not permit her to behave again with such excessive zeal. His Eminence is in complete agreement, and they have determined ways to deal with her.

"The details have not yet been communicated to us by His Eminence, but he is in good spirits and is confident that all will be well. So great is our confidence in him and in the wisdom of His Holiness that we do not doubt that the Queen will, at long last, be muzzled."

Clement and Azzolino began by pretending to accept Kristina's fraudulent claims of victory for the Church at face value. When she crossed into Italy early in November, 1668, she sent an equerry ahead to Rome to announce her coming, and the man was greeted with the pomp and ceremony accorded a representative of a reigning monarch. The Pope gave him a gold medal, Azzolino presented him with a silver medal, and he returned to Kristina with glowing tales of his reception.

He was followed by an envoy from the Vatican, who was traveling with a suite of twenty retainers. The nobleman met Kristina on the road, his trumpeters greeted her with a fanfare, and he informed her that the Pope would be happy to defray the expenses of her journey through the Papal States. Hungry for recognition and honor, Kristina consented graciously.

Cardinal Azzolino rode out to meet her at the town of Narni, and after she had kissed his ring, he drew her to her feet with his own hands and announced to the large crowd gathered to witness the spectacle that Her Majesty was a heroine. "The Cardinal," Mathilde writes in her *Memoirs*, "made a moving address and dwelt at length on the victories the Queen had won for the Church in Sweden. His words were so solemn and his manner so earnest that, had I not known otherwise, I would have believed him; but the people, being unfamiliar with the true state of affairs in the North, were deceived and cheered for a long time. Her Majesty was overcome and wept with joy, whereupon the Cardinal and his attendants withdrew so that she could compose herself. Later the Cardinal gave a dinner in her honor, and then left for Rome, promising that other glories awaited Her Majesty. She was pleased and kept me awake for long hours that night, speculating on the nature of the honors."

When Kristina arrived at Castel Nuovo, a magnificent palace owned by the Vatican, twenty-four Cardinals were on hand to welcome her, and three of the Pope's nephews came forward to give her His Holiness' personal greetings. A banquet was held in her honor, and she was hailed repeatedly as the Minerva of the North. The excitement of her first visit to Rome was revived; the members of her entourage had never seen her in better spirits.

Her arrival in Rome was a triumphal procession. She rode in the Pope's private carriage, followed by sixty coaches carrying the members of her entourage and the cardinals and other dignitaries who had ridden out to meet her. Each coach was drawn by six matched horses, and the citizens of Rome lined the streets to watch the parade. An escort of Papal cavalry and Swiss guards prevented the crowd from spilling into the road, and the Papal artillery fired a salute of one hundred and one guns. No detail was overlooked.

The procession made its way to the Vatican, where Pope Clement received the Queen in a private audience. They conferred for the better part of an hour, and Clement solemnly thanked Kristina for all of her efforts on behalf of the Church in Sweden. He told her he was sorry that she had failed in her attempt to become the ruler of Poland, but hinted that the glories that awaited her would provide her with far greater compensation. Azzolino joined them in the final minutes of the audience and he spoke in the same vein. The elated Kristina received the Pope's blessing and departed for her own palace.

There, reality awaited her. Two members of Azzolino's staff, who had been making a thorough study of her financial affairs, confronted her quietly with the news that she was heavily in debt. She owed her bankers in Hamburg considerable sums and she had left a string of other debts all over Europe. The payment of her Swedish allowance was in arrears, and she was urged, gently, to send a firm letter to the Regents in Stockholm. The letter was dispatched the following day, and in it she revealed the depths of despair to which she had actually sunk.

"I wish," she said plaintively, "that you would either send me the money that is due me or teach me how to live without it. Nobody pays me, but everybody expects to be paid."

A day or two later she paid a visit to Azzolino, who received her in his office at the Vatican and carefully maintained the façade that all of her affairs were in order. Nevertheless, he suggested that she hire two representatives to establish permanent residence in Stockholm and take charge of her financial matters there. "The Queen told me," Mathilde notes in her *Diary*, "that Cardinal Azzolino believes it beneath her dignity to negotiate in person with those who owe her money. She agrees, and will send two men of the Cardinal's choice to Stockholm."

Azzolino was treading on wafer-thin ice, but he also persuaded the Queen to appoint a new household treasurer, a man in whom he had complete confidence. This gentleman, whom Kristina called "my ogre," but whose name has not been recorded for posterity, was Swiss, but little else is known about him except the vigor and determination he demonstrated in discharging his duties. There were large stacks of bills that had to be paid immediately if Kristina was to preserve her credit standing, so he paid no attention to her agonized protests and insisted that she sell two paintings, a statue, and a necklace of diamonds and sapphires.

She could not bring herself to part with the treasures, so her "ogre" disposed of them for her and, giving her no chance to squander the money, paid her most pressing obligations. For the immediate future, at least, she was relatively solvent.

Clement and Azzolino had not yet revealed their plans for her, so Kristina returned to her favorite pastime — intrigue. She tried to create enmity between the other losing candidates for the throne of Poland, and a letter she wrote to a count on the staff of her old enemy, the Prince de Condé, was typical.

"Had justice governed the decision," she wrote, "the crown would indubitably have gone to the Prince de Condé, who, of all the candidates, was the most worthy of it. It is to the eternal discredit of his opponents that they schemed to eliminate him, knowing, as they did, that he was a man who stood high above them. They have earned their Fate, and in time will be required to pay for their folly. Be that as it may, however, His Highness' worth and his glory may well console him for the injustice which Fortune has done him."

She sent similar letters to friends, relatives, and supporters of each of the others who had lost the Polish throne, hinting in each case that the man had been the victim of a deliberate conspiracy. Her secretaries delivered copies of the letters to the Vatican, and both Clement and Azzolino now realized that neither age nor travel had made her wiser. They had hoped to arouse her interest in wholesome pursuits gradually, but an incident that occurred less than a week after her return to Rome made them decide they could not afford to wait.

Kristina met an English bishop, who acknowledged the introduction to her with cool civility and then turned away. She felt she had been snubbed and inquired into the matter. Discovering that the bishop held firm convictions about the murder of Monaldeschi, she insisted on reviving the whole nasty affair by sending him a letter. Not satisfied to conduct a private correspondence with the bishop, she ordered her secretaries to make twenty copies of the communication and circulate them.

The tone of the self-justifying letter was belligerent, harsh, and uncompromising. "Monaldeschi," she wrote forcefully, "was a monster. He forced my hand and practically compelled me to have him put to death, by the blackest treachery that a servant can display toward a master. I did not order his execution until I had convicted him of crime from letters in his own handwriting. He confessed his guilt in the presence of the Prior of Fontainebleau, who heard him confess his guilt. The Prior knows that I caused all the sacraments the wretch could receive to be administered to him before he was executed.

"Any man who accuses me of barbarism or neglect of duty is disloyal to the Church, to himself, and, above all, to God."

The angry bishop was hastily summoned to the Vatican, where Cardinal Azzolino spent the better part of a morning soothing him. The Pope then received him in private audience, and the bishop apparently was mollified, for he did not reply to the letter. Those who hoped to see Kristina become involved in a new feud were disappointed when the bishop quietly left Rome on a special mission. Clement was taking no chances and was nipping scandals in the bud.

Soon after the bishop left, Kristina was called to the Vatican, and the Pope received her in private. "His Holiness suggested to me," Kristina later wrote in her *Memoirs*, "that I establish the most brilliant salon of scholars, men of letters, and artists that the world had ever seen. It was the most sensible idea that I ever heard any Pope express, either publicly or privately."

The plan aroused her wild enthusiasm, but, recalling the day in her old age, she could not refrain from making a typically sardonic comment in her *Memoirs*. "Of course it must be admitted that the thought did not originate either with the

Pope or with Cardinal Azzolino. Both knew that I had maintained such a court in Stockholm. I must give Clement his due and admit that he meant well. In all candor, however, I am compelled to observe that the Church must certainly be governed by the Holy Spirit, for since I have been at Rome I have seen four Popes, and I swear that not one of them had common sense."

In spite of her derogatory personal views, she accepted the Pope's suggestion and threw herself into the project with all of her inexhaustible vitality. The times were ripe for the creation of such a salon, as the description of Clement's court by a contemporary historian indicates.

> Every day there was some fresh and ingenious spectacle to be witnessed. One day it was the reception of a foreign Ambassador; another day, the promotion of a new Cardinal; always some entertainment, conducted on a lavish scale.
>
> His Holiness devoted the morning to worship and the afternoon to public affairs. He permitted nothing to interfere with his duty to God or the Church. But as soon as his daily dinner — a sumptuous repast — was over, the Papal party repaired to the theater or the opera house, or listened to a serenade by an orchestra of excellent musicians, whose entertainment was diversified by part-songs and symphonies.
>
> The Pope, who was generous and benevolent, inspired his nephews with these qualities. It is small wonder that the reign of Pope Clement has been called a Golden Age of the Papacy. There was no suggestion of miserliness about the noble lords of his household, as had been the case during some previous reigns; on the contrary, many lived beyond their means.
>
> The ladies wore magnificent French gowns, or attired themselves as Amazons, in imitation of the Queen of Sweden. Each tried to dress better than all the others, with the result that there was as much exaggerated luxury at Rome as at any of the temporal Courts of Europe.

Public comedies were introduced at Rome for the first time during the season of Carnival. A large box of extraordinary magnificence was constructed at the theater for His Holiness, and when he was not in attendance, it was always occupied by the Queen. It held fifteen or sixteen persons, and there were always ten or a dozen Cardinals there, keeping Her Majesty company.

Kristina should have been content, but her pride was still too great. Cardinals were princes, and as any one of them might inherit the throne of the Church, she dealt with them accordingly. But members of the Roman aristocracy had reason to complain bitterly, and a member of one of the city's ancient noble houses said, "She treats us as though we were her domestic servants."

Pope Clement put her in her place, but only for the moment. Kristina attended an outdoor entertainment, accompanied by a large entourage, and was annoyed because Princess Colonna's private box was as spacious and as prominent as her own. The Queen went to the Vatican the following day and protested vehemently. Clement listened to her in silence until she stopped for breath, and then he remarked with gentle sarcasm that inasmuch as the common people were admitted to public spectacles, he saw no reason why the nobility should be excluded from them.

It was fortunate that few aristocrats were interested in the arts, and Kristina's new "academy," which met twice each week at her palace, flourished from the start. Birth, rank, and fortune meant nothing; there was only one qualification for membership — "noble sentiments." There were fourteen members, each a man knowledgeable in his field, and the rules were simple: members were forbidden to praise each other's works, and no one was allowed to eulogize Kristina. Her attitude from the outset astonished those who knew her. She announced at the first meeting that aside from "a rather extensive knowledge of many tongues," she was not talented, and that she felt privileged to contribute her house and hospitality to the group.

It was her intention to listen and learn, she said, and she expressed the hope that the members would not lose patience with her and become vexed if she asked questions they considered simple. Rome buzzed when she opened the membership to women, too, declaring that only an interest in the arts and a positive desire to write poetry were required. Literature and ethics were the principal topics of conversation at the meetings but gradually, as the society expanded, other subjects were added. Scientists and philosophers attended, women who were afraid the Queen might snub them soon learned better, and the group achieved such renown that scholars in other parts of Europe began corresponding with Kristina.

The dream of a lifetime had been realized. Clement and Azzolino had done their work subtly, and it is doubtful that Kristina knew they were responsible for the success of the academy.

Her personality began to change at last, and she grew softer and less demanding as the society absorbed her interest and time. Her correspondence during this period indicates that she was mellowing rapidly, and nothing is more indicative of her new character than a brief letter she wrote to a bishop who was engaged in archeological work as a hobby and who asked her for help. "I am sending you two hundred and fifty ducats," she said. "I fear it is less than you deserve and far less than I should like to give. But my blushes will avenge you. Please say nothing about my little contribution to anyone or I shall be mortally offended."

Vincenzo da Filicaja, one of the most gifted young poets in Italy, was a member of the society, and not yet having achieved fame or found a patron, he lived in poverty with his wife and two small sons. Kristina could not afford to support Filicaja, but she ordered his sons educated at her expense, on condition that neither he nor his wife mention her generosity to anyone. She wrote to him, "I do not want to be obliged to blush at the thought of having done so little for a man whom I esteem so highly."

Filicaja wanted to write an ode in her honor, but she refused to grant her permission, and her note to him does not sound like the Kristina who had been the cause of incessant gossip for a generation. "Pray do not think that I want you to praise me," she said firmly. "Whoever put that thought into your head has done me a great wrong. You must not waste your precious time or your great talents on one who can only appreciate beauty but is incapable of creating that which is beautiful."

She became so engrossed in the affairs of the society that she no longer bothered to attend the theater or other entertainments, and when she was not meeting with the group, she visited individual members in their studios or laboratories. She became a student of astronomy under the most distinguished scholar in the field, Giovanni Cassini, professor of astronomy at Bologna, who was spending the winter in Rome. She called upon him and asked if he would become her instructor. Cassini, a brilliant, temperamental man, had heard of Kristina and was suspicious, but tentatively consented to let her observe him at work.

He soon discovered that she was an enthusiastic pupil, and subsequently wrote in his *Memoirs*, "It is a pity that so fine a mind should have been wasted on a queen and woman. Had Her Majesty been born a male, she would have become one of the great scientists of this or any other age. She grasps all that she is taught, she shows infinite patience and her humility sets a rare example for my son. When I offer her compliments, her face grows red, she stammers and seems ill at ease, but she forgets herself when she studies the stars."

Kristina was thrilled one evening when she was studying in the observatory the Pope had set up for Cassini in Rome. The astronomer discovered a comet, thus establishing his reputation for all time, and Kristina was so pleased that she wept. The professor wanted to name the comet in her honor, but she refused. "I am one who has tasted few glories in this world," he quotes her as saying. "I do not deserve celestial immortality."

Clement and Azzolino, still guiding her quietly, suggested that Kristina should become an author. The Cardinal told her that her life had been unique and that she should tell her own story for posterity. She agreed, reluctantly, and started work on her autobiography, a task that occupied her attention intermittently for the rest of her life.

But she displayed greater enthusiasm for a small volume which she called *Aphorisms*, and devoted considerable labor to the project. However, she was not satisfied with what she had written, and states in her *Memoirs*, "My poor words were so foolish, so awkward and so dull that I consigned them to the fire."

Nevertheless, the idea of writing a book of aphorisms took root, and later in her life she returned to the task. It is difficult to think of Kristina as a shy woman, but she would not publish the volume while she lived, and after her death it was neglected and gathered dust for more than two hundred years. Perhaps no one ever insisted more loudly that kings and queens ruled by divine right, but she associated with enough creative artists to be aware of her limitations as an author.

Possibly the most significant character development she displayed in 1669 was her indifference to gossip. Not even the subject of Monaldeschi's death could arouse her ire, and when she heard that talk about it had been revived in Westphalia after a member of her literary society had visited the German state, she made a weary notation in her *Memoirs*, "How ridiculous is all this nonsense about Monaldeschi!" she wrote. "All Westphalia may believe him to have been innocent if it chooses. The opinion of Westphalia is a matter of supreme indifference to me. I am responsible to my conscience and to God, not to public opinion."

She allowed her hair to grow longer, she stopped dressing in men's clothing, and it was noted that she not only attended church services regularly, but listened to the sermons. Some Roman aristocrats began to call her "Kristina the Meek," but she paid no attention to their slurs, and demonstrating a calm that was new to her, went about her business serenely, antagonizing no one.

Those who thought she had reformed and would tolerate any abuse soon learned otherwise, however. Late in 1669 it was announced that Clement IX was ill and would not recover. The Pope sent for his friends to bid them farewell, and he received Kristina in an audience that lasted so long it taxed his failing strength. She left the Vatican for her palace, weeping, and was not seen in public again until he died, a week later.

Then, suddenly, she entered the arena of world affairs again, and plunged into one of the most hectic periods of her life.

XII: 1669–1676
DUSK

The death of Clement IX marked the beginning of a frantic seventeen weeks for Kristina. Members of the College of Cardinals retired into the inner recesses of the Vatican and, following a formula that had been practiced for centuries, began the deliberations that would end only when they had elected a new Pope. Twice each day they cast ballots in the Sistine Chapel, and until they agreed on a new Pope they saw only each other. They were permitted to receive letters, which were censored, and even their food was broken into small bits before it was served to them for fear political connivers on the outside might try to send them secret messages that would influence them.

The French and Spaniards each proposed candidates, the Austrians straddled the fence, and the Italians were divided into a number of factions. No one knew who was favored. The circumstances were made-to-order for Kristina who, having failed to obtain the crowns of either Naples or Poland for herself, now determined to win the greatest crown of all for Azzolino. She conferred with him in the Vatican before the cardinals retired, and Azzolino, a realist, tried to dissuade her. He was only forty-seven years old, far too young to inherit the triple crown, and he lacked the active support of any major group. Only if his colleagues could decide on no one else might they turn to him, and that possibility was so remote that he refused to consider it seriously.

Nevertheless, the election was of great importance to him for spiritual and personal reasons. The strength of the Ottoman

Empire was growing in the East, the Protestant nations of Europe were becoming increasingly powerful, and Azzolino was one of a band of serious young princes of the Church who were convinced that Catholicism had to meet the challenge by acting promptly and vigorously. Consequently he wanted to keep his position as Secretary of State, but knew he would be reappointed to the post only if he threw his support to the right man. So he wanted no electioneering on his own behalf.

But Kristina would not listen to reason. He had been her best friend at a time when everyone else had deserted her, and she insisted on returning the favor. She knew what was right for him, even if he was too myopic to see for himself. Never before had she been given such a splendid opportunity to exercise her talents for mysterious intrigue, and before she left the Vatican she horrified Azzolino by pressing a piece of folded paper into his hand and telling him it contained a secret cipher. She planned to work for his election on the outside, she declared, and would write to him in a code that no one else would understand.

She went to work in a crisp, authoritative fashion when a large crowd gathered to watch the final procession of the cardinals as they made their way to their cells. It was rumored that the scholarly Cardinal Vidoni stood the best chance, and Kristina commented loudly as he passed her, "There have been so many rumors one doesn't know what to think, but I feel certain that Cardinal Vidoni won't be elected."

Many of the bystanders, knowing that she was a good friend of so many members of the Sacred College, were impressed.

Later that same day she sent one of her agents to rent a small palace overlooking the Vatican, where she established an office, keeping several secretaries busy writing letters to foreign envoys — special representatives of Catholic kings who had hurried to Rome — and other influential men. Each night she gave a dinner party for dignitaries favoring one faction or another, and she pounded incessantly at the same theme: the Conclave was deadlocked; Azzolino was the only man to whom all factions could turn.

She kept her favorite informed of her activities, and during the four months the College of Cardinals met and balloted, she sent him the incredible total of one hundred and twenty-three letters, all in cipher.

The Queen's labors were wasted. It was true that the cardinals were unable to reach a decision, and the atmosphere inside the Vatican became increasingly tense. The Spaniards and Austrians formed an alliance, but were blocked by the French, who enlisted the aid of the so-called "independents" — cardinals from small nations — and a number of the Italians. Powerful men who had grown accustomed to every luxury, shivered in their cold cells, ate their unappetizing chunks of food apathetically, and made every effort to end the deadlock.

At no time was Azzolino given serious consideration, and neither he nor his friends tried to win the Papacy for him. His one indefatigable supporter was Kristina, whose fervor remained undiminished even though various nobles tried to tell her that her favorite could not win. One by one the eligible candidates were eliminated, and finally the exhausted cardinals compromised by electing a man everyone had virtually ignored from the outset, eighty-year-old Cardinal Altieri, the last living member of an ancient Roman family.

He, feeling himself unworthy and saying he wanted to die in peace, refused the honor. His colleagues, uniting at last, spent the better part of a day imploring and arguing, and, in the end, according to legend, placed the crown on his head in spite of his protests. Resigning himself to the inevitable, the old man adopted the name of Clement X, in honor of his predecessor, who had given him the red hat.

When the white smoke was seen rising from the chimney where the ballots were being burned, word spread rapidly that Cardinal Altieri had been elected and a huge crowd gathered outside. Persons of distinction were admitted to the Vatican, and the first to kneel before the new Pope was Kristina, who had worked so hard for someone else.

Clement X changed nothing. He paid little attention to the social life of Rome, and the theater and opera continued to flourish. He instituted no reforms of note, was unimpressed by the menace of the Turks or the growth of Protestantism, and allowed several Catholic monarchs, chief among them Louis XIV, to consolidate the authority of temporal powers over religious institutions. Azzolino kept his post as Secretary of State, but soon discovered that he had become a figurehead. Clement X, who knew nothing of the world and had been happiest as parish priest, grew increasingly senile and the real ruler of the Church became his adopted nephew, Cardinal Paluzzi-Altieri, a man of meager talent and unlimited personal ambition.

For six years the influence and strength of the Church declined, but Kristina enjoyed one of the happiest periods of her life. She created no scandals, became involved in no disputes, and lived calmly in her palace, surrounded by her art treasures and books. Her learned society occupied most of her time, she attended the theater and opera regularly, and she lived precisely the sort of life she had said she wanted when she abdicated. She received her pension more or less regularly from Stockholm, presumably because she behaved herself, and she stopped making a nuisance of herself in public. Roman nobles accepted her as a gracious and charming lady. For the first time in her life she became plump. Her hair hung in long curls, she gave up men's clothing permanently, and, to all outward appearances, her spirit of rebellion had burned itself out.

She admired Bernini, both as an artist and as a friend, and he visited her palace frequently. She was the first to recognize the genius of a young composer, Alessandro Scarlatti, and gave him every encouragement. Eventually she financed his studies by creating a new post, that of music master to her household, and he moved into her palace but was given no duties to perform. She heard of anatomical experiments being conducted by a gifted young physician, Vincenzo Bellini, and sent him a purse on condition that he write her no letter of thanks. She admired Carlo Maratta, the foremost painter of the day, and when she learned he was in debt, commissioned him to paint her portrait, even though she hated posing. When Maratta was finished, she gave him four thousand crowns instead of his usual fee, three hundred.

There was no author, artist, or scientist in Italy who did not know and respect her. The Papacy had enjoyed its Golden Age, and now it was Kristina's turn. She had become a serious critic, an astute judge, and young men came to her palace in an unending stream for advice. Cardinal Azzolino remained her friend and continued to supervise her finances, other members of the Curia were frequent callers, and her life was both full and rich.

"Never," wrote Mathilde von Echner in her *Diary* shortly before the Queen's fiftieth birthday, "have I seen Her Majesty so much at peace with herself and the world."

Clement X died in 1676, and the Sacred College elected

Cardinal Benedetto Odescalchi, a pious, farseeing Lombard, as Pope. Adopting the title of Innocent XI, he went to work with a vengeance, and the whole world soon learned that the Church had a new master worthy of respect. It is necessary to understand something of this extraordinary man's character and achievements in order to see his relationship with Kristina in proper perspective. Austere and scrupulously honest, wholeheartedly devoted to the Church, and a man whose closest friends called holy, he hated petulance and fraud and wanted, more than all else, to revive the glory of Catholicism.

Azzolino, now nearing sixty, supported Innocent completely and approved of the reforms which the new Pope instituted. It was immoral, Innocent said, for gambling to flourish in his capital, and nobles were forbidden to play games for money in the city. Most actresses, he declared, were loose women, so he revoked the permit, which Kristina had been influential in persuading Clement IX to grant, which allowed women to appear on the Roman stage. He rebuked the Jesuits, who had been acting as a law unto themselves, and he issued orders to halt the sale of Church offices. He cut the expenditures of the Vatican staff drastically, refused to permit extravagance of any sort, and sent a firm letter to Louis XIV, with whom he was to maintain a running feud, reminding the King that sovereigns were not immortal and that the Church was the custodian of royal as well as common souls.

Innocent stopped merely talking about conducting a war against the Turks and began to prepare in earnest for such a struggle. He lived long enough to see the Ottoman invaders halted before the gates of Vienna, and troops bearing the Papal banner recover Hungary for Christendom. However, in spite of the strength of his beliefs, he was no bigot. He was horrified by the persecution of Protestants in France, and condemned

King Louis in the strongest terms. When James II made a clumsy and abortive attempt to restore Catholicism as the official religion in England, Innocent opposed him, saying that the attempt was stupid and that it would have no effect except to arouse the hatred of the English people for the Church. In brief, let it be noted that Innocent was one of the strongest, wisest, and most influential of Popes.

Kristina, long accustomed to living as she pleased, began to bristle. Her life had been serene during the reigns of Innocent's two immediate predecessors, but her dormant sense of rebellion flared again when she was told how to behave. The wisdom that she had accumulated was forgotten, and she discovered that she was as incapable of bowing her head at fifty as she had been at twenty. Friends tried to tell her that she was fighting a losing battle, but she listened to no one, and even Azzolino could not persuade her to submit gracefully to higher authority.

Her dispute with the Pope erupted unexpectedly. He had been a friend for many years, and as she apparently expected their close relationship to continue, she ignored the first minor inconveniences that changed the pattern of daily living. She was sorry to see actresses disappear from the Roman stage, and she was mildly annoyed when she received word from the Vatican that she was expected to set an example for the people and that the silk draperies lining her box at the opera should be replaced with a less expensive fabric.

She could not believe that Innocent was intent on reforming the morals of the civilized world and, expecting him to relax his restrictions after he had been in office for a time, she cheerfully accepted the initial regulations. Innocent, who had been observing her for years and understood her nature, was as pleased as he was surprised, and offered her a gift of twelve thousand crowns as a reward for her obedience and humility. He hoped to encourage her, but he misjudged her.

A new law caused her to revolt. The Pope issued a stern decree in which he said that the dress of ladies was shocking and extravagant; even those who could afford to buy costly gowns should find other, worthier ways to spend their money, and he deplored current styles, which featured low-cut dresses and bare arms. Kristina made no protest, but invited the Pope to call on her at his convenience. When he arrived at her palace, she received him in a shapeless, ragged, long-sleeved dress that she had bought from a peasant woman. She had expanded her court in recent years to include several ladies, and all of them made their obeisances similarly attired.

Members of the Papal entourage were horrified, but Innocent chatted pleasantly and pretended to be unaware of anything out-of-the-ordinary. Two days later he published a document congratulating the Queen on the zeal she was displaying in trying to obtain support for the campaign against the Turks. Thinking she had won, she praised him, but changed her tune when the courier who was supposed to bring her the gift of twelve thousand crowns arrived at her palace from the Vatican. He brought no money, but handed her a brief note in which the Pope thanked her for contributing the entire sum to the holy war.

She became wildly angry, and the Kristina of old reappeared in the furious letter that she wrote to Azzolino. "My acceptance of the twelve thousand crowns which the Pope offered me was the one blot on my life," she declared sarcastically. "I only accepted it as a mortification in order to humiliate my pride. His Holiness' gracious goodness in taking it away from me in circumstances of such glory proves that I have found favor in his eyes and am worthy of his trust.

"This is his reward for the poor services which he has permitted me to render him. The favor is worth more to me than a thousand kingdoms, and I pray to God to preserve me from the vanity which I might naturally feel in it.

"Would that one hundred thousand crowns a month could be taken from me, so that my merit in rejoicing might be greater!"

The battle was joined, and Kristina refused to attend a diplomatic reception at the Vatican. Azzolino, no longer Secretary of State but still an influential member of the Curia, asked her to reconsider, but she refused. Then he suggested that she plead illness, but she offered no excuse, preferring to snub the Pope publicly. Innocent had more important matters on his mind and he ignored her rudeness.

But Kristina's insistence on keeping up this feud continued to create repercussions, the most important of which was totally unexpected. Mathilde von Echner, tired of a long life of turmoil and caprice, announced that she intended to return to Sweden, and resigned from the Queen's staff. The angry Kristina swept out of the room without speaking a word when she heard the news, but when the resignation was reported to Azzolino, he was disturbed.

"His Eminence called on me," Mathilde recalled in her *Memoirs*, "and asked me to reconsider my decision. He acknowledged that I had served Her Majesty faithfully for many years and he said he knew I must miss my own home and the opportunity to practice my own religion in public. But he expressed the fear that the Queen would become less balanced if my influence on her was withdrawn.

"I replied that I did not exert an influence over her, nor did anyone else, and he was ruefully forced to agree. He made an attempt to reconcile Her Majesty to me, but she refused to see me, and I left Rome for Stockholm without bidding her good-by."

Subsequently, Kristina realized she had behaved disgracefully and wrote an apologetic letter to her old friend. Thereafter they corresponded, and although they frequently mentioned the idea of Mathilde visiting Rome at some future time, the journey never materialized and the two women never saw each other again. Mathilde went to live at her brother's estate outside Stockholm and remained there until she died. She was active in the social life of the Swedish capital, but she refused to discuss her former mistress and commented that although she was annoyed by the curious, she kept a vow she had made and answered no questions. She wrote her *Memoirs*, which she finished in 1686, but in a sense she remained loyal to the Queen, for the book was not published until 1692, three years after Kristina's death. Mathilde's *Diary*, which she had not written for publication, did not come into print until fifty years later, when the husband of one of her great-nieces published an edition in Paris.

The *Diary* makes it plain that Mathilde was relieved to be home again and that she enjoyed living her own life in her own way. She missed the excitement of Kristina's court, but there were compensations, and she was happy.

Kristina does not mention the departure of her principal lady in waiting in her *Memoirs*, and only through the letters she sent to Mathilde is there an indication that she missed her old friend. However, she was too busy feeding the flames of her new feud with Pope Innocent to think of anyone except herself.

Showing neither discretion nor common sense, she became immersed in one of the most ridiculous and futile battles in which she had ever engaged. She decided that her master of the horse, a man named Del Monte, should be addressed as, "Your Excellency." The idea was absurd, but she sent an official letter to the Vatican, requesting that this honor be accorded the man, and similar communications were dispatched to all foreign embassies and legations in Rome.

The Vatican was a very busy place, so Kristina's demand went unanswered. She interpreted the silence as a personal affront and sent a second letter, addressed to the Pope. Innocent, who began his day at dawn and worked far into the night, ignored the request. The envoys followed his example, and the frustrated Kristina seemed unable to create a controversy over this trifle. But she created an opportunity to bring the issue into the open at a quiet reception given at the Vatican for the new Portuguese Ambassador. He, unfamiliar with the details of the affair, was startled when she accosted him and requested that he and the members of his staff grant the honors she deemed essential to the dignity of her master of the horse. The Ambassador, a trained diplomat, replied that he would study her request.

The following day a messenger delivered a written rebuke from the Vatican, and the sting was particularly painful because the reprimand was signed by Cardinal Azzolino. "When Her Majesty behaves with the decorum expected of one who has attained her high station," he wrote, "she will be respected by the whole world."

XIII: 1677–1689
NIGHT

Kristina's most violent dispute with Innocent XI began in 1677, lasted for two years, and ended when the Queen won a victory of a sort. Once again her "prestige" was at stake, and she sparred because of what she regarded as a principle.

In Rome, as in any capital, the houses and surrounding grounds of the chiefs of diplomatic missions were considered the property of the nation that owned and maintained the embassy. Papal laws did not apply in these quarters, and the envoys, their families, and the members of their staffs obeyed their own national laws. Ambassadors and members of their suites were also immune from arrest, a diplomatic privilege that has survived to the present day.

Through the centuries there had been considerable abuse of the right in the city of Rome, where crime flourished. Ambassadors gave sanctuary to those whom they chose to protect for political purposes, and gradually, as the custom spread, many criminals took advantage of the situation. Pope Innocent, anxious to transform Rome into a model capital, decided to restrict the privilege of sanctuary, and when he first announced his plan, his most enthusiastic supporter was Kristina.

She took the attitude that she had always enjoyed the right accorded to diplomats because she was a queen; actually, the question was academic, as she had never granted sanctuary to anyone. Nevertheless, she wrote a strong letter, which her secretaries copied and circulated among the legations. "The Pope's proposal is very just," she declared. "I willingly make him a gift of my privilege, never abused and freely granted to me by his predecessors, reserving to myself only the right to protect my personal attendants."

The Vatican was willing to overlook her careless statement, and although several cardinals, Azzolino among them, reminded her privately that she had never been granted Papal diplomatic immunity, she received no official communication on the subject, probably because she had addressed her letters to the envoys rather than to the head of the Church.

Aware of her oversight, she corrected it at once, sending Innocent a letter which she had her secretaries copy for the ambassadors. "I confess," she said with a display of humility that must have surprised the Pontiff, "that I am only offering to cede a right which already appertains to Your Holiness. But, then, we can offer God Himself nothing but what He has given us, and God not only accepts such offerings, but rewards them, in His infinite goodness, with immeasurable and eternal benefits. For my own part, I ask nothing from Your Holiness, but only beg Your Holiness to accept the offering as an example which, perhaps, will not be without its utility to the Holy See."

An ordinary man might have been fooled, but Innocent was too shrewd. Kristina, frightened by his severity, was trying to make amends for her many discourtesies to him by leading the parade, and would claim credit when the envoys accepted the Pope's decision to restrict their rights. A Papal secretary acknowledged receipt of the letter, but no direct reply was written. Presumably the Holy Father failed to appreciate Kristina's authoritative observations on the subject of God. On the other hand, he may have been stunned; certainly no one else in Christendom had dared to inform him of the nature and extent of God's power.

In any event, the French Ambassador spoiled everything for Kristina. Had the envoys accepted the Pope's proposal without dissent, Kristina could have posed as the champion of the Vatican, and it would have been difficult to discount her influence. But the Ambassador from Louis XIV, reflecting his King's arrogance, sent a haughty note to the Vatican, saying that he was not guided by precedents, but set them. Then, in curt, undiplomatic language, he refused to agree to the curtailment of his prerogatives. His tone was so insulting that Innocent excommunicated him, and Louis retaliated by refusing to name a new ambassador and insisting that his disgraced but unrepentant envoy remain at his post. "Those who represent us at courts abroad, be those places temporal or spiritual, command our respect and love," the King of France said haughtily.

Other rulers were bewildered by the dispute and could not decide whether to follow the example of France or retain the support of the Church. Kristina was not confused, however. Louis had shown her the path to follow, and she not only walked in his footsteps, but soon passed him on the road. She was no less an absolute monarch than the Sun King, and, determined to prove it, she became embroiled in one of the most scandalous incidents in her long career.

On Easter Sunday, 1677, the Papal constabulary, which was responsible for maintaining peace in Rome, found a criminal for whom they had been searching. He was a wine merchant who had cheated his customers by watering his product, and many citizens had filed complaints against him. He was recognized in church and escaped, but the constables followed him as he dashed wildly through the streets. The chase took place near Kristina's palace, and by luck rather than design he tried to hide in her coach house. But he could not lift the latch, and the constables, reaching over a hedge into the Queen's property, fastened a rope around his neck, dragged him out, and arrested him.

A crowd had gathered, and, being Romans, they cursed the constables. Kristina, returning from Mass at St. Peter's, arrived as the uproar reached its peak. She listened to what had happened and, according to her own account, lost her temper. "I might hush this matter up, but I shall not," she said. "The Pope is treating me too badly, and I shall take this opportunity of showing him that he is mistaken if he expects me to tolerate such treatment."

Encouraged by the crowd, she sent several of her gentlemen to obtain the release of the prisoner, and the nobles rode off at a gallop. They surrounded the donkey cart in which the wine merchant was being carried to prison and demanded that he be released into their custody. The constables, accustomed to obeying kings and queens, released the prisoner without a protest, and Kristina gave the man sanctuary in her palace. A huge throng applauded her, and she came out onto the steps to make a speech.

"I have done no more than that which is my right," she told the people. "The prisoner had reached my property in his flight from the constables, and I granted him sanctuary. There the matter rests, and there is nothing more to say."

There was a great deal more to be said, however, and a delegation from the Vatican called on her that afternoon to say it. Her anger mounting, she treated the Pope's emissaries disdainfully, and, giving them no chance to speak, lashed out at them for a quarter of an hour and then dismissed them. "Her Majesty spoke to us as a Queen," the officials said in their written report. "She informed us that all had been done at her orders, that she took full responsibility for the affair and was prepared to do it again under the same provocation."

She also refused to release the wine merchant to the constables. The cardinal who was governor of Rome was her next visitor, coming to see her late in the day, and she gave him the same reply. Azzolino and two other cardinals went to her at dinnertime, but left her palace hurriedly, without joining her for a meal. That night the lights burned late at the Vatican.

The next morning the Pope struck with all his might. He instituted criminal proceedings against Kristina's gentlemen, charging them with obstructing justice and interfering with his constables. The nobles were in hiding behind the barred doors of Kristina's palace and refused to appear in court, but the trial was held that same day and each was condemned, *in absentia*, to ten years in prison. The Vatican press quickly printed placards announcing the results of the trial, and these posters were nailed on boards in every quarter of the city. That night the watch was doubled, and the citizens, smelling trouble, stayed at home.

Kristina's fury continued to soar, and early the next morning she sent a long letter to the president of the tribunal that had condemned her retainers. "So you call this justice!" she exclaimed angrily. "You dishonor yourself and your master. I am sorry for you, and I shall be still more sorry for you when you are a cardinal. Meanwhile I promise you that those whom you have condemned shall not, by God's grace, die yet awhile, and if they do die any but a natural death, they shall not die alone."

The Pope could not tolerate such a demonstration of insubordination, and a Vatican courier delivered a private note to the Queen, telling her she had two choices: either she could submit to Papal authority or she would be charged with fomenting sedition against His Holiness.

Kristina wept, recovered, and replied by taking a stroll through the streets of the city, surrounded by the gentlemen who had been condemned. All were armed, and Kristina expected a public demonstration in her favor. But the people looked at her in fearful silence from their windows, and she was disappointed when several squads of Papal constabulary whom she encountered on the street pretended not to see her or her escorts.

The incident, magnified out of proportion, was threatening the dignity of the Papacy, and no one understood the situation better than Innocent. He sent Azzolino and another cardinal to the Queen's palace that night, and Kristina's old friend explained some cold, hard facts to her. She would apologize to the Pope immediately, in writing, or she would be excommunicated and expelled from Rome. Having burned her Protestant bridges behind her, she had nowhere to go. However, Azzolino said, Innocent was as merciful as he was stern. If she would admit His Holiness' authority, she and her retainers would be pardoned, and the Pope would issue a public statement acknowledging her status as a queen.

Under the circumstances, Innocent was acting generously, but Kristina failed to sympathize with his position. She had no alternative, however, so she agreed, and Azzolino wrote a statement for her. In it she apologized completely and said that she had given offense unintentionally. Being Kristina, she felt compelled to add a few words: She hoped, she said, that His Holiness would give strict orders that she should be treated more respectfully in the future, as she would rather die than submit to affronts.

The Pope's reply was superb. He was much impressed by the spectacle of edifying humility on the part of a person of exalted station, he wrote, and he assured Kristina that she would be treated with all the respect due her. But, he added, with uncompromising firmness, he was a reigning sovereign and as such he had the right to punish a criminal, whoever he might be.

Kristina admitted temporary defeat and surrendered the wine merchant to a captain of the constabulary. The following day, still smarting, she attended church, escorted by the gentlemen who had been condemned. She was disappointed when no attempt was made to arrest them, but the Pope had won all that he had sought: he had established the principle of his supremacy, and the wine merchant was in prison. So, instead of prolonging the dispute, he sent Kristina a huge basket of peaches, a rare treat, as they were out of season.

The receipt of the basket prompted a remark that has endured through the ages. "The Pope needn't think that his gift will lull my suspicions," Kristina said. "On the contrary, I shall be more on my guard then ever."

Innocent sighed quietly when the comment was reported to him, and his reply became even more famous. "Kristina is a woman," he declared, "and behaves as such — irrationally."

The Pope obtained the consent of virtually all the foreign legations to limit the privilege of sanctuary to practicing diplomats and their blood relatives. Then, having won the victory he had sought from the beginning, he devoted himself to other matters. But Kristina continued to brood, and a year later she finally had an opportunity to even the score.

A young woman who was being held against her will in a convent, managed to escape and appealed to the Queen for protection. Kristina promptly granted her sanctuary and made the girl her personal chambermaid. The facts of the case have become frayed, and it is difficult to evaluate them. Whether the girl was of "doubtful reputation," as the irate cardinal insisted, in whose jurisdiction the convent was located, or whether she had been imprisoned unjustly, as Kristina insisted, is impossible to tell.

The Queen tried hard to make a major issue of the incident, and stated publicly that had the cardinal who demanded the fugitive's surrender not been a personal friend, she would have had him thrown out of her palace. Pope Innocent was too busy to worry about a girl who may or may not have been a delinquent, and he told the cardinal to forget the case.

Kristina was elated. Her persistence had been rewarded, and she had won the final triumph. The young woman remained in her employ, and as there was no more reason to display belligerence, the Queen subsided. She had fought her last battle.

The remaining years of Kristina's life were peaceful, and she finally fulfilled the promise of brilliance she had demonstrated fitfully through the years. The Reverend Thomas Burnet of Yorkshire, a distinguished Anglican scholar who visited Rome in 1681–82, after publishing a treatise that caused considerable excitement in the academic world, was curious about Kristina and sought an introduction to her. She charmed him, he became a frequent visitor to her house, and much that is known of her last years was written by him.

"I cannot imagine," he said, "what manner of person she may have been in her youth, and it is not easy to picture this grey-haired lady, very small, fat and round, with a double chin, as an Amazon. She may have been what others say about her; I know only that she is profoundly wise, very humble, sincere in all things, and she worships God with all of her heart. I do not agree with her religion, but I wish that all members of my Church shared the deep faith in the Almighty that she has acquired."

Shortly before his return to England, Burnet wrote of her again in glowing terms. "At the Queen of Sweden's, one learns all the news relating to Germany and the North. This wise Princess, who will always reign among those who are endowed with wit and learning, keeps up in her antechamber the finest Court of strangers in Rome. The civility and great diversity of matters furnished by her conversation make her among all the rare sights of Rome the rarest."

In the last decade of her life, Kristina became a real magnet for artists and scholars of every land, and, as the trappings of wealth and royalty came to mean less to her, the financial problems that had plagued her for so many years ceased to burden her. When she received only a portion of her allowance from Sweden, she sold a painting or a jewel in order to maintain her household, but she said frequently that she had never disposed of a book for profit and that she would die with her library intact.

Encouraged by authors, she spent several hours each day at her desk, writing. Her *Memoirs* remained incomplete at the time of her death. Some portions were changed frequently; others were mere fragments; and some periods in her life received no mention. Her *Aphorisms*, which she first entitled *Sentiments*, show two distinct strains. Her religion influenced her profoundly in her last years, so she devoted many pages to a contemplation of her faith, but she was still a worldly woman and could not resist writing epigrams and maxims in the manner of the Duc de la Rochefoucauld and other cosmopolitan French authors, who were setting the current fashion in literature.

The religious portions of her *Aphorisms* are worth noting, for it becomes obvious that her faith had developed and matured. She was a Catholic by conviction now, not caprice, as her opening statement indicates: "There is, beyond question, a God who is the unique source and the ultimate end of all things."

Many of her sayings are commonplace, and she frequently falls back on platitudes, but it must be remembered that she had fought and won a terrible inner battle that had lasted a lifetime, and her observations represented the convictions she had formed as a result of that struggle. A few examples will suffice to show what she had become:

"Even if God did not reward virtue, one should practice it for its own sake."

"Civility and kindness are becoming, even to the great, who must put the less fortunate at their ease."

"Nothing that is not honorable is useful."

"Economy is necessary for all people, but regardless of one's station, he who practices it must be inspired by motives that are noble, not sordid."

"A prince should love the brave, but should detest the boastful and the brutal."

"It is far better to deserve good fortune than to possess it."

"There is no rule without its exception; our judgment should guide us in doubtful cases."

"The doctrines of the Pope are infallible; one is rightly amazed to find persons professing and calling themselves Christians who have their doubts about this visible Head of the Church."

The Kristina who had waged war with Innocent XI over the privileges of diplomatic sanctuary could not have written the last statement. But the character of the Queen was not completely changed in the last years of her life. She still showed flashes of wit and independence, of rebellion, and, in spite of her willingness to compromise, she clung to the principles of a social nonconformist. She, who had never married, dared to write, "Every woman who wants to enjoy herself needs a husband; in fact, she cannot do without one."

In a more ironic mood, she wrote, "Women only marry in order to acquire greater liberty. The unmarried woman who takes a lover loses her reputation, but the married woman gains a lover. Therefore women would rather have aged husbands than none at all."

Having lived as freely as a man, she sympathized with the opposite sex when she wrote, "Socrates said: 'Whether you marry or refrain from marrying, you will be sorry.' For my own part, I believe that any man who marries will infallibly regret it, but I do not see why anyone should regret having remained single. Experience makes me a judge of that."

Other passages demonstrate her undiminished hostility to the institution of marriage. In one of the more vehement, she said, "One needs more courage to expose oneself to the evils of marriage than to those of war. I marvel at the intrepidity of those who marry; but this terrible contract is currently entered into without consideration of its importance or of the engagements to which it commits one."

"Many husbands and wives are virtuous, and claim credit for their virtue," she wrote acidly. "I have the highest respect for those who are chaste through real virtue, but those who are chaste only because their temperaments are cold are never good for anything."

It is clear that she felt the same distaste for marriage that she had shown as a young woman, but her attitude toward love had changed. She devoted many pages of her *Aphorisms* to the subject, and her enthusiasm was unrestrained. In her discussion of love, she demonstrated her greatest wisdom, and certainly she proved that she had learned much from her own experiences.

"Sensual enjoyment is not necessary to the existence of love," she said candidly, "but it is almost an essential to one's perfect happiness."

"Love is possible without possession," she declared in another frank confession of her values, "but complete happiness is not."

Perhaps she was referring to her unrequited love for Azzolino when she said, "When the hope of sensual enjoyment has to be abandoned, one suffers terribly, but still one continues to love." Several nineteenth-century biographers quoted this statement as "proof" of her love for Azzolino, but the reed is too slender to support a firm foundation.

As idle speculation reveals nothing new about Kristina's life, it is preferable to read her comments on love for their own sake, and nothing indicates her nature more clearly than the comment, "The unique purpose of love is to love and be loved. It makes no other claim."

"Love," she said subsequently, enlarging on the theme, "embellishes the beloved object and makes it more and more worthy of love with every passing hour; but the love of those who do not know how to love is madly importunate."

"Fidelity in love is not so much a merit as a necessity," she declared in another passage, with which marriage counselors of a later era would agree. "It is the touchstone which distinguishes the true love from the false."

She made a number of similar observations which are as valid today as they were when she wrote them. "Absence does not destroy true love; and time, which destroys everything else, has no power over it."

And another: "True love is chaste. Nothing pleases it, and nothing moves it, except the beloved object."

Inevitably, her concept of love confirmed her faith in God. "When a heart is capable of loving," she said, "it is impossible that it should not, sooner or later, come to love God, who alone is capable of bringing all its desires to fulfillment."

It is neither surprising nor inconsistent with Kristina's basic character to discover that even in her last years, she thought like a sinner one moment and a saint the next. Eschewing convention, she wrote, "The passions are the salt of life. One is only happy or unhappy in proportion as one does them violence."

But she denied these sentiments on the next page, and her tone was solemn as she wrote, "The goodness and the felicity of God are the most just and worthy subjects of our joy and consolation. If God had only created us as brands to be burned eternally in hell, He would nonetheless deserve our love and adoration.

"To be completely happy in this world and in the next, we must dispense with everything except God.

"Nothing can fix the affections of our hearts; it is only in God that they find peace."

She left no doubt that she was speaking of herself and the sincerity of her faith in this passage: "There are some hearts so fortunately born and so happy that they never set their affection on anything but God; there are others who only arrive at the love of God after everything else has disgusted them. The former are enviable; the latter are less fortunate. But it is better to love God late than never. Yes, it is infinitely better."

The murder of Monaldeschi continued to weigh on her conscience, and she referred to the infamous incident obliquely, at some length, in her *Aphorisms*: "One never repents of having pardoned offenses; one always repents of having punished them, however just the punishment may have been. On reflection, I have concluded that a great heart cannot exact vengeance when it is weak, and ought not to exact it when it is strong. One should only avenge oneself by conferring benefits; any other kind of vengeance, however just, is unworthy of an heroic soul."

It is significant that the next sentence, set off in a paragraph alone, was heavily underscored: "It is better to pardon the guilty than to punish the innocent."

Later in the *Aphorisms* she brought up the matter again. "One ought to pardon every man who confesses his fault and surrenders at discretion. Every crime is a rude penance for him who has committed it. Where our own actions are concerned, it is much easier to deceive others than to deceive ourselves."

Early in 1689, she suffered a stroke, and although she recovered, it was clear to her that the end was near. She summed up her philosophy in the final pages of the *Aphorisms*, which she wrote with a shaking hand.

> One ought to fear the smallest sin more than one fears death.
>
> Our true glory and happiness depend only upon the last moments of our lives. All the rest passes like smoke, which disappears, carried by the wind. It is only at our last hour, be it happy, or be it terrible, that God will reveal us to ourselves as we really are, and as we shall have to be, throughout all eternity, in the sight of God Himself and of His Universe.

The Universe is a great and glorious temple, and the earth on which we dwell is its magnificent altar. God, for His own glory, brought this great and beautiful earth out of nothingness, but it is His will that all shall return thereto. Let us submit to His eternal decrees and let us be fully persuaded that it is just that all things should perish for His glory and greatness.

When our turn arrives, let us adore this Infinite Being, who alone exists and who alone is worthy to exist. When our turn arrives, let us adore this Infinite Being with perfect resignation and have no fear of death, because God is just.

Early in April, 1689, she became ill again, and the physicians told her what she already knew — the end was near. Kristina signed her will, leaving her books and paintings to the Church and her personal property to the servants and attendants who had remained faithful to her. Cardinal Azzolino was named as her executor.

Summoning her failing strength, she sent a message to Pope Innocent, asking pardon for the affronts which her pride had forced him to bear and begging for absolution and his blessing. Innocent would have gone to her himself, but he, too, was ill, so he sent Cardinal Azzolino, Kristina's oldest friend, with a Papal blessing. The Cardinal administered the last rites, and at dawn Kristina died.

Church bells tolled in Rome for twenty-four hours to mark her passing, but in Sweden, where Charles XI ruled with the strong hand of an absolute monarch, few remembered the Queen who had abdicated thirty-five years before, and fewer cared. Mathilde von Echner wept, a few old men went to the Storkyrka and prayed, and the King signed an order halting the payment of the eccentric old lady's allowance.

At various Courts, old men and women with long memories revived stories of the past, and younger people, who had never heard her name, were fascinated. Kristina, whose exploits had electrified her own generation, lived again in legends and, like the Queen herself, became ageless.

SELECTED BIBLIOGRAPHY

Bain, F.W. *Queen Christina of Sweden*. Cambridge, England.

Bain, R.N. *Scandinavia*. Cambridge, England.

Barine, A. *Princesses and Court Ladies*. London.

Bertrand, M.L.E. *Louis XIV*. Paris.

Bildt, C.N. de. *Kristina*. Stockholm.

——. *The Woman and the Myth: Christina of Sweden*. London.

——. *The Catholic Encyclopaedia*, C.E. Herbermann (ed.). New York.

Echner, Mathilde von. *Diary*. Paris.

——. *Memoirs*. Paris.

Gribble, Francis. *The Court of Christina of Sweden*. London.

Kristina. *Aphorisms*. London.

——. *Aphorisms* (A selection). London.

——. *Correspondence*. London: Privately published.

——. *Letters to Cardinal Azzolino*. Paris.

——. *Memoirs* (A fragment). London.

Mann, H.K. *The Lives of the Popes* (13 volumes). London.

Marny, A. de. *Oxenstjerna*. Paris.

Mentz, G. *Louis XIV*. Bonn.

Montpensier, Anne Marie, Duchesse de. *Memoirs*. Paris.

Motteville, Françoise de. *Memoirs*. Paris.

Murat, Princesse Lucien. *Christine*. Paris.

——. *La Reine Christine de Suéde*. Paris.

Scott, D.D. *The Popes of Rome* (4 volumes). London.

Stevens, J.L. *History of Gustavus II Adolphus*. New York.

Williamson, Theodore. *The Seventeenth Century*. New York.

——. *Seventeenth Century Scholars & Scholarship*. New York.

A NOTE TO THE READER

If you have enjoyed this book enough to leave a review on **Amazon** and **Goodreads**, then we would be truly grateful. The Estate of Noel B. Gerson

Sapere Books is an exciting new publisher of brilliant fiction and popular history.

To find out more about our latest releases and our monthly bargain books visit our website: **saperebooks.com**